90 0666595 6

D0477370

Unive

Subject

http

E
F

Beyond Betrayal

Taking Charge of Your Life after Boyhood Sexual Abuse

Richard B. Gartner, Ph.D.

WILEY

John Wiley & Sons, Inc.

Copyright © 2005 by Richard B. Gartner. All rights reserved
Foreword © 2005 by William S. Pollack, Ph.D.

Published by John Wiley & Sons, Inc., Hoboken, New Jersey
Published simultaneously in Canada

No part of this publication may be reproduced, stored in a retrieval system, or transmitted
in any form or by any means, electronic, mechanical, photocopying, recording, scanning, or
otherwise, except as permitted under Section 107 or 108 of the 1976 United States Copyright
Act, without either the prior written permission of the Publisher, or authorization through
payment of the appropriate per-copy fee to the Copyright Clearance Center, 222 Rosewood
Drive, Danvers, MA 01923, (978) 750–8400, fax (978) 646–8600, or on the web at
www.copyright.com. Requests to the Publisher for permission should be addressed to the
Permissions Department, John Wiley & Sons, Inc., 111 River Street, Hoboken, NJ 07030,
(201) 748–6011, fax (201) 748–6008.

Limit of Liability/Disclaimer of Warranty: While the publisher and the author have used
their best efforts in preparing this book, they make no representations or warranties with
respect to the accuracy or completeness of the contents of this book and specifically dis-
claim any implied warranties of merchantability or fitness for a particular purpose. No warranty may be created or extended by sales representatives or written sales materials. The
advice and strategies contained herein may not be suitable for your situation. You should
consult with a professional where appropriate. Neither the publisher nor the author shall be
liable for any loss of profit or any other commercial damages, including but not limited to
special, incidental, consequential, or other damages.

For general information about our other products and services, please contact our Customer
Care Department within the United States at (800) 762–2974, outside the United States at
(317) 572–3993 or fax (317) 572–4002.

Wiley also publishes its books in a variety of electronic formats. Some content that appears
in print may not be available in electronic books. For more information about Wiley products, visit our web site at www.wiley.com.

Library of Congress Cataloging-in-Publication Data:

Gartner, Richard B.
    Beyond betrayal : taking charge of your life after boyhood sexual abuse / Richard B.
Gartner.
        p.   cm.
    Includes bibliographical references and index.
    ISBN 0-471-61910-8 (cloth)
    1. Adult child sexual abuse victims—Psychology.   2. Adult child sexual abuse
victims—Rehabilitation.   I. Title.
    HV6570.G37 2005
    362.76'4—dc22

                                                                    2004025803

10   9   8   7   6   5   4   3   2   1

UNIVERSITY OF PLYMOUTH

9006665956

I dedicate this book to the memory of my parents,
Mae and Ben Gartner. Their generosity, love, and vision ensured that
I got the education I needed to write about complex topics. Their
confidence, pride, and faith in me made all the difference.

I also dedicate this book to the memory of my agent, Jed Mattes.
He cared extraordinarily about the power of books, and his
unwavering confidence in the need for this book outlasted the fear
and distrust of many doubters.

WITHDRAWN
FROM
UNIVERSITY OF PLYMOUTH
LIBRARY SERVICES

Contents

Foreword

For years clinicians and the general population believed that a man or even a boy as a *victim* of sexual abuse was an oxymoron. The reasoning went that males weren't those who were hurt and betrayed as a result of sexual mistreatment, incest, sexual criminal behavior, and/or abuse—they were the abusers, the predators. It is indeed true, unfortunately, that men and boys do perpetrate sexual abuse. Equally true is the painful fact that men and boys are the victims of it as well. Some of the striking clinical writing of pioneers working with abused boys and men abused as boys finally brought this mental health epidemic out of the closet.

Indeed it was the pioneering groundbreaking clinical work of Dr. Richard Gartner that first opened our eyes to this hidden crisis of male-based pain. He was the one who informed the world of clinicians that by the age of sixteen up to one in four boys has experienced some form of unwanted direct or indirect sexual contact with someone older. In his highly regarded professional text, *Betrayed as Boys: Psychodynamic Treatment of Sexually Abused Boys*, he revealed how the effects of abuse on boys are distinctly different from the effects on girls. Gartner explored the sense of betrayal by one's supposed protectors within a context of the pathways to "normal" masculinity. He showed how many of the male-female differences result from the negative admonitions, emotional straitjackets, and myths we place on boys growing up in our culture, which I also explored in my own book, *Real Boys*.

No clinician who read *Betrayed as Boys* could ever approach the treatment of boys and men, especially those betrayed by sexual abuse, in the same manner again. I do not believe it is an exaggeration to state that Dr. Gartner's work led to the saving of countless emotional lives.

As the twenty-first century arrived, headlines were filled with horrific stories about clergy sexually abusing young boys for decades, a scourge that still haunts adult male victims. As a society, we began to see that this was merely the tip of an iceberg. We finally saw that boys were victims of sexual abuse at the hands of a myriad of adults—male and female—who betrayed their trust and responsibility. And now it was out in the open and we were finally talking about it in the press. The issues went way beyond blame and adjudication; the most important issues were the effects of the betrayal and how we could help male victims heal from the abuse as well as bring knowledge, succor, and support to the males, females, adults, and children who love them.

In his new and important book, *Beyond Betrayal: Taking Charge of Your Life after Boyhood Sexual Abuse*, Gartner takes his work out of the treatment setting directly to the victims of boyhood sexual abuse and those who love them. In this book—one of the finest self-help books for male victims of sexual abuse—he allows their heretofore hidden voices and stories of pain and recovery to be heard and respected. He outlines the symptoms of the problem, discusses the differences between cases when the abuser is male and when the abuser is female, and shows how this betrayal affects a healthy sense of self and healthy sexual development.

Dr. Gartner does not leave those touched by abuse with just a cogent explanation of their problems; in *Beyond Betrayal* he shows men and boys in recovery how to move beyond their experiences of betrayal, take charge of their lives again, learn how to heal, experience a full range of emotions in a safe manner, and redefine themselves as full people. Importantly, as well, Dr. Gartner shares his wisdom for loved ones and the families who live with men struggling with betrayal. *Beyond Betrayal* molds a model of healing, bringing us all to the shores of relief and change.

I only wish *Beyond Betrayal* were published years ago. I am very happy it comes to us now. It is a must-read for all victims of sexual abuse as boys and for their loved ones. It is necessary, practical, well written—and yes, a life-saving book. I urge you to read it and use its wise suggestions. I am honored to be allowed to introduce *Beyond Betrayal* to you.

William S. Pollack, Ph.D., author of *Real Boys* and
Real Boys' Voices; director, Centers for Men & Young
Men, McLean Hospital, Belmont, Massachusetts;
assistant clinical professor (psychology), Department
of Psychiatry, Harvard Medical School

Acknowledgments

I have been fortunate to have had many inspiring teachers, and I thank them all. From my primary and secondary schools: Marjorie Levi, Dorothy Giebel, Anna Ford, Rose Zeiber, Gussie Berson, Rachel Ehrlich, and Jacob Luria. From my college and post college years: Sid Perloe, Bob Butman, Joel Davitz, Rosalea Schonbar, John Coie, Arnold Krugman, Richard Kramer, Marilyn Mendelsohn, Andy Ferber, Phil Guerin, Tom Fogarty, Harry Mendelsohn, Ben Wolstein, Paul Lippmann, Janet Jeppson, Marylou Lionells, Philip Bromberg, Darlene Ehrenberg, Bertram Schaffner, and Dale Ortmeyer. In some measure, they each contributed to this book.

Others have affected my thinking through their writings. I have never met some of them while others are dear colleagues. I want to acknowledge the influences of David Lisak, Mic Hunter, Mike Lew, Richard Hoffman, Bill Holmes, Ken Adams, Stephen Grubman-Black, Matthew Mendel, James Cassese, Nicholas Groth, John Briere, David Finkelhor, Jane Gilgun, Patrick Carnes, Bessel van der Kolk, Judith Herman, Christine Courtois, Jody Messler Davies, Mary Gail Frawley-O'Dea, Laura Davis, Ellen Bass, Richard Kluft, Linda Williams, Karen Hopenwasser, Michelle Price, Stephen Knoblauch, Sue Grand, Judith Alpert, William Pollack, Terrence Real, Jack Drescher, Richard Isay, Martin Moran, Muriel Dimen, Adrienne Harris, Virginia Goldner, Karen Maroda, Julia Cameron, Steve Mitchell, Lew Aron, Donnel Stern, Stuart Pizer, Salvador Minuchin, Jay Haley, Sandor Ferenczi, and Harry Stack Sullivan.

Haverford College instilled in me a respect for scholarship, an ethical compass, and a desire to do service.

The William Alanson White Institute for Psychiatry, Psychoanalysis, and Psychology broadened and deepened my respect for the meaning of interpersonal relationships. Further, it has supported my efforts to bring concepts from interpersonal and relational psychoanalysis to their practical application in aid of people betrayed by those closest to them. I am especially grateful to Marylou Lionells, who as Director of the White Institute showed visionary support for the Sexual Abuse Program I founded there, and to her successor, Joerg Bose, with whose support the service continues to flourish. I am also deeply appreciative of the many individuals in the service who stimulated and encouraged my thinking throughout the eleven years I served as its director.

I also thank the many, many members of MaleSurvivor: National Organization against Male Sexual Victimization who have sustained me through the years. They have been among my dearest personal and professional supports.

I want to thank three people for their contributions to specific areas of the book. I hope my free adaptations of their ideas have done them justice. Howard Fradkin suggested exercises for part two. John O'Leary kindly shared with me thoughts about ways to heal without the use of professionals; they appear in altered form in chapter 12. Ken Singer generously gave me permission to revise two of his papers, *Breaking the Cycle of Self-Defeating Behavior* and *A Consumer's Guide to Therapist Shopping*. The originals appear on the MaleSurvivor Web site and their revisions appear in chapters 11 and 12 respectively.

I further thank Michelangelo Castellana, Fred Tolson, Larry Morris, Don Wright, Sue Shapiro, Elizabeth Hegeman, Ernesto Mujica, Olga Cheselka, Eli Zal, Murray Schane, Rick Goodwin, Mikele Rauch, Chris Turner, Julie Jarett Marcuse, Sarah Stemp, Jill Bellinson, Helene Kafka, Tina Harrell, Daniel Gensler, Martin Walker, Emily Garrod, and Anton Hart. In different ways, they each helped me understand.

My thanks to my late agent, Jed Mattes, who wanted this book published, and to Fred Morris, his successor, who skillfully shepherded it through its later stages. To Tom Miller, my editor at Wiley, for immediately understanding why this book is needed; to John Wiley & Sons for agreeing with him; and to Lisa Burstiner and the staff at Wiley for making the production easy. Thanks also to Michelle Sidrane, Diane Ruben, and Jane Chelius for their practical help in starting this project.

Mark Blechner, Sandra Buechler, John O'Leary, and Mary Gail Frawley-O'Dea have all been amazingly generous, openhearted friends and colleagues. Each of them has read and commented on my work over the years, and helped me become the writer, clinician, and thinker I am.

Walter de Milly stayed as close to this book as one could imagine. His tact, skill, humor, and literary suggestions have been myriad.

I feel exceptional gratitude to my Viceroys: Mark Blechner, Sandra Buechler, John O'Leary, Annie Rosen, and Bob Watson. We have met weekly since 1983. They know my secrets, they forgive my failings, they support my strengths. What more could one ask for in one's most trusted colleagues?

My particular thanks to my precious friends and family for reading, commenting, forgiving, allowing, asking, understanding, supporting and loving: J, J, E, and D, and Rick, Julie, Bob, Gloria, David, Eric, John, Renee, Mike, Ziva, Ken, Leonore, Margaret, Marilyn, Shelley, Mark, Michelle, Alan, Mary Gail, and Dennis. I am truly blessed.

I hope that by now J knows my feelings, stronger than ever.

Finally, I thank the many men and their loved ones whom I have known over the years—those whose stories appear in this book and all the others who trusted me enough to open up to mc. You have helped me understand male sexual victimization in the most personal way. I can't name you here, but I hope you know who you are.

Introduction

If you've picked up this book, chances are you or someone you know was sexually victimized as a boy. You're not alone. Research suggests that by the age of sixteen as many as one in six boys has had unwanted direct sexual contact with someone older. (When you add in those who had indirect contact—such as someone exposing genitals to the boy—it's about one in four.)

One in six! This is higher than the rate of prostate cancer among men, yet we rarely talk about it. When we do talk, shame or embarrassment often stops us from speaking openly and frankly.

At the beginning of the twenty-first century, scandals involving sexual abuse of boys by Catholic priests received tremendous media coverage in the United States. The stories were terribly sad, and the efforts by some in the Church to cover up the abuse were shocking. But after those revelations, it suddenly became possible to talk openly about sexual abuse of boys. The topic has entered the public discourse.

In the 1980s, when I first started thinking about the effects of boyhood sexual victimization, hardly anything was known about it. A few books about molestation of girls mentioned that boys were also abused, but the books often gave the impression that sexual abuse of boys rarely occurred and that boys were similar to girls in their reactions. The sexually abused men who were coming to see me, however, were different in important ways from sexually abused women I'd seen or read about.

I wanted to figure out how sexual victimization was unique for boys and men. What I discovered is that boys and men face problems related

1

to a group of myths, *none* of which is supported by research but many of which are generally believed. These myths include the following:

- Boys can't be sexually abused.

- Women don't abuse sexually.

- Sexual abuse is always overt.

- Only sissies and weaklings allow abuse.

- Unless violence is used, victims who don't say no to abuse must have invited it.

- If a boy feels sexually aroused, he's an equal partner in abuse.

- Sexual abuse turns a boy gay.

- Sexually abused boys almost inevitably grow up to be sexually abusing men.

This book is the result of my work as a psychologist, a psychoanalyst, and an advocate for sexually abused men. It is written especially for sexually abused men and those most affected by their trauma: their partners and loved ones.

I usually use the word "you" as I write, addressing myself to a man who's been sexually abused, but my ideas are equally important for his loved ones and those who want to help him. Also, I use "he" and "him" when referring to victims of sexual abuse because this book is about male victims. Since boys may have female as well as male abusers, however, I refer to victimizers sometimes as "he" and sometimes as "she."

I want to thank the many sexually abused men who have given me permission to tell the stories that appear both in this book and in my previous writings. Their willingness to help other men this way is moving and admirable. I hope I have done my part by telling their stories well while disguising their identities. I have changed details when I felt this would not compromise the truth of a man's experience and I have changed all names.

As I prepared this book, many people recounted to me how male sexual victimization affected them. To convey the depth and breadth of the problem—and the reason why this book is necessary—I let them speak for themselves by quoting them at the beginning of each part of the book. The words of these courageous individuals will set the stage for the book you're about to read. They tell you about the devastations of sexual abuse for boys and why there is reason for men to hope for a better life.

The men in this book have experienced despair, secrecy, and isolation. They have worried about manhood and sexual orientation and agonized about developing intimate relationships. On the other hand, they bravely decided to face inner demons. They moved beyond the past by confronting it and attaining a better sense of trust, resolution, and connection. You can also work to achieve this. That's what this book is about.

PART ONE

BETRAYAL'S WOUNDS

Mason, a married man whose self-involved mother left him in the care of a sexually abusing guardian for months at a time, talked about guilt and the pretense that he used to make believe he wasn't damaged by his experience: "We cling to survivor's guilt in a perilous, condemning culture that doesn't understand nor want to understand this unmanly affliction. I don't blame those who can't or won't grasp the gravity and ugly, persistent reality of our wounds. It's a primal, fear-filled reaction. God knows how many of the afflicted have died from the burden of pretense. The energy we must exert to 'be men,' to 'get over ourselves,' to 'not indulge the pain of past events'! The strength required to maintain this facade is crippling."

Nolan, a married man who from age eight to nineteen was forced by an older brother to have sex, described his rage: "I was deeply depressed and suffered bouts of intense road rage. All I wanted was for the pain to stop. I was actively contemplating suicide. I picked out a method and a location. I felt that the only people who didn't have problems were in the graveyard."

Zane, a gay man who was covertly abused by several family members, then raped by a scout leader, wrote about how he hid his pain: "All I could see was that I was basically a good fuck and a friendly guy who smiled *all* the time. Denial can be a powerful friend. That's how I learned to survive my childhood."

Guillermo, brutally raped for years by an older boy he'd idolized, had an ever-present sense of danger: "Every day, I feel I'm standing on the fifty-yard line in a huge football stadium. I'm all alone. There are sixty thousand people in the stands. All have rifles, and all are aimed at me. When and where the shot will come from, I don't know. But it will come!"

Steve, a married man, had been repeatedly molested by a man who was his Cub Scout leader, neighbor, and barber in a "chapel" the man constructed in his basement. The "confessional"-like scene left Steve devastated: "My mother saved my Cub Scout uniform. Today, when I hold that tiny uniform up against my forty-year-old body, I'm crushed by the smallness, the frailness of my body then, by the humiliating abuse it survived, and by the tremendous emotional weight this polyester shirt and pants still carry."

Luis, primed for abuse, then sexually assaulted by the director of a summer camp, described his agony: "Why did he choose me? What made him pick me out of all the boys in the camp, out of all the boys in the world? I was different now—damaged goods. I had nightmares. I shut down sexually. I kept the secret. I suffered in silence."

For years, Miles was abused by multiple teachers at his boarding school. A married man, attracted to and in love with his wife, he compulsively searched for sex with men, always feeling the hold his abusers continued to have on him: "I thought my teachers—these men who hurt and abused me—liked me and cared about me. I didn't know why I was always sad. Sex was constantly on my mind. Wherever I was, wherever I went, shopping malls, libraries, movies, beaches, and parks, I looked deep into the faces of strangers and searched for anonymous sex. I often felt sick afterward, but I couldn't stop. I frequently thought that I was possessed by the very devil. One day, I told a friend I was gay. I offered evidence of what happened in boarding school. 'But those were adults,' she said, 'and you were a child. You were molested.' 'No,' I denied, 'they didn't molest me. They didn't hurt me.' But her words stayed with me. Like the quietest of whispers, they haunted me until I found a therapist specializing in childhood sexual abuse."

1

Trust and Betrayal

Trust

There is potential for great beauty in the emotional currents that run between adults and children: the adult's power can be expressed as love, while the child's dependence is the beginning of trust.

As a child learns that the people who provided for him yesterday will take care of him today, he learns not only that people affect him but that the same people affect him in the same ways, day after day. He's learning how people behave with one another. He doesn't know what the word *relationship* means, but he knows what a mommy is to him, or a daddy, or a teacher, or a cousin, or a coach. He doesn't know what the word *trust* means, but he is able to feel it.

By the time he reaches adulthood, trust not only gives him an expectation that people will behave in specific ways but also that people will be *who they are*, especially in relation to *who he is*. He learns who people are by remembering *who they've been*. He learns to trust in the enduring qualities of a person and a relationship.

That's the way it ought to be. The idea of relying on a person to *be* that person and to treat you for who you are is fundamental to the nature of trust. According to the *Random House Dictionary of the English Language*, trust is "the firm reliance on the integrity, ability, or character of a person." The word *trust* derives from words meaning help, firm, strong, comfort, support, and confidence. These words add up to what we know as love.

Trust is so important that you sense its presence or absence in virtually every one of your relationships. Of course, you can put limits on the trust you place in others. Often, these limitations are obvious and well defined by the role someone plays in your life. For example, you may trust your banker to keep your money safe, but you wouldn't necessarily trust her to design a new suspension bridge.

There are other reasons you sometimes limit the trust you place in others. For example, you aren't likely to trust someone who has lied to you or harmed other people. Fortunately, as an adult living in a free society, you can usually protect yourself from this type of person by exercising your rights and powers. You may live where you want, call law enforcement authorities for assistance, assert your constitutional rights, seek help from friends, and decide who you want to take care of your emotional and physical needs.

Your efforts may never be completely effective, but you possess the freedom as an adult to try to arrange your life so that you're surrounded by people you trust and you're protected from those you don't. You can accomplish this by reducing your dependence on untrustworthy people and increasing your reliance on those you can trust.

But what about a child? He has little choice about how to arrange his life. He isn't always able to protect himself from people he doesn't trust. Because he's completely dependent on those who are responsible for him, he trusts out of necessity. He trusts people to take care of him, to be who they are, to remain who they've been, to love him for his own good, to be attuned to his needs, and to cherish him as a person of worth.

When a child hopes for these things and they happen, then love and trust have worked their magic. They've combined into something beautiful. The child thrives. He begins to understand love and character. He grows in his relationships, believing that people are usually good and honorable, that authorities most often use their power to benefit others. At the same time, he learns, often with the help of these same benevolent authorities, to understand the difference between those who are trustworthy and those who are not.

Does a parent have to raise a child perfectly in order for him to thrive? Of course not. All parents make mistakes. Everybody has moods, and there is no blueprint for raising the perfect child or being the perfect parent. We do our best, knowing that sometimes we'll fail, hopefully in minor ways that won't damage our children. When relationships between adults and children—although sometimes imperfect—are basically honest and free of exploitation, children are well equipped to overcome life's difficulties with resilience, promise, and a capacity to love. This is not to say, of course, that all children who are not sexually abused have happy lives. Any child, however, needs to develop some capacity to trust in order to face life's inevitable troubles, and sexual abuse interferes with attaining this ability.

Throughout your life, people will come and go, but you want to make sense of all of your relationships, however temporary they are. This may be as simple as understanding that your mailman is, indeed, a mailman. In your more enduring and personal relationships, however, there is more to figure out.

This need to understand others begins in childhood, when you learn to make sense of your life. If you had nonabusive relationships with your parents and caregivers that encouraged trust, you could make sense of them. You knew you would be taken care of. If you were raised under these circumstances, you developed a strong heart filled with a sense of self-esteem, competence, and the belief that you're worth loving. You could look forward to a basically trusting relationship with the world, a sense of optimism, even a faith about life itself.

But maybe your earliest relationships didn't make sense. If your developing heart was broken by someone who you needed to trust, then it may be hard for you to get along in the world. Your current relationships may seem mysterious and tricky to manage. You may even have difficulty understanding your relationship with your own self.

Betrayal

Even if everyone else in a boy's life loves and cherishes him, sometimes a single adult can wreak havoc in his heart and soul. If this happened to you, you may have been imprinted with the belief that no one in the world is trustworthy, that the character of life itself is false. Maybe you came to believe that life means being hurt, lied to, or exploited. Worse, this belief may have made you vulnerable to what you fear most: You may consciously or unconsciously send signals to others that you *expect* to be abused. Then ill-intentioned people may perceive you as a walking victim and select you for mistreatment.

If you were abused as a child, betrayal is your life's core issue. It ravages your self-concept as a man, especially if the betrayal was sexual. It affects how you behave with your family, your parents, your partners, and your friends. Recovering from your betrayal must involve not only you but your relationships. Without understanding and help from those who love you, the prospect for your recovery and growth is diminished.

Betrayal is the violation and destruction of trust. Lying is an obvious and direct form of betrayal. But trust is also violated when an adult uses his relationship with a child to satisfy his own needs without regard for the child's needs. The adult may subject the child to violence, adult sexuality, or otherwise treat him as less than human. She may violate the child's trust by trying to take something from him that the child can't give. When any person who is ordinarily expected to protect a child from harm instead reverses his role and demands an "adult" relationship from the child, he destroys trust.

There are at least two kinds of trust between people. The first is formal, as in a written legal agreement or an oath of office. This is *explicit trust*. The second is unspoken and expected. This is *implicit trust*. It exists when it's so naturally part of a relationship that no contracts need to be signed and no words need to be spoken. A suckling infant, for example, doesn't need to ask his mother if he can trust her not to drop him. A parent trusts a teacher to educate a child. A boy trusts his coach to respect the boy's ownership of his own body.

If an adult used you when you were a boy to satisfy his sexual urges or romantic (i.e., "boy-loving") fantasies, that adult stopped treating you as a worthwhile, developing person. This betrayal may have led you to develop a tragic understanding of the way the world works. If you were physically abused, you learned that violence is a normal part of relationships. If you were sexually abused, you learned that in at least some relationships what people really want is your body. You may have deduced that your primary function in life is to provide sex to those who need it. You may have assumed that when anyone gives you affection, it's just a prelude to your having to "put out." You may have figured out that the only way you can get attention, protection, nurturing, and "love" is by offering your body for sex.

Betrayal creates immediate pain as well as a hurt that lives on. On the one hand, you may feel pain without any conscious memory of what caused it. On the other, the pain creates harmful connections, demolishing parts of life that ought to give you satisfaction: friendships, good feelings toward the people who care about you, and loving, intimate relationships.

No matter what form betrayal took, no matter how seldom or how often it happened, it challenged and changed your perception of yourself as you grew into manhood. Your whole world may have shifted in cataclysmic ways. The connections you make with other people, in love, friendship, authority, and dependence, may all have been damaged by suspicions and fear. You may feel completely unable to control your own states of consciousness. At times, you may experience the intrusion of powerful, unwanted thoughts and feelings that leave you confused, afraid, and depressed.

Sexual Betrayal

When we talk about adults' sexual misuse of children, we often use such expressions as *sexual abuse*, *incest*, and *sexual trauma*. In a moment, we'll talk about what each of these terms means. While all of them indicate some form of sexual violation, none conveys the great range of human experience suggested by the term *sexual betrayal*.

MAURICE: Doing Good Means Feeling Bad

Looking back at his life with hard-earned insight, Maurice said his sexual betrayal by his father created a pattern that kept him from flourishing in any endeavor. This was most apparent in school, but it also affected his career. "Even if I liked my teachers and employers, at some point in the relationship I developed a resentment that I didn't understand," he told me. "Even if I knew they were sexually harmless toward me, even if I knew that what they wanted me to do was legitimate and for my own good, anything I did for them still felt bad. It was awful! It didn't matter whether I really thought they were sexually interested in me. It still felt like I had to 'put out' for them."

It's not surprising that this intelligent, gifted man never "excelled" in school. He dropped out twice, finally graduating with a mediocre record. It was only years later that Maurice made a connection between the bad feelings he experienced when doing good things for himself and his childhood betrayal by a father who fed him, protected him, and encouraged him to be good in life, all the while violating him sexually.

Sexual Abuse

Abuse is a potent form of betrayal. It occurs when one person exploits another. Abusers take advantage of their power in a relationship to satisfy their own needs without regard for the needs of the person being abused. For example, a drug dealer who tells his young brother to carry drugs across the street is endangering his brother in order to satisfy his own needs.

Sexual abuse (or sexual molestation) occurs when someone uses her power and control to coerce someone else to engage in sexual acts without regard for the other person's will or needs. If you were sexually abused, your abuser cared more about satisfying his own desires than about the fact that you were still developing and your development was being put at terrible risk.

Your abuser may have believed she loved you. But genuine love isn't simply a desire to be with a loved one. It certainly isn't a sexual desire *for* that loved one that ignores the loved one's needs and priorities. Loving someone requires sensitivity to what he needs in order to thrive in life and a willingness to temper your own wishes if satisfying them would harm him.

Why do people sexually abuse children? What is this need they have? Sometimes, of course, it's about sexual desire. But for many abusers sexual longing isn't an important factor. Sexual behavior may mask many motives. For example, adult abusers may be prompted by insecurity. They attempt to feel more secure by exercising power over someone who is weaker. Other abusers, unable to soothe themselves without being sexually aggressive, choose children because they're easy targets. There are also adults who feel an inner urgency to have a deeply personal connection with children, sometimes because they themselves are psychological children. Sometimes these adults have sadistic fantasies and may brutally act out their own early betrayal on a helpless child. But others yearn for something they can't have: a child lover. Children can't be lovers in the adult sense, not in the real world.

Sexual abuse can be violent when force and coercion are involved. But sometimes it seems loving. Some abusers create an atmosphere that seems safe. If the abuser senses a boy is attracted to him on some level, the abuser may appeal directly to this desire. It will appear that a seduction is taking place, even a mutual seduction. The boy may fall in love with his seducer, and the seducer may believe he is in love with the boy.

Understanding seductive experiences is complicated. Many men believe that as boys they had loving, pleasurable, nontraumatic sexual initiations from adults. I don't dismiss this possibility. If this describes you, though, look at the rest of your life. Do you exhibit symptoms of sexual abuse described elsewhere in this book? Have you suffered from compulsions or addictions? Have you been able to maintain intimate relationships? Are they exploitative in some way? Think through your situation before deciding whether you were abused.

Abusers who don't try to seduce a boy directly may groom him slowly, perhaps over many months. Through grooming, they gain access, authority, and control over the boy. They may even groom the boy's family, convincing parents that it's safe to leave their child with this adult. We'll see in chapter 5 how Seth's abuser attached himself to a family with numerous sons, then abused several of them.

During grooming, the abuser may offer a relationship that the boy desperately needs, or show him pornography, sexualizing the relationship. An atmosphere of secrecy about what they are doing may be established. Gradually, physical contact is introduced. By the time overt sex is introduced, it may seem to be a natural outgrowth of all that came before. The boy may feel he should go along with it—even if he doesn't really want to—because he's gone along with previous sexualized activities. Or he may feel increasingly aroused by grooming behaviors (as well as from his own hormones), so sex feels welcome.

If you were abused, maybe you grew up believing you agreed to it or were even responsible for it. Maybe your abuser said you wanted it. It was easy for her to conclude this if you needed love and affection. In fact, in order to get what feels like love, you may have been willing to engage in sex. You may have even believed that sex is love.

But a child can't freely consent to sex with an adult. Children don't have the capacity to give informed consent to sexuality with adults. After all, it's hard enough for an adult to comprehend the meaning of a sexual encounter. Look at all the books, theories, movies, and everyday conversations between adults trying to understand sexual relationships. Children can't participate as equals in dialogues like these. They're simply not developmentally prepared to understand the consequences of a sexual relationship with an adult.

Adults encountering problems in a relationship can address them, and, if necessary, change or even end the relationship. But if you were dependent on your abuser for protection or survival, you couldn't just declare, "It's over. Take a walk." And it would be hard for you to find ways to express your feelings if you were afraid of punishment, abandonment, or the safety of your family.

ANDREAS: Sex under Threat

Andreas was abused by a ring of child molesters for several years starting when he was eight. He can't forgive himself for obeying these men when they ordered him to wait at a convenience store at the same time every week so that they could pick him up and continue their sessions of sexual abuse. Weighed down by years of self-blame, Andreas asked himself why he met them weekly, why he never doubted their authority over him. Only after several years of therapy did he admit that his abusers warned him time and again, "We'll kill your mother if you don't show up!" No wonder he was terrified! But, although he acknowledged that he believed his mother's life was endangered, he nevertheless blamed himself for returning weekly for more abuse.

Sexual Excitement during Abuse

If you experienced any sexual pleasure or desire during your molestation, you may blame yourself for the whole episode. But sexual behavior involves stimulating nerve endings that transmit pleasure. It excites the part of a child's brain that eventually develops his adult sexuality. As a little boy, however, you couldn't understand this. You couldn't understand that when your penis is rubbed—however it happens—you'll feel pleasure. Not knowing any better, maybe you grew up convinced you were responsible for what happened.

For these reasons, all sexual acts between children and people who have power over them are sexually abusive. This is true if the adult's power is legitimately recognized by other adults, as in the cases of babysitters, teachers, and parents who molest children. It's equally true, however, if your abuser was just older, bigger, or more powerful than you. For example, a seven-year-old might obey a teenage neighbor who invites him home simply because he's older and authoritative.

No matter how willingly you seemed to participate in sex acts, if the other person had power over you, it was an abusive situation. Willing or not, you were abused by having the natural developmental unfolding of your sexuality violated and hurried into awareness.

Occasionally, men tell me they weren't hurt by their childhood sexual experiences with adults, and sometimes even that they enjoyed them. They may be right, but even seemingly consensual situations may turn out to have long-term negative effects. For example, many gay men report that when they were children they enjoyed having sex with an older man and even initiated their encounters. However, there can be both subtle and obvious aftereffects to adult–child sex. It may be decades before a man looks back and realizes, for example, that his life-consuming, insatiable, and ultimately unfulfilling need for anonymous sex began at an early age when he was molested by a school counselor who paid attention to him when no one else would.

That's why adult–child sex is always abusive. There's no way for an adult to know whether a particular child—even if he seems happy to participate—will be affected negatively by taking part in sex acts. And the very last person we can expect to be objective about the needs and best interests of a child is the adult who sexually desires him.

Incest

Incest is perhaps the most psychologically catastrophic form of sexual betrayal. It can have even more far-reaching consequences than sexual abuse by adults who are unrelated to the child. This is especially likely when incest occurs regularly, often for years.

Even more destructive to the boy is that he's living in a family that somehow supports incest. When the abuser is a parent, the child grows up chronically trapped in at least one twisted primary relationship. Stories about men abused as boys by their fathers appear throughout this book; abuse by mothers is discussed in chapter 7.

While the dictionary may define incest as sex between blood relatives, in the reality of a boy's world it can be perpetrated by any older person who holds a position of power, trust, and protection over him. If you felt a family-like connection to an older caretaker who sexually betrayed you, the molestation may have been as traumatic as if you'd been betrayed by a blood relative: a shattering of the natural trust you had in the adults who cared for you.

Sexual Trauma

Trauma is different from abuse. Abuse refers to what a victimizer does to a child. Trauma is the effect of the betrayal on the child. Sexual trauma specifically refers to the traumatic effects of abusive sexual behavior.

We usually think of trauma as a visible, physical injury, such as lacerations and bruising received in an automobile accident. We cannot see the human brain or psyche, but that doesn't mean they're invulnerable.

Far from it. They respond to betrayal in many ways, affecting your perception of the world and of yourself.

Trauma is a reaction to an overwhelming life experience that the brain cannot process. Traumatic events are unusual, often coming without warning. They surpass a person's capacity to deal with them, disrupting his frame of mind and psychological stability.

Some symptoms of trauma—such as the feeling that everything is unreal or dreamy—may appear immediately. Others—such as suddenly experiencing powerful feelings for unknown reasons—may not emerge until years later.

Sexual trauma, because it involves sexual acts, inflicts deep injury on a child's sexuality. Even if no coercion or force is used, the child's sexual development is traumatized. This means that traumatic symptoms are especially likely to affect the victim's capacity for intimacy and sexuality.

Betrayal by Caretakers Who Are Not Relatives

In recent years the news has been filled with revelations of sexual abuse by caretakers other than relatives. Following are just some examples.

Clergy

Historically, clergy have been more trusted than any other adults outside the family. They're often seen as individuals with a special relationship with God who therefore can be relied on to take responsible care of anyone put under their protection. If you grew up in a religiously observant family, perhaps you were taught that the religious authorities in your life were so completely trustworthy that they were almost incapable of misdeed. They may have become substitutes for family, and you may have addressed them as "Father," "Mother," "Sister," and "Brother." They may have even become stand-ins for God, people whose commands seem to come directly from heaven.

When an authority on whom a family bestows such trust, reverence, and familial closeness betrays a child, the extent of damage can seem infinite. It's hard to imagine feeling more abandoned, isolated, and worthless than a boy who believes in God, but also believes that God betrayed him.

The more a boy believes in the familial implications of calling someone Father, Mother, Sister, or Brother, the more incestuous are the acts committed during sexual abuse. So, many victims of priests are psychologically dealing with the equivalent of incest.

For these reasons, abuse by clergy can be as devastating as incest. Through incest, the relationship of a father or mother to a son is compromised or twisted beyond remedy. So can the relationship between a boy and God be distorted and shattered if he's molested by a spiritual authority. Add that to the other wounds caused by sexual exploitation, and his suffering will be vast.

Without the sense of unity and love that so many religions offer, a boy betrayed by a member of the clergy may become spiritually isolated and cynical. When Lorenzo went to the Church seeking help because he was confused about previous sexual abuse and his sexual orientation, he was molested by a priest. He completely lost his spiritual bearings. As he put it, "It was a terrible thing to do. They knew how fucked up I was about sex with all those men and how unsure I was about being gay. I went to them for sanctuary, and they just helped me party. In those days, I really believed in the Catholic Church. No more."

There are no easy answers for a boy or man who was betrayed by clergy, but this does not mean there are no answers. His spiritual nightmare does not have to last forever. We'll talk more about sexual victimization by clergy in chapter 5.

Health Professionals

Adults who have power and influence over a child set up a tragedy if they use their position to molest him. Because health professionals are sought out for advice and answers when a child is abused, they're among the last people you'd expect to be capable of betrayal. Yet it happens. It happens to children who were previously abused and to those who were never traumatized before. If health professionals engage in sexual activity with a patient or client, they are of course committing a crime. But they're also committing a terrible ethical and moral breach.

These betrayals can occur in the offices of physicians or mental health professionals. But nurses, nurses' aides, dentists, chiropractors, massage therapists, and other health professionals are also entrusted with the health of their patients. All of these professionals have enormous power over their charges and so the potential for an abuse of power is always present. Fortunately, this rarely occurs, but when it does the betrayal can be terribly damaging.

To add to the potential for catastrophe, people in distress are at a heightened risk for becoming romantically infatuated with people who betray them even as they seem to heal them. When the air clears and the professional goes back to her life, the abused boy or man is left stranded, doubly victimized, and far less likely to ever trust a professional again. Overcoming skepticism and anger toward health professionals can take years. In the meantime, the original wound of betrayal remains open and raw.

Scoutmasters, Teachers, Coaches, Nannies, Babysitters, Godparents, and Camp Counselors

The list of potential abusers goes on and on. All of these people have positions that invite the trust not only of children but of their parents. They all have positions of authority over the child. Through betrayal, all of them can damage a child deeply. Most of these individuals are, of course, worthy of trust, and are committed to ensuring young people's health and well-being. In fact, for many children in distress and at risk of losing their life's direction completely, a relationship with such a person is a wonderful and helpful influence, perhaps a lifesaving connection. But overcoming the devastation caused by the few who betray children in their care is often as difficult as overcoming "real" incest.

Sexually Abusive Behaviors

Sexually abusive behavior takes many forms. Some would be obviously abusive to anyone who heard about them. Others are subtler and at first might not be considered sexually abusive by an onlooker or even by the victim.

Sexual Abuse with Touch

When sexual abuse involves physical contact, it's called *contact abuse*. Contact abuse can range from the seemingly accidental brushing of a hand against a fully clothed child's genital area, to sexual kissing, to actual penetration by a finger, an object, or a penis. Adults who molest children can be very adept at creating situations that allow them to make physical contact with a child. Masked as expressions of kindness and nurturing, molestations can occur when bathing a child, dressing him, playing games with him, tickling him, sleeping with him, teaching him, holding him, or keeping him warm.

But how is appropriate, loving touch different from acts of sexual abuse? In most cases, the child knows. If it happened to you, you knew. You started to feel uncomfortable with the contact. You may have even suspected that the adult was making up an excuse to touch you sexually. There was no real nurturing purpose in the contact, and you sensed this. The adult focused more on the physical act than on you as a person. He may have ignored your signals that you were uncomfortable with the touching. The acts may have been hidden from other adults' view. She may have warned you not to talk about what happened. Or he may have found a less direct way to let you know to keep things secret. For example, an adult may not verbally acknowledge what happened but instead make believe you misinterpreted a loving touch.

In extreme cases of contact abuse, the adult physically forces a child into submission. Even to think about this can be disturbing. Regardless of whether force was used, contact abuse criminally violates a child's integrity.

Sexual Abuse without Touch

Sexual abuse doesn't necessarily involve physically touching a child. For example, adults having sex in front of a child is a form of *noncontact abuse*. It is similarly abusive to encourage a child to have sex with others, or photograph him for sexual purposes, or show him pornography, or engage him in sexualized or seductive talk. Adults may also sexually abuse a child when they take too much interest in bath time, especially when the child is old enough to bathe himself. Too much attention to the child's sexual development, his sexual organs, or his private sexual behavior (asking him to describe how he masturbates, for example) can all be sexually abusive behaviors that don't involve physical contact. They may not be legally criminal acts, but they are destructive nonetheless.

Covert Abuse

Adults who are interested in children for sex can be creative in the ways they obtain their pleasure. They may create a sexualized atmosphere so subtly that it's hard to accuse them of anything: a knowing look, a secret smile, a slightly sexualized walk. Abusing covertly helps maintain a fiction that they're doing nothing wrong, assuaging the guilt they'd otherwise feel.

A child, however, is powerless to ignore the adult's efforts, and he may feel uneasy, embarrassed, angry, or afraid even though the adult isn't touching him. He may feel especially disturbed because there's no specific thing the adult did that he can point to as sexually abusive, yet he has a queasy feeling about the relationship. This kind of covert abuse is difficult to pin down. Yet the child knows and he hurts.

Recovery

It's natural to want to recover from betrayal, and quickly. But recovery takes time. It requires patience with yourself. It calls on you to forgive yourself for your failures, accept your progress, and find ways to voice what you've never spoken about before.

Nothing has to be done immediately, nor can it be. There's no way to know what your life will be like when you've recovered. And there's no way to avoid discouragement and setbacks along the way. But the possibilities for human development don't lie in the past. Possessing a will to recover, to take charge of your life again, is a great indication that it's possible for you to succeed at it.

2

Sexual Abuse and Manhood

In our culture, men mustn't be victims. Men mustn't be penetrated, violated, subdued, or otherwise forced into submission. They're taught to be in charge of themselves. So it's difficult for men to ever visualize themselves as being victimized.

This is a paradox. On the one hand, it's good, because a psychologically healthy man doesn't see himself as a victim. On the other hand, being unable to see yourself as a victim now prevents you from remembering what it was like to be a victim as a boy. And until you're able to accept your childhood victimization, you won't recover from it.

The cultural rule that men shouldn't be victims may have left you feeling your manhood was threatened, if not permanently weakened or damaged. So it's natural for you to feel intense inner conflicts. Every betrayed boy reacts uniquely to anxieties about masculinity, but if these reactions remain unexpressed and unarticulated, he'll encounter great difficulties in adulthood.

For example, you may hurt yourself or others through physical, sexual, or emotional aggression. Or maybe you've given up and become passive. In that case, it's more likely you'll somehow be victimized again. Another way of dealing with anxieties over your masculinity is to stay so busy that you never experience the fullness of life and the joys of relationships. You may go back and forth between deep, troubled reflection and periods of proving how masculine you are. You may wonder if you're gay, or if your betrayal "made" you gay. You may harbor deep feelings of hatred toward homosexuals even if you are gay.

21

No matter how you responded to sexual betrayal, what happened to you as a boy is unhappily intertwined with how you experience life now. But this pervasive injury to your humanity can be healed. That's what this book is about. It's about taking charge of your masculinity and your life.

Three Images of Man

Your troubles and anxieties probably don't arise from sexual abuse alone. One way to look at the complications rooted in sexual abuse is to contemplate the following three mental images:

1. The man you know you are

2. The man you want to be

3. The man the world expects you to be

These images can evoke profound feelings and desires, affecting every dimension of your life. In many men, these mental figures are at relative peace with one another, but if you were betrayed, they may clash with agonizing severity.

Early in life, you figured out what a man is supposed to be. You learned the rules to follow, the passions to explore, and how to behave in various situations. The world offered masculine heroes to emulate, from Superman to your school's quarterback.

If you grew up as most men did, you felt you should be a hero who played by the rules, sought the truth, protected the weak, and stood up to evil. These heroes were mythic in stature, supremely confident and able. Whatever an ideal man did, he did well. He was supposed to appreciate and safeguard women. In return, they would be attracted to him. He was in control, competent, and powerful.

Men receive recognition for taking charge and exerting power, whether by handling a truck, handling a disagreement between employees, or handling a life-or-death emergency. These are the qualities of masculinity as defined by our culture. No matter what's best or natural for any individual, these qualities are expected of every boy and man.

If you met the world's expectations, you were rewarded. If you ran the fastest, you received a ribbon. If you caught the largest fish, your photo was taken with it. If you opened a door for a girl, you had reason to believe she would appreciate your gallantry and reward you with a smile.

If you haven't met the world's expectations as a man or if you believe you can't meet them, your confusion and doubts can slide down into depression. And then your behaviors can hurt you.

From the time you were a boy, you compared yourself to others. You wanted to know how you were like or unlike your friends, your heroes, and the man you wanted to become. As you made these comparisons, you made realistic adjustments. You tested yourself and compromised and adapted, developing skills and accepting your limitations. Sometimes you encountered challenges and embarrassments, but you sorted them out, absorbed them into your life experience, and moved on. This is how you matured. This is how your masculine identity evolved.

Becoming a man takes on a life of its own. For many boys, it's a process filled with hope, pleasure, and adventure. It's as if their original childhood hero is at one end of the earth, and the boy is at the other. They slowly move toward one another, becoming more similar. The boy becomes more proficient, and the hero becomes more human.

That's what happens if his life goes well. Journeying toward manhood, he finds self-acceptance. He finds a balance between the man he is and the man he wants to be. The balance may not be perfect, but he is comfortable with it. Pleased and proud, he sees a resemblance between himself and the masculine ideal he learned early on.

But maybe he's very unlike that masculine ideal. Sometimes a boy realizes he's not interested in meeting the world's expectations. Sometimes a boy realizes he's gay, but none of his heroes were. Sometimes a boy's heroes were women. Sometimes he has disabilities that prevent him from reaching his ideal. Sometimes things happen to him that he believes couldn't happen to the man he wanted to become.

Betrayal of Manhood

Your early heroes weren't weaklings who gave up easily. Your hero would never submit to another man or allow his body to be used to pleasure someone else just because that person was stronger or older.

The world gives medals to men for subduing prey, not for being subdued. We're told that the best men win. As a general once said, in war there's no second prize. It's clear: a real man can't be a victim.

So if you were sexually abused, where does this leave you? As a boy, maybe you felt pulled apart. Your three images of man were caught up in an impossible conflict: Maybe you disliked the boy you were. Maybe you felt you couldn't become the boy you wanted to be. And you very likely felt you couldn't develop into the man the world expected you to become. These conflicts may have left you feeling cut off and lost. You were disconnected from the man you were becoming. You were detached from your self—the self who felt hope about growing up, the self with strength, will, determination, and a sense of discovery.

If you were betrayed, you had to find ways to resolve your conflict. You had to find out how to be at home with yourself and the world. Every betrayed boy finds his own way, but few ways are easy or ideal.

ISAAC: Giving Up on Growing Up

Isaac tried to solve his problems by trying not to grow up. He changed his reality by thinking of himself as a boy instead of the man he was.

At forty-five, Isaac radiated a sweet, boyish charm. He understood relationships as an early adolescent might. His friendships lacked complexity and depth, and he found it difficult to understand people's behavior. Molested a dozen different times as a boy, he'd read self-help books in order to understand himself. But he didn't gain any real insight from them. Employed in a low-level position that didn't use his intellect, abilities, or education, he remained financially and emotionally dependent on his stepfather. He was unhappy, but he didn't know why.

One day, Isaac was late to a session. He held his head low and looked at me with apologetic puppy eyes.

"You seem like a little boy now," I said. "Like you're expecting to be punished."

"I do," he said. "I feel like I'm ten years old. It's weird." He said he didn't really know how to be older than a teenager. In his own mind, most adult men were like the many older boys or men who'd abused him, all of whom he assumed were straight. He felt he'd have to behave abusively if he were a "regular" heterosexual adult man. In contrast, he saw gay men as societal victims. He wanted to be neither gay nor a victim but was terribly afraid he was both. So he retreated to a seemingly asexual, innocent adolescent posture.

Gender Identity and Sexual Orientation

Many boys grow up imagining a not-very-real world in which there are men and women, and that's that. Men would understand how to be masculine and women knew how to be feminine. In a world like this, a boy would easily balance his three images of man. By the time he was grown, he would feel manly and masculine.

But this is not how things are. For any boy, sexuality and gender may be a struggle, especially regarding sexual orientation and gender identity. For sexually abused boys, this struggle can seem impossible to resolve.

Sexual Orientation

Sexual orientation is the predominating erotic desire for either the same or the opposite sex. Everyone has some degree of attraction to both sexes, but by the time they reach adulthood most people have stronger consistent desires for either one sex or the other. Most men are heterosexual, meaning they are predominantly attracted to women. A smaller proportion are homosexual, meaning they are predominantly attracted to men. Bisexual men are attracted to both sexes.

Many men who were sexually abused as boys feel uncertain about their sexual orientation. Abused homosexual and bisexual men have a lot of the same questions about masculinity as abused heterosexual men. We'll come back to concerns about sexual orientation in chapter 6.

Gender Identity

Most people feel like their biological sex. If you have a male body, you probably feel male. Possessing an internal sense that you're one sex or the other is called gender identity. Most people's gender identity feels so natural that it seems their outward appearance and internal sense of gender are the same.

Yet gender identity is actually learned. Gender is our culture's definition of masculinity and femininity, the *social* qualities of being a man or a woman. Rather than instinctively knowing what your gender is, you're taught about it. Being masculine may feel instinctive and innate to you, but the qualities that define gender vary from place to place and time to time. That's how we know that many gender characteristics are learned, not genetically inherited.

In American society, using makeup is characteristically feminine, and playing professional football is characteristically masculine. Interestingly, it's often easier for a woman to cross over to masculine behaviors than for a man to cross over to feminine ones. Women may play soccer or even drive bulldozers without being stigmatized much, but how many men wear makeup? Some do, but how many would be comfortable with others knowing about it?

The characteristics that define gender can change over time: Ulysses S. Grant wore a dress when he was a baby. So did the most macho American president, Theodore Roosevelt. This wasn't because they had strange parents. Dressing baby boys in pinafores and petticoats was customary during the nineteenth century in the United States.

At first glance, our culture allows only two real possibilities when it comes to men's and women's roles: men are masculine and women are feminine. We're sometimes rigid about this. You can see this in adolescent boys, who are often inflexible about masculinity and femininity as they try to fit themselves into the world of men and women. They're likely to get confused and angry if, say, they see a boy wearing an outfit with ruffles, like the ones Quinn's mother made for him (see chapter 8).

Masculine Gender Identity

When you were a toddler, you didn't know the difference between men and women. Like all very young children, you exhibited both masculine and feminine characteristics. But you grew up and learned what it means to be a boy. As you confirmed your masculine identity, you may have rejected anything feminine about yourself.

Some psychologists believe that a masculine identity is developed by warding off threats to it. This is why adolescent boys often spend lots of energy trying to meet the masculine expectations of their peers. They may develop sports skills or learn about cars. And some of them even beat up other boys they perceive as effeminate or gay. Boys who do this may feel shaky about their masculinity, so they try to prove they're "real men" by attacking those they perceive as "unmale."

Fighting off feminine traits and bolstering masculine ones doesn't stop when we become adults, although we're usually not aware of it. Social pressures persist throughout our lives. As an adult, you may feel pressured to show other men that you're "masculine." Some men do this in symbolic ways, like identifying with a sports team, escorting beautiful women, or being successful businessmen. If you feel you've succeeded in matching your gender identity to cultural expectations of masculinity, the three self-images we've talked about are more likely to be at peace. The more at peace they are, the less you're likely to worry about your masculinity.

Men and Femininity

Homosexual men, especially those comfortable with being gay, may feel more flexible about their gender identity than heterosexual men. They may be more comfortable with traditionally feminine characteristics than most straight men. As a group, they're more at ease blending masculine and feminine gender traits and interests than heterosexual men.

Each individual is different, however. Whatever their sexual orientation, some men will only be comfortable with traditional masculine characteristics whereas others will be relaxed about conventionally feminine ones. A homosexual man with a predominantly male gender identity will think of himself as masculine and will fit easily into, say, the world of sports. A gay man with a predominantly female gender identity, in contrast, may feel more feminine and may be unconflicted about an interest in makeup and hairstyling.

Some biologically male individuals have a well-formed female gender identity. These men—whom we call transgendered—are psychologically female. A transgendered man feels like a woman on the inside. He perceives himself as female. Usually, he'd rather be referred to as "she." Some transgendered people undergo surgery, hormone treatments, and therapy, with the goal of completely becoming a woman.

It's also possible for a heterosexual man to identify with women without being transgendered. He may take on some mental and perhaps even physical characteristics of women but not feel female. He may still be sexually attracted to women, feel heterosexual, and want to be a man in a relationship with a woman.

CORY: A "Young Lady" Flowers as a Man

When Cory, a gifted researcher, came to me, he was depressed, unable to work, and feeling suffocated in his marriage. He had no specific memories of sexual abuse, nor did he regain any while in therapy. Nevertheless, he felt strongly that his mother had sexually abused him.

He felt nauseated when he was near her or even when he thought of being touched by her.

Yet he also strongly identified with his mother. He and his sisters grew up exceptionally well behaved and high-achieving in school. Cory bitterly said, "My mother controlled all of us through strict rules. She brought us all up to be ladies. She pointedly warned us about the outside world, particularly about the untrustworthiness of men, including our father."

She told him in extravagant detail the horror she felt during sex on her wedding night and afterward. "At the same time," he told me, "she'd complain to me that my father was unable to satisfy her sexually!"

He spelled out his dilemma: "My mother taught me over and over that men were scary and awful. Then one day I was fourteen and I had hairy knees and broad shoulders and I was fucked—I was one of Them."

Cory felt he disgusted his mother now: his smells, his sweatiness, his bulk, the sexual thoughts he might be having. His burgeoning sexuality also revolted him. He considered entering the priesthood as a solution to his agony.

"By the time I was a teenager," Cory said, "I could hardly relate to either sex. I certainly couldn't bond with other boys. I didn't feel like one of them. The few people I could relate to were girls, and even then, it was awkward for me." Throughout high school and college, he had few meaningful relationships with men. As he put it, he "remained one of the ladies."

After he married, problems developed. Whenever he and his wife had sex, he'd freeze up emotionally, cutting her off. One night while they were having sex, she caressed his back in a certain way. He suddenly saw his mother's face on her and bolted upright in bed, weeping and shouting, "Don't touch me!" He decided to begin therapy.

In treatment, he voiced the anger he'd repressed about his masculine and feminine identifications—anger he'd felt would make his mother label him "a rough, hairy killer." Expressing and confronting this anger allowed him to move on. He felt freer to develop his masculine identity and began to go to a gym, develop his physique, and wear clothes that revealed his attractiveness and maleness.

Over time, he felt less driven to react to the needs of his mother and others like her. This allowed him to see that his wife wasn't at all like his mother. In fact, she wanted to talk meaningfully with him about his gender anxieties. Their ability to communicate and discuss their anxieties strengthened their marriage.

Masculinity and Victimhood

Admitting victimhood can feel like confessing to not being a man. "Being a man" means being powerful, in control. This idea is so deeply embedded in our language that when used as a verb, the word *man* means "be in charge" (as in "Man the ship!"). The need to "be a man" makes many sexually betrayed men feel responsible for their victimization. But, of course, little boys don't have the power to stop sexual predators.

Maybe thinking you haven't lived up to the "requirements" of masculinity left you feeling flawed. As one sexually abused man put it, "I have a sense of being ruined, a foundation of shame I take with me everywhere." Another bitterly told his psychologist, "I'm not a man, I'm a victim." It's as if you can be either a man or a victim but not both.

Accepting having been sexually victimized means you have to give up the belief you were in control. Giving up that belief is particularly tough if it was formed around the time of the original abuse. Once it was formed, it was probably as frozen in place as your memory of sexual betrayal. As you were being betrayed, you may have quickly made the mental adjustments necessary to believe you'd arranged the abuse. That would be more acceptable than believing you were a victim. It's hard for a man to rethink such a fundamental idea, especially if he's believed it for thirty or forty years.

BROOKE: Redefining an Old Self-Image

Brooke Hopkins, a college professor who has written with great frankness about his childhood betrayal, reflected on how different his experience seemed from more common stories about adult men molesting young girls: "The standard roles were reversed," he wrote. "I was the active party, while my mother's role was almost completely passive." He'd thought this way for decades. After all, when his mother came to his bed, as he saw it, she sleepily "allowed" him to touch her sexually, meaning it was his idea.

But as a reflective adult trying to free himself from betrayal, Brooke reminded himself that he didn't choose to sleep with her. She came into his bed at her own initiative, surely knowing better. And his father permitted it to happen, night after night, week after week.

Brooke forced himself to rethink the circumstances of his abuse. Accepting that he'd been a "passive" boy—a victim of his own mother—took time, maturity, and self-honesty. His long struggle to change his mind about events from decades earlier shows us the power of cultural expectations that boys and men are the active partners in sexual activity.

Five Paths to Masculinity

The three images we've talked about—the man you are, the man you want to become, and the man the world wants you to be—all have their own demands. If you were sexually betrayed, these demands are in conflict. As long as they're in conflict, you will be in conflict, too.

How do you end this conflict? You must negotiate with these images, redefine them, and accept them. If you're an adult, these images have been around a long time, so your work won't be easy. Until now, you've struggled to be a man, however you defined manhood. The course you took was largely based on who you already were when you were abused. You probably didn't understand this, but your choice of paths started to be defined the moment you were betrayed.

Although every man's path is unique, there are five common paths men take when trying to resolve abuse. They can be so ingrained that they're not really choices. Rather, they reflect how you've responded to conflicts among your self-images as a man. All of these paths have pitfalls, and most of them ultimately fail.

1. Altering Reality

In order to feel masculine, you may have altered your perception of reality. Maybe you rearranged the world as a sort of "first aid" for yourself.

One way to do this is to deny the abuse occurred at all. As Seth, whom we'll discuss in a moment, said to his abuser the next morning, "Last night never happened!" But this works better for a boy than a man.

As you grew older and rethought what happened, maybe you started to deal with it another way. Rigidly maintaining that nothing happened can push you to have dissociative episodes—bewildering, painful, frightening states of mind in which things usually associated with one another are disconnected. We'll discuss this in chapter 4.

Sometimes men rewrite history, changing troubling experiences so that they seem benign or pleasurable. Research shows that boys often say their abuse was unwanted if they're asked shortly after the incident. (Of course, most boys are not asked because they don't reveal they were abused.) They soon shift their feelings, however. Later, boys often say their abuse was a positive experience, or at least not negative. They may even boast how lucky they were to have been sexually initiated early. (We'll talk more about this in chapter 7.) Only in adulthood do they connect current life problems back to their victimization.

JARED: Remembering How It Really Felt

As a seven-year-old, Jared met a seventeen-year-old who engaged him in sex. Jared told me this made him feel happy and loved. He'd been a very lonely little boy.

But was he loved? He revealed a disturbing fact while describing these feelings of acceptance and love. When they were almost discovered having sex, his abuser put Jared out a window to wander home alone at night, crying—hardly a sign he cared for Jared. Then he abruptly stopped their "friendship." Jared was heartbroken.

Jared was delighted and thrilled to be befriended by this teenager. He was inconsolable about how things ended. Yet he later remembered his experience as a happy one. He'd had to rework his idea of what it meant to be a victim. Feeling "loved" was how he explained things to himself.

Jared reacted to his abuse by changing his recollection into something less toxic to reassure himself that he had control of his life. But as an adult, he endured severe difficulties in his relationships, always expecting to be abandoned by people he cared about. With bravery and hard work, he eventually saw what really happened, how unhappy he'd been, and how much he hadn't been in charge of his life.

2. Giving Up

Some betrayed boys give up trying to be masculine as defined by our culture. They become passive and isolated. If you took this direction, maybe you settled for jobs and situations below your abilities. Maybe you gave up your capacity for anger. Your lack of aggression may have set you up for further victimization, reinforcing the idea that you're a victim who can't win. Recall how Isaac remained boylike well into his forties, making himself an easy sexual victim.

Sexually abused men who give up on masculinity may feel sexual anxiety around other men, even men they believe aren't sexually interested in them. They may be uncomfortable undressing in locker rooms, urinating in public lavatories, participating in traditional masculine activities, or even being alone with other men. They may lead isolated, lonely lives, with few if any same-sex friendships.

Why would a man have sexually based wariness and revulsion about men with no sexual interest in him? He might believe his masculinity has been destroyed, nothing can make it right again, and the piece of him that makes him male is missing. So he feels exposed around other men, afraid they'll see he's not a "real man." Fearing this would expose him to further humiliation, ridicule, and shame, he avoids relationships with other men to ensure he won't be disgraced.

SETH: Passively Fearing Other Men

Seth felt a continual sense of contempt from men, especially men in groups. Although frightened of men, he also longed desperately to be accepted by them and treated like an equal.

Seth's fears propelled him into a self-fulfilling cycle that worsened over time. Because of his insecurity, his behavior communicated his sense of helplessness. Picking on vulnerable people is one way men use to prove their masculinity to themselves, so some men took this as an invitation to mistreat him, making him feel even more threatened and insecure.

For example, Seth's job required him to drive from one place to another. One day, he discovered his car was missing from a company parking lot. When he asked his coworkers where it was, they smirked knowingly at one another. He knew they were lying when they claimed they didn't know what happened to his car. He tried to treat it as a joke, but they started to get nasty, especially when he flushed and eventually wept in exasperation and helplessness. The men derisively mimicked his crying as he got angrier and angrier. Finally, they told him they'd lent Seth's car to another worker who needed to take his wife to the hospital.

Seth felt as he had since childhood—that men who considered him odd and unmale had turned him into a victimized fool. He'd always felt a sense of apartness because of his interest in solitary, artistic activities and his dislike of team sports. This feeling intensified after his molestation.

When he and I met, he felt panicky and had difficulty staying in the room with me. He had to struggle to let down his guard in his therapy group for sexually abused men. Eventually, though, he overcame his fears and began to feel accepted. He said with elation that he finally belonged in a group of men rather than being the odd one out.

Seth's positive experiences in his men's group led to his becoming more relaxed and assertive with men in other areas of his life. This helped him to develop a general ease and sense of camaraderie with men that he'd never experienced before.

3. Fighting Blindly

Men in our culture are expected to fight back. Some betrayed boys and men fight back without knowing or caring why. They may resort to extreme measures to convince themselves that they have authority over their lives. They're not reflective about their behavior, even when they hurt someone else. This creates problems for them both internally and in their relationships.

As they struggle for a sense of masculinity and for power and control over their lives, they may identify with their abusers so that they can bond, feel stronger, and find safety. Bonding with other men helps them feel mutually invincible.

Men are especially likely to identify with their abusers if they believe being a victim means being feminine. That's intolerable to them. They calm their fears by becoming excessively "masculine," or *hypermasculine*.

A hypermasculine man may be a tyrannical boss at work or a demeaning dictator at home. He may be a sexual conqueror, a Don Juan constantly proving to himself what a stud he is, callous to the feelings of his sexual partners, eternally demonstrating to himself that he can dominate others.

These men often become addicted to gambling, alcohol, drugs, work, and even exercise. It's not uncommon for them to be sexually compulsive, always on the hunt for more encounters. Worse, they can be sexually predatory, becoming abusers themselves. (We'll talk more about this in chapter 9.)

A man like this tries to be the masculine ideal: independent, competitive, resilient. He may have outbursts of anger and rage, but otherwise he expresses few emotions. He leads an action-filled life, too busy to permit himself self-reflection. He's rarely able to empathize with other people's feelings. He may be so engaged in activities that "prove" how manly he is that the rest of his life suffers.

He doesn't make connections between how he deals with the world and the boyhood betrayal he suffered. When he denies childhood victimization and fights off pain and shame, he rarely makes progress. Unfortunately, he's not likely to enter psychotherapy, for he cannot bear to feel needy, as people often do when they start treatment. One way or another, he's likely to be antisocial, so he often gets in trouble with the law. Men like this are often found in prisons, eager to fight and brawl.

Fortunately, most men who were sexually abused are not like this. Most actually become more empathic than nonabused men. Over time, they often become less constrained by the rules of masculinity than other men.

4. Fighting Reflectively

If you've been conscious of your betrayal, you may engage in an endless struggle, on the one hand attempting to "be a man" rather than a victim, and on the other trying to deal with your abuse. You may at times endeavor to become supermasculine and at other times become self-reflective and emotional. Reflective men seem to be the most ready to seek help and engage in psychotherapy. This seems to occur most frequently when they're in their thirties or forties, the time of life when sexually abused men are most likely to attempt to confront their histories directly. They've discovered the hard way that denying, ignoring, or soothing their pain through compulsions and addictions just doesn't work. Many of the men described throughout this book find themselves on this path.

PETER: The Throwaway Boy

When Peter was ten, his uncle Luke started to invite him for car rides. Uncle Luke showed him pornography and gradually taught Peter to masturbate himself and Uncle Luke. This went on for several years. Peter was never sure why he went along with this. The pornography was exciting, but he didn't really like his uncle, who often gave him the creeps. Still, there was something about Uncle Luke's wink and smile as he invited Peter to come for a ride that made Peter feel grown up, one of the guys. But afterward, Uncle Luke would disappear without a word as soon as he dropped Peter off at home, leaving Peter feeling soiled, disgusted, and disgusting.

Most of the boys in Peter's large extended family became very troubled young men. One committed suicide, and others were alcoholics or drug abusers. Few fulfilled the promise their intelligence and education would suggest. As an adult, Peter came to believe that before Uncle Luke died, he probably abused most of these cousins.

As in many families where incest exists, no one talked about the problem, even though Peter believes his father sensed what was happening. Silence allowed the abuse to continue. And it only made things worse for Peter: he felt his parents permitted the abuse.

During adolescence, Peter started drinking and quickly got involved with drugs. From there, it was an easy transition to small-time drug dealing. The police picked him up more than once, although he was never arrested. He got into serious fights with other drug dealers in which he could easily have killed someone or been killed.

By seventeen, Peter was a chronic, severe alcoholic and drug abuser. His family pressed him to go to rehab, and to his credit, he agreed to go and stopped both drinking and drugs. Yet, despite having finished an advanced degree and starting a lucrative career, Peter's life didn't reflect his potential. He had an excellent salary but he lived in a grungy apartment. He tracked his investments incessantly. When he had trouble going to sleep at night, he'd soothe himself by counting his money and imagining how he'd spend it on houses, vacations, and cars. But he never bought those things. He was afraid to spend his resources, so he stayed in his threadbare apartment, living like a mole.

While careful about staying away from alcohol and drugs, Peter became sexually compulsive. He picked up prostitutes and enjoyed watching them "humiliate themselves" by servicing him. He felt whole and healthy in comparison to them, yet afterward he felt dirty and degraded. When he wasn't having sex with prostitutes, he obsessed about them, or prowled through areas they frequented, or went to massage parlors and topless bars, or planned the next time he would pick one up.

Peter acquired a sexually transmitted disease but didn't get treatment for a long time. He thought of himself as a kind of throwaway, almost like a packet of ketchup you'd get with a fast-food hamburger, a man without worth. When he had girlfriends, he became uneasy and apprehensive if they got close to him emotionally. He constantly found reasons to pull back from them during intimate moments. Each of these affairs ended badly.

"I'm always great at the beginning," he told me. "I know how to make myself charming and attentive. We have fun, and each time I really believe things will be different. But I can't do the long haul. I always feel she's too much in my space, or trying to exploit me for my money. It makes me start to take things out on her, making her back off from me enough so I can breathe. But then that's it. The beginning of the end."

Although superficially friendly to everyone, Peter had only one friend, a man he'd originally met as a teenager in rehab. "I always think people wouldn't want to know me if they knew how far I sank. It doesn't matter that I seem to be doing okay now. I know damn well that inside I'm as sick a puppy as I ever was. So I keep my distance."

Peter was discontented with his sparse, isolated life. He yearned to feel close to a woman, to marry and have children. "I want to live out the American dream—a house in the suburbs, white picket fence and all, coming home to my loving wife, three children, and two dogs." He had dreams about being a man who could manage relationships, a man who wasn't frightened and vulnerable when he got close to someone.

The difference between the life he was leading at age thirty and the life he wanted to lead made Peter commit to examining himself in depth. He struggled to stay close enough to his current girlfriend so that they could work out a mutually satisfying relationship. He even told her about some of his struggles. While she was sympathetic about his boyhood abuse, she pushed him to stay emotionally involved with her as he faced his past. She was willing to give him breathing room but didn't let him use his past as an excuse to stay away from her. Their relationship was stormy as they dealt with the contrast between her easygoing attitude toward money and his frugality, the numbness he often felt during sex, and other complicated problems.

With time, Peter learned to track how he pulled back from his girlfriend by going to massage parlors and topless bars or using work commitments to keep his distance from her. He wasn't always able to stop himself from these pullbacks, but his need to stay remote gradually became less urgent. His sexual compulsion continued, but he was more in control of when and how often he acted on it.

In his therapy, Peter saw unmistakably how his sexual compulsivity resulted from being overstimulated before he could manage adult sexual feelings. He recognized how his frozen feelings in relationships dated back to Uncle Luke and to his family's denial of problems. Although his parents pressured him to start rehab, they never acknowledged their inability to protect their children from Uncle Luke. Peter never confronted them with what his uncle did, but he did develop more direct relationships with them.

In turn, this helped him develop other relationships of substance. He found male friends with whom he was happy to spend time, although in small doses. Four years after starting therapy, he and his girlfriend married. He knew he still had inner work to do, but he felt ready to proceed toward being the man he wanted to be and living the life he wanted.

5. Redefining Masculinity

The final path you can take after betrayal involves changing your idea of what a man should be. You can redefine masculinity in a realistic way that reflects both your own identity and a new masculine ideal—a way that's more forgiving, more enlightened, and more human.

To redefine masculinity, you must understand where your own feelings about masculinity come from and why they exist. Let's look at some of our culture's rules:

- Men are mentally and physically tough.

- Men are never penetrated or subdued.

- Men are always in control.

- Men are powerful.

- Men can't be victims.

- Only women and weaklings are penetrated.

You've been aware of these rules since early childhood, but you don't have to accept them. Rules can change.

You have the right and the power to create your own definition of masculinity that is just as valid as anyone else's. So far, you may have distorted your experience to reassure yourself of your masculinity.

- Maybe you decided that your early sexual experience was a sexual initiation or rite of passage rather than abuse, especially if your abuser was female.

- Maybe you denied you were penetrated or otherwise victimized, reassuring yourself how masculine and powerful you are.

- Maybe you learned to control other people (and thus feel more powerful) by manipulating them.

Recovering from boyhood sexual betrayal requires that you take a long look at yourself and see how you tried to assuage your pain by bolstering your masculinity. Then you must develop new, more flexible conceptions of masculinity.

Your Many Masculine Selves

The depth and virtuosity of the human spirit give us the ability to express ourselves in diverse ways. You can shift your state of mind from one moment to the next, depending on what you're doing, who you're with, where you are, and how you feel.

For example, you may wake up in bed next to your partner or spouse. At that moment, you're primarily a lover. Then you go into the kitchen to make breakfast for the family and fluidly change into being a nurturer. Soon you're dressed and off to work, where you quickly become a breadwinner. At work, you shift rapidly over the course of the day from being a worker to being a supervisor, to being a coworker's friend, to being all the roles your job requires. In a sense, these states of mind are like different selves that make up a totality of your one self. We'll talk more about these selves in chapter 4.

Of course, you're probably recognizable to yourself as the same person and rarely think about the different selves you are over the course of the day. This is because in most cases you can make transitions smoothly, without deliberation. Healthy adults readily shift among the different people they need to be in life—for example, from neediness to assertiveness, or from sexual dominance to sympathy, depending on what's happening at the moment.

But betrayed men often have only limited selves available to them. These are often selves that relate to the world in very specific ways. One self may believe all men are predators. Another knows only one way to get its way: by acting seductively. See if you recognize any of these "masculine" selves within you:

- The inexpressive, emotionally flat self

- The compulsive, endlessly busy self

- The needy self
- The victim self
- The controlling self
- The feminized self
- The sexually conquering self
- The supermasculine self
- The angry, abusive self
- The boy self

Rigidly keeping to selves like these and being unable to shift to others doesn't allow you to live fully, to adapt and change as you move from one life situation to another. It's not only limiting but unhealthy and even hurtful. It's as if you have only ten words in your vocabulary that you must use no matter what you really need to say. If you knew only ten words of Chinese, how fully could you experience life if you moved to China? And how fully—and fairly—would the Chinese experience you?

The capacity to express multiple qualities is a sign that you're psychologically at peace with yourself. Healthy men and women move with ease among their many selves.

If you were betrayed as a child, you may lack that effortless ability. It may feel like there's a jagged edge between different ways of being, a chasm between your selves that's hard to bridge. If so, know that it's possible to move between your different selves. One way to begin is to create your own definition of masculinity.

Your New Masculinity

To find peace, reinvigorate your life, and live more fully, you need to independently define for yourself what it means to be a man. This requires courage. You must see your three self-images clearly and look at your old heroes without the boyish awe that made them both surreal and unalterable. You must understand that mythical heroes never existed and that the real-life heroes you may have worshipped are as human as you are.

You must accept that *every* person has both masculine and feminine characteristics. Your definitions of both genders can change without causing the world to fall apart.

Many men I've seen originally took refuge from their internal pain in behaviors that numbed them. Trapped by masculine gender expectations and dazed by the trio of man images fighting within them, they became addicted: to alcohol, drugs, overeating, gambling, pornography, or other compulsive sexual activities. Peter, and as we'll see later, Abe, Devin, Keith, and Patrick, went through prolonged periods when they used addictions to cope with their overwhelming inner worlds. In the short term, these addictions soothed and numbed their problems without challenging their self-concepts as men. Over time, though, these men's lives deteriorated to the point of crisis or despair before they finally left behind much of their pain as they discovered a new kind of masculinity.

If you take this path, you'll have to set aside some ideas about men and women. You'll decide for yourself what gender really means and whether it makes sense to live by rules set long ago by tribes of spear-throwers. You'll consider whether some characteristics you once thought of as solely feminine can also be masculine.

A wise psychiatrist named Harry Stack Sullivan once said, "Everyone is more simply human than otherwise." As you consider gender, you'll realize that many qualities are neither masculine nor feminine but simply human. The abilities to acknowledge fear, be vulnerable, and express emotions are neither masculine nor feminine. They are human capacities. People who have these abilities are more fully human. The truer we are to our humanity, the better it is for us and for others.

Redefining what it means to be a man involves questioning traditional ideas. You'll have to analyze whether victimization makes a statement about the victim's masculinity or femininity. You'll come to understand that sexual abuse results from the moral turpitude of the perpetrator, from the abuser's desire to use power over another person, and from the victimizer's need to soothe his or her own anxiety in a particularly terrible way.

Maybe you'll decide men can express emotional pain and still be men. Maybe you'll learn to encounter your sexuality, sexual orientation, and gender identity without having to numb yourself out.

In short, you'll use your life experiences more fluidly and express yourself more fully. You'll be a man more naturally in charge of your life than you were when you were desperately trying to control it all the time. You'll learn to absorb your childhood experiences without disabling yourself.

It's painful to face those ordeals, but it's necessary in order to heal. Recovery requires letting the trauma become just another part of your history, as when you broke your arm as a boy. Your sexual betrayal will be there in the background like everything else that happened to you. But it won't painfully occupy center stage all the time, seizing you unexpectedly with terror or rage. Instead, memories may reemerge from time to time in a simpler, less disturbing way, then recede again like any ordinary memory, allowing you to proceed with your life. It's that ease between one mental state and another that's your goal.

While fluidity is the objective, getting there is a complicated, challenging task. Entering psychotherapy can be especially difficult for men. For some of us, getting help is an acknowledgment of weakness. We don't want to feel like we're incapable of running our lives. It can be embarrassing, even humiliating, to sit with a therapist, wondering if he or she is making judgments, evaluating you, uncovering your secrets. But overcoming this reluctance may be your first step on a new path toward a life where the real test of a man is how fully human he can be. Getting there is worth the trip.

3

Boundaries in Relationships

In a relationship, a boundary is where you "end" and another person "begins." Boundaries are borders defining your personal space. Your boundaries have developed as you've matured and learned who you are. With time, you can also learn to change them.

Boundaries can shift from one situation to another. In a crowded elevator, you may feel some discomfort, signaling that your boundaries are, by necessity, temporarily compressed. But if you want privacy and go into a room to be alone, the room's walls become your boundaries. People coming into the room—especially if they know you want privacy or they don't knock before entering—are crossing your boundaries. This may feel like a violation.

Boundaries enclose more than just your body. Your private thoughts occur within your personal boundaries. So do your private conversations. Perhaps this is why in the age of cell phones it can be unsettling to overhear one side of a person's private conversation—you are unwillingly violating that person's boundaries. And, of course, that person is violating your boundaries by talking in your space when you want quiet.

When people's houses and apartments are burglarized, they'll often say they feel raped. This is because their boundaries were violated by the burglar. Your private spaces—your home, your car, your office— constitute boundaries even when you're not in them.

Much of the courtesy between people is a matter of respecting boundaries: knocking on a door before entering, being quiet while someone sleeps, not smoking around nonsmokers, not staring at someone undressing in the locker room, not keeping a friend on the phone for a long chat when you know his dinner is on the table. The word *courtesy* itself is derived from the Latin word *curt*, meaning "yard" or "enclosure." To be courteous is to be respectful of another person's enclosure.

The role you're expected to play in a relationship dictates the relationship's boundaries. Your banker, for example, cashes your paycheck for you. You don't expect him to advise you on how to manage your cholesterol levels or to ask about your sex life. The bus driver you only know by the name on her badge is expected to drive the bus. You don't expect her to follow you uninvited into your house, open your refrigerator, and help herself to a beer. You don't even expect her to *ask* if she can have a beer, unless you've demonstrated you want to be her friend. Your discomfort in these situations signals that your boundaries have been disregarded, imposed upon, threatened, blurred, or violated.

Boundary Violations

People respond to boundary violations in different ways. You may recognize some of these reactions:

- Shock
- Indignation
- Rage
- Fear
- Disappointment
- Disillusionment
- Feeling like giving up
- Loss of self-confidence and self-esteem

- Depression
- Confusion
- An urge to fight
- An urge to flee
- Tension
- Stress
- Blushing
- Dissociation

If you were sexually abused, your boundaries were discounted, muddied, weakened, confused, and assaulted. It's bad enough when an adult has his boundaries violated. It's worse when a child, whose boundaries are not yet even fully formed, has them intruded upon. It's hard to build your own house if someone else comes in and moves the walls to suit himself, or puts in doors where you want windows, or decides to build a tennis court in the exact spot you intended to plant a garden.

If your developing boundaries were routinely violated, you've probably had difficulty developing into an independent, self-determined person. Maybe you feel steered or influenced by others to act according to their wishes and expectations, regardless of your own needs. Maybe you have trouble sorting out your real relationship with another person. Maybe you disclose too much personal information about yourself to the wrong people. Maybe you shut out intimate friends or even withdraw from human contact.

Perhaps you have a hard time deciding what your personal boundaries should be and then establishing and protecting them. This sets up problems in your relationships.

Boundaries within the Family

Every family has its own style of dealing with boundaries, from the way family members respect one another's personal space to their expectations of each other according to their ages and generations. For example, parents are responsible for making rules and decisions that affect their children. These create a kind of boundary that shifts in nature as the child matures and is allowed to give more input into how these rules and decisions are made.

Parents need a different kind of boundary with one another. If they have a good relationship, parents can maintain an ebb and flow between intimacy and individuality. They know how to relate intimately when they want to, but can also pull back smoothly from each other when they have separate needs and desires.

Sometimes, family members distort the boundaries between them by ignoring their fundamental roles in the family structure. For example, a parent may treat a child as a spouse, or one spouse may treat the other as a child. When this happens, it means boundaries have been inappropriately drawn, usually with negative effects. If some members of a family regularly violate and disregard others' boundaries, problems arise. No one maintains a strong, healthy identity.

Every family member needs private time and space. Children need it in order to learn they can take care of themselves. Parents need it in order to maintain separate identities and nurture themselves. In creating this privacy, however, they also teach their children by example how to establish and preserve relationships. Children who don't learn they can be independent won't become independent adults.

If parents allow a child to come and go into their bedroom at will, the child won't learn that people need privacy. Nor will he learn how to be independent. Closing the bedroom door helps children learn to grow up and take care of themselves.

Incest and Boundaries

Incest is an extreme form of boundary violation. This criminal behavior profoundly affects a child's personality, especially if the abuse goes on for an extended period. Unfortunately, this is exactly what happens to many boys, and they suffer repeated boundary violations.

If this happened to you, it may markedly influence how you relate to others. Maybe you can't be flexible in relationships. Maybe you see others in a distorted manner, overemphasizing their failures and misinterpreting their intentions. Maybe you idealize them, failing to see them as ordinary human beings. Or maybe you allow yourself to be recurringly victimized in everyday life.

Maybe you have difficulty maintaining close and intimate friendships or good relationships with employers and coworkers. Relationship problems affect your outlook on life. They isolate you, feed your anger, deepen your sense of hopelessness, and reinforce your inner sense that you're a victim.

It's possible for boundaries to be violated even when incest doesn't involve physical sex. For example, you may have felt seductive energy from a parent or other family member. Or you may have been exposed to sexual activities or pornography when you needed your sexual thoughts to be private and of your own choosing. If you faced situations like these, you may have as much trouble with boundaries in adult relationships as people who suffered actual physical sexual abuse in childhood.

Distorting Parent–Child Boundaries

As a child, your key relationships were with your parents or other primary caretakers. If boundaries between you and them were distorted or violated, it's important to consider how that happened.

Reversing Roles

One way a parent may violate or blur a boundary is to reverse roles. For example, rather than nurturing you, your parent may have demanded to be nurtured. If you learned you must unfailingly please or take care of a parent, you were obeying an unspoken command to sacrifice your own needs for the wishes and desires of that parent.

Even if your parent or other caregiver only expected you to take care of his or her nonsexual needs, this could still have been inappropriate. Ira wasn't sexually abused by his mother. But her need for attention and nurturing taught him to take care of women. So when his unhappy older sister initiated sex play, he agreed even though he wasn't really interested. Later, although he wasn't especially attracted to her, he became his professor's boyfriend when she asked him to think of her as a woman rather than a professor. You'll learn more about Ira in chapter 7.

Another kind of role reversal may have occurred if your parent asked you to become more like a spouse than a child. Marital problems between parents can affect boundaries throughout the entire family. Sexual energy that would ordinarily flow between your parents might have been misdirected toward you. This may have been worse if one or both of them abused alcohol or other substances to relieve stress. Or if your mother received no affection from her husband, perhaps she inappropriately sought it from you. If so, you became a substitute husband and friend.

If this happened, maybe you felt great love as well as anger or hatred for your parent/abuser. If you were ambivalent, you may not have been aware of both sets of feelings. Or if you were aware of them, you may not have recognized their contradiction, which we'll discuss in chapter 8.

KEITH: Mom Was My Drinking Buddy

Keith was ambivalent about being his mother's substitute spouse. But he went through a period when he only allowed the positive side of his feelings for her into awareness. During that time, though, she disregarded her role as a mother and encouraged him to be her confidant and drinking buddy. As he healed, he saw he'd also been very angry at her.

When Keith was six or seven, he heard about a movie that had naked women in it. He asked his parents if he could see it. When they asked him why, he said he wanted to see these naked women. His father offered to show him his *Playboy* magazines instead, while his mother said, "If you want to see naked women, why don't I take my clothes off and you can look at me?"

He felt confused and repulsed. He didn't want to look at *Playboy* with his father and he certainly hadn't asked to see his mother naked. But at his age, he didn't have the language available to explain any of this to them. Instead, he felt shamed by his request, although he didn't know exactly why.

"I learned from the incident that it was wrong of me to want to see the movie," he told me, "but I didn't understand the reasons." He never again discussed sexuality of any kind with either parent.

Keith's mother had been sexually abused by her own father. She was bitter about her relationships with him and her philandering husband. "My mother hated men, really hated them," he said. "I wonder how that has affected me?" During therapy, he began to understand the answer to this question as he realized how he shied away from doing "manly" things that would remind his mother of his maleness. But then he resented having to give up his masculinity for her.

When a boy's boundaries are violated, he may experience difficulty separating his own self from the people who take care of him and/or abuse him. This is called *merging*. Keith merged with his mother. Shortly after divorcing his father, Keith's mother began to pick Keith up from high school in her car, bringing along a six pack of beer to share with him. She was chronically depressed, angry at men, needy, and heading toward alcoholism. Keith became her drinking companion. In doing so, he lost her as a mother.

Keith often got into trouble. He had a severe drug and alcohol problem from the time he was twelve. He drank; used pot, LSD, and mescaline; and at age fifteen moved on to virtually any drug he could find.

By the time he was sixteen, he was drinking every day, often with his mother. "Me and my mom were kicked out of a bar together—we were getting rowdy and they finally decided to ask me for my ID. Then my mom got mean and started hitting them. We were soon out on our asses."

Keith was "completely addicted" from age eighteen to twenty-three: "By eighteen I realized I was an alcoholic. I drank more and more viciously. I'd easily drink a quart of vodka at a time. I'd wake up in the morning and take speed to get rid of the DTs, then I'd drink continuously all day, then at night I'd take coke to prevent blackouts." At twenty-three, he entered a detox program and succeeded in giving up drugs and alcohol.

Once he controlled his addictions, Keith realized how ambivalent he felt about his mother. Although it had been fun to be drinking with her when he was a teenager, he was angry that she encouraged him to abuse alcohol, made him her companion, drew him into her neediness, and failed to act like a mother. He understood that much of his misbehavior as a youth had been his way of acting out his anger toward her. Over time, he continued to improve and began a rewarding career.

Competing for a Son's Loyalty

When parents don't get along, they sometimes erect rigid boundaries between themselves to the point where they try to ignore one another completely. Instead, they turn their attention to their children in ways that violate the children's boundaries. Each tries to recruit the child to his or her side.

DAVID: Taking Sides

David was put in the terrible situation of feeling forced to take sides against each of his parents on behalf of the other. At twenty-three, he was dealing with this in a way that was at once ingenious and nearly tragic.

When I met him, David had just been released from a psychiatric hospital and was still suffering from severe depression. He was experiencing mood swings, chronic boredom, and emptiness. He was impulsive with money. He hadn't been able to even begin making long-term plans for his life. He was spending most of his days at home in bed, rarely attending classes at junior college, going out most nights to clubs and discos, and usually returning home drunk early in the morning.

David's parents were both Holocaust survivors whose entire families had been murdered. They met and married in a displaced persons camp after World War II. Born in a small village in Eastern Europe and with few cultural pretensions, David's father had nevertheless trained as a professional. David's mother originally came from a wealthy family in a large cultural center. A teenager at the beginning of World War II, she'd attended a finishing school and was tutored in music and art.

David's parents had apparently been a mismatch from the beginning of their marriage. By the time David entered the psychiatric hospital, their marriage was filled with contempt, bitterness, and barely contained fury. David's mother was chronically depressed, while his father was exceptionally controlling. Each was in a rage at David for his inability to care for himself. Meanwhile, however, each parent also had a special relationship with David, an alliance against the other parent. They blamed each other for David's problems, and each tried to enlist David to take sides.

Despite his anger at David's irresponsibility about money and his own characteristic tightfistedness, David's father continued to supply his son with money for his nightly jaunts into the club scene. He even bought David a new car, all the while complaining that David's expenses would be his ruin. He also often asked about David's experiences with girls, leering and winking at him in a way that excluded David's mother. For her part, David's mother complained of chronic back pain and fatigue, yet she continued to make David's bed every day, cleaned his room, and massaged his bare legs and back.

When David was around both parents, he remained quiet and withdrawn. But when alone with either of them, he came to life and shared private jokes, often about the other parent.

The boundary violations that occurred in this family didn't involve blatant sexual acts, but David's relationship with each parent involved erotic elements. His mother massaging his bare legs and his father leering and asking about details of his sex life were both violations of the boundaries that normally define a parent's role with a twenty-three-year-old. The bitter distance between mother and father and the close ties each of them had with David also distorted the family boundaries.

David became much better after I told the family that his behavior was a self-sacrificing way to keep them together. His depression and inability to mature were his way to force his parents to relate to one another. His parents resisted the idea that their son was sacrificing himself in order to save the family. But they began to react in more healthy ways, and David improved tremendously after I repeatedly congratulated him on his skill at keeping his parents together. Over a long time, David joined others his own age in starting a life for himself.

The Effect of Boundary Violations on Everyday Life

Relationships require boundaries. When they're missing, people feel merged together, unable to act for themselves. At the other extreme, boundaries can be too rigid. If you have rigid boundaries, it's hard to accept the give and take of relationships.

Healthy people are able to adapt their boundaries as they move through life. They accept that people are human and that every human makes mistakes. They accept that on occasion they'll bear the brunt of someone else's insensitivity, greed, or anger. At the same time they feel internally strong and able to swiftly recover from life's complications. They don't allow themselves to become perpetual victims.

If you were sexually betrayed, a criminal trespass was made into the sovereign territory of your mind, body, and soul. Your boundaries were attacked. Perhaps you've grown up without fully repairing them.

Maybe you have difficulty seeing how you fit into the world. Maybe you have trouble recognizing other people's boundaries and respecting them. Maybe you feel different without understanding why. Any physical or psychological touch from another person may be overwhelming, even if you recognize the other person is well meaning.

You may not know how much to disclose of your inner life and to whom. Abe, whom you will read about in later chapters, said, "I always spill the beans too much and always regret it."

Getting close to someone can be threatening and uncomfortable. Seth, whose story we discussed earlier, seemed friendly enough in the company of others. But he said the only place in the world where he felt truly safe was in his canoe, "alone and with lots of water between me and the next nearest person."

Beau, whom you will read about in chapter 6, was raped and severely abused both sexually and psychologically by numerous people. He noticed he never had his disabling anxiety attacks when he was alone in his room, "just me and the four walls," weekend after weekend. But he was terrified that having to go to these lengths to preserve his boundaries meant he was destined to be alone the rest of his life.

You may give up your autonomy. Andreas, whom we discussed earlier, functioned superbly at work but at great inner cost. "My boss said to me, 'Why do you think you keep getting the employee of the month award? You never say no!' After he said that, I fell apart." Andreas saw how his superiors often made inappropriate requests. His compliance was a psychological repetition of his boyhood betrayal, when he'd meet his abusers' demands, returning to them week after week for further molestation. Musing on his tendency to lose himself in others' requirements and needs, he said, "I do what others want and do what others want, and then when I look in the mirror there's no one there."

Sometimes boys can even create boundaries within their own flesh. In Quinn's young adulthood, he'd been athletic and muscular. Women were attracted to him, but this only made him feel uptight and bewildered. Unable to manage these complicated relationships, he built up a wall of fat that saved him from them by rendering him both unattractive and unapproachable. His weight was an armor he'd built up for two purposes: First, his massiveness made him a man who no one would likely confront or abuse. Second, his weight protected him from being an object of desire. (You will read about Quinn in chapter 8.)

Fortunately, you can learn at any age to re-form your boundaries. Keith, who had to separate from his mother to get sober, at first created ultra-rigid boundaries to keep her alcoholism out of his life. Later, he realized that they weren't necessary or appropriate with most other people. He learned he could create more flexible boundaries, allowing himself to live with greater ease and develop healthier relationships.

Your childhood boundary violations aren't the sole cause of all your problems. Developing healthy boundaries, however, is critical to restoring the life and integrity you deserve. Fortunately, you can learn how to reclaim your territory. You can learn how to develop and maintain healthy boundaries.

Using Daydreams

Sometimes a boy who can't define and protect his borders in the real world builds boundaries in his fantasy life. His experiences prevent him from maintaining the boundaries he needs, so he builds them inside his head as a way of keeping some sense, however small, of himself as a separate person.

If you were sexually betrayed in boyhood, you may have spent a lot of time daydreaming. Perhaps your fantasies have developed to the point where they practically have a life of their own, taking over your mind even when the real world needs your attention. If you've spent much of your life daydreaming, you may find that when you're with another person (intimately or otherwise) your mind is somewhere else. Your daydreams may be intense and powerful, but they can negatively affect your real relationships and, in turn, your feelings about yourself.

PATRICK: Watching the World from a Tower

Patrick is a charming and articulate gay man. But when he first came to me, he was very depressed. He felt lonely and isolated. He had a hard time in relationships. He had frequent nightmares about strangers breaking into his room. And he was obsessed with impersonal sexual fantasies.

The fifth of nine children in a middle-class family with two alcoholic parents, Patrick is himself a recovering alcoholic, as are several of his siblings. As a teenager, he'd had an extended sexual relationship with his three-year-younger brother. Then, at seventeen, he'd actively attempted (but failed) to initiate sex with his father. He later learned that his brother had also attempted unsuccessfully to seduce his father during the same period. When he and his brother were adults, they'd once had sex together with a third man. This brother died of AIDS two years before I first met Patrick.

As he saw me over time, Patrick began to remember details of his early childhood. When he was only two or three, "the monster" would come into his room at night and fondle him. Later, he remembered that the monster was his father and that he'd often raped Patrick orally, banging his head against walls during the rape, then leading him crying back to bed after ejaculating in his mouth. Patrick also began to recall memories of being anally assaulted and penetrated by a twelve-year-old brother when he was six.

One day he had a vague sense of his mother there afterward, wiping his mouth or anus clean but saying nothing about the molestations. He was never sure whether this was a memory or a fantasy. This often happens when adults are trying to remember the murky details of their childhood. If you have a clear sense of having been abused, it may not be so important whether the specific details surrounding an event occurred exactly as you recall them. What matters most is how you experienced the abuse and how those experiences lodged in your psyche.

Patrick's impression that his mother cleaned him up conveys how he experienced his mother's role in the abuse. By not protecting Patrick, she was silently participating in incest. In her own way, she'd cooperated with his father's transgressions. She facilitated them passively, not opening her eyes to what was happening. If so, the "memory" about her cleaning up after him might have been a fantasy that conveys how her not seeing his hurt made her part of the problem. Alternatively, she may have really cooperated actively, in which case the memory was just that—a memory of how she knew but didn't protect Patrick.

In the memory/fantasy, Patrick's mother seemed loving to him as she cleaned and soothed him. He came to realize that this had only made him feel guilty. He felt he was the bad one for being angry at her. And because he was the bad one, he had no right to protest what happened.

Sometimes boys who were sexually betrayed will build psychological walls as they grow up that allow them to develop without exposing them to further hurt. Patrick did this. He built walls in his fantasy life. One fantasy was that he was inside a construction site surrounded by a plywood fence. There were holes in the plywood, and men urinated through these holes. He couldn't see these men, except for their penises. This both excited and frightened him. The fantasy allowed him to have sexual thoughts but keep them completely impersonal. He didn't feel the hurt of betrayal, but he was isolated and removed from other people.

In another fantasy, Patrick created a tower where he lived completely cut off from the outside world. His food was delivered to him through a mechanical device. He could watch the world, but he didn't have to participate in it. This fantasy made Patrick feel protected, but it also made him feel extremely isolated and lonely. He created an alternate personality, a child companion named Paddy who lived in the tower with him. No one in the world but Patrick knew about Paddy. This imaginary little boy kept him company but also became the part of Patrick that contained all his childhood terrors. Patrick was able to function better in the world by giving all these terrors to Paddy. Eventually, Patrick was able to come to terms with his need to protect himself in the fantasy tower he'd built. He and Paddy opened a hole in the tower and ventured out.

4

Not Knowing What You Know, Not Feeling What You Feel

If you were sexually abused, you may have lived in constant dread of what your abuser might do to you the next day. Maybe you feared that if people found out, you'd get in trouble, or you'd be responsible for splitting up your family or causing scandal. It's hard when you're a kid to live an ordinary existence—to go to school, involve yourself in sports, get interested in dating—when you're filled with rage and there's no way to talk about it or vent it without hurting someone else or yourself. It's hard to be in constant pain, to wonder whether someone really loves you or simply wants to use you.

It's too much for anyone to bear. Adults have enormous difficulty regaining serenity after betrayal. For children, it seems impossible. Yet if it happened to you, somehow you survived. You're here, you're safe, and you're reclaiming the tranquility you deserve.

How did you survive? When you were a boy, how did your mind respond to the impossible? How were you able to think about the unthinkable? Perhaps your mind dissociated many of your experiences.

Dissociation

Dissociation is the opposite of *association*. It means to sever or disconnect one set of mental contents from other sets. When certain thoughts, feelings, memories, sensations, behaviors, and knowledge would normally be associated with one another, dissociation "deassociates" them.

When you dissociate, your mind disconnects an unpleasant memory from the feelings you had about it, or detaches some of the facts from others, or separates the memory from your awareness altogether so that you don't have to think about it while you go about the business of your life. Dissociation takes the ingredients of a trauma and freezes them in time and space. This prevents them from combining and overwhelming you. Instead, the frozen memory elements remain out of contact with your consciousness, protecting you from a devastating emotional experience.

You can dissociate more than feelings and facts. You can also dissociate behavior—your physical actions. This explains why someone might comment on your facial expressions, for example, in a way that contrasts to feelings and thoughts filling your mind. One man told me that people often came up to him and said, "You have such a nice smile." This surprised him, because often when this occurred, he was concentrating on unpleasant and difficult problems. In fact, the more he smiled, the less happy he was likely to be. As a child he'd hid the truth of his unfolding tragedy by smiling.

Everybody dissociates to some degree. Daydreams occur in a dissociated state of mind. So do other everyday experiences such as a driving trance. Have you ever noticed when driving a car that you don't remember having driven the last twenty miles? You've been dissociating. The automatic act of driving—even turning corners, stopping at lights, passing cars—was disconnected from your conscious thoughts. This freed you to, say, use your mind to figure out a thorny problem as you drove.

Associations

As you go through life, your mind records your experiences. It's as if your brain were constantly writing down your life story, adding one sentence after the other. Anytime you want, you should be able to go back and read your story. Of course, no one recalls every detail of his life. Still, you know your own story remarkably well. You have a pretty good understanding of where you came from, how and why you got where you are today, and where you want to go.

Your story is the basis of who you are. It's the core of your personality, the way you perceive the world, the way you think. It provides you with your sense of your self.

As your mind records your life story, normally it does a good job of keeping things in place. It creates associations between them. This is how you can think of the word *sea* and easily associate it with *water* and *saltwater* and perhaps *waves* or *storms* or *ships*. You could go on forever, associating *ships* with *ocean liners* and from there perhaps the *Titanic*.

Associations help you make sense of the world. Understanding one thing requires relating it to another. After all, the idea of a ship makes no sense unless there's also water. Allowing yourself to perceive the relationships between people enables you to understand them. The more you understand one person's relationship to another and to you, the better you'll function in the world.

Associations allow you to make your way through new situations. For example, you may have never climbed a particular set of stairs before, but since you've climbed other stairs in your life, you know exactly what to do, even if the new stairs are a slightly different width and height. Your mind automatically associates one set of mental contents with another, taking past experiences, and, without any conscious effort on your part, making them part of your new ones.

How Trauma Affects Memories

If an experience is painful or overwhelming, your mind may not associate all the traumatic parts into your life story. It may put the entire trauma into a kind of closed container somewhere in your mind. Or it may take the trauma apart as it's happening, disconnecting each piece from your life story, even disconnecting one piece from another. These disconnected pieces may include records of your physical sensations, the images you see, the words that are spoken, or any of the other details of the experience: the temperature, the feeling of the sheets, the pattern of the cracks on the plaster, the clouds in the sky, anything you may feel, see, think, or do at the time.

This is how you can live through an entire childhood of trauma and not remember the bad parts. If you dissociated during the trauma, you may *only* remember the harmless parts: the clouds, the cracks in the plaster, the texture of the sheets. You concentrated on them to exclude the hurt.

It would be great if you never had to remember the bad parts. Unfortunately, though, "deleting" the bad parts creates new problems.

You *need* to know your life story. If you don't, severe difficulties may arise.

Without knowing your full life story, you might not be able to solve problems you thought you already worked out. You might repeatedly put yourself in a position to be victimized, without noticing that victimization always follows specific behaviors. People may react to you in seemingly peculiar ways, because you're not fully aware of how you've behaved with them in the past. Things that shouldn't confuse you might leave you perplexed, even depressed. When things in your life go well, you may still be haunted by a feeling of incompleteness or a sense that something important is missing.

The parts of your trauma you dissociated from awareness don't just fade away. They may intrude into your consciousness at the worst times, sometimes with the intensity they would have had if you'd allowed them into awareness when they first occurred.

Suppose that when you were first learning how to write the letters of the alphabet your teacher yelled at you when you couldn't form the letter *A* with your yellow pencil. If you dissociated the entire event, you wouldn't be able to write an *A*. But if you dissociated only your *feelings* at the time, you could still write down all the letters of the alphabet, except years later as you are writing the letter *A* you might be overcome with a strange sense of embarrassment or hurt without knowing why.

When your teacher yelled at you, the full experience didn't become part of your life story. You remembered how to write an *A*, but your embarrassment got separated from that memory. Instead of being digested by your mind, it went into a kind of unmarked box, where it remained in its original power. The rest of your mind doesn't recognize the box's contents. But now, whenever you write the letter *A*, or perhaps even when you simply hold a yellow pencil, your mind gets flooded with the awful contents of that box. You feel embarrassed, but don't know why.

If you were sexually abused as a child, there may be times when the boxes containing the parts of your past experiences suddenly open up and overwhelm you. You may experience sensations, feelings, moods, flashes of memory, and impulses without understanding why you're having them, where they came from, or how they fit into your self. Dissociation explains why you can become like a different person at times or why you have more than one set of seemingly disconnected thoughts going on at once.

Traumatic Dissociation

Usually, dissociation is an everyday kind, such as zoning out while driving, but it also accompanies trauma. It often begins as a person enters a hypnotic state to avoid shock during a traumatic event. You may have experienced this state as an adult during some deeply disturbing period of time. The world feels surreal and dreamy. You might feel disconnected from your body, as if you were floating above yourself. This is nature's way of allowing you to mentally process the facts of a situation without being overwhelmed with pain.

Traumatic dissociation can be helpful, even lifesaving. For example, if you were in a burning building and needed to escape, if you allowed yourself to experience the full extent of your danger you might just stand there in a panic. By dissociating your fear, however, you might be able to make better decisions about getting out safely. So dissociation is a creative, adaptive response to traumatic situations.

If you were sexually betrayed as a boy, you may be conscious of some of the facts of your betrayal, but this doesn't mean you're aware of everything you experienced or did. As a result, you may sometimes experience certain feelings without being able to attach them to memories. You may feel simultaneously good and bad about certain people or events in your childhood without sensing any conflict. This is because your good feelings are disconnected from your bad ones.

If this sounds impossible, consider a child who is abused every night. He learns to dissociate his terror and proceed in the daytime as though he lives an ordinary existence. This enables him to go on learning and building up competence in the world while his traumatic reactions to abuse remain encapsulated in another part of his mind. He may even grow up remembering a good childhood, unaware of the missing parts of his life story until years later.

Not everyone possesses the same capacity to dissociate. A boy who can't dissociate his terror may be so paralyzed by his feelings that he's unable to learn in school, relate to others, or develop other skills he needs in life. Boys who don't dissociate enough have a harder time growing up and staying out of trouble. Because the memories and anger are in the forefront of their mind, they may be more apt to hurt others or act out their rage in other ways. This explains why so many criminals have histories of physical and sexual child abuse. (Later on in this chapter you'll read about how some men become criminals for another reason: their inability to put dissociated experience into words.)

Dissociated Experiences Return

How do you know if you dissociated as a boy? How would it feel now? You may sometimes have a sense of dreaming while awake, except that your waking dream feels like a nightmare. This flashback experience can be intense, frightening, and disorienting. It may also be embarrassing, because dissociated feelings may be triggered in harmless, innocent situations.

You may experience sharp, intense feelings that have no relationship at all to your current environment. The people around you may have no clue about what you feel. You may feel paralyzed and exhausted afterward. Because it's so difficult to articulate your experience, you may not find words to describe what happened. You may be afraid you're going crazy. You may not be able to share your experiences with others, or if you try, you may feel frustrated because no one seems to understand.

When dissociated memories return, those that come back first may seem to have nothing to do with abuse. Yet they may produce anxiety and distress. Patrick recalled "yellow roses all around me" without understanding why this recollection made him so anxious and frightened. Eventually he remembered that the roses were images from the wallpaper in the living room of the house he'd lived in as a very young child, and he'd concentrated on them while being molested. Focusing on the wallpaper was his way of hypnotizing himself, creating an inner experience of leaving his body during the abuse.

Memory fragments don't always return to awareness at a comfortable pace. Sometimes they rush into consciousness, catching you off guard and overwhelming you with their unexpected power.

Brooke Hopkins writes about how when he was in his twenties he was suddenly inundated one night with memories of his sexual abuse by his mother: "I vividly recall how involuntarily they came back—how dumbstruck I was as I watched those memories come out, almost perfectly intact, the almost physical excitement I felt as that whole portion of my childhood continued, with just a little renewed pressure, to unfold."

Naturally, you may fear what might happen if you allow dissociated experiences to enter your conscious state. Each step presents new strains and reasons to put brakes on the process.

It's frightening not to know what newly recovered memories will bring with them. Abe recounted the story of Bluebeard, one of his childhood favorites. He remembered Bluebeard telling his wife that she was free to go anywhere in the house she wanted as long as she didn't open a certain door. Eventually, curiosity got the better of her and she opened it. Behind the door she discovered the dead bodies of the previous wives who Bluebeard had killed.

Abe was frightened about what dead bodies he would find if he opened more doors to his experience. I pointed out that opening up these doors had saved the woman's life: she knew what she was up against and saved herself. Abe hadn't thought about this before. Taking it as his cue, he went on with his difficult interior self-exposure. You'll hear more about Abe in chapter 8.

Severe Dissociation

In most cases, sexually betrayed individuals experience relatively mild forms of dissociation. But in extreme cases, dissociation can lead you to hear voices in your head, or to "wake up" at times in places or situations you don't remember getting into. In these cases, dissociation has created multiple selves or multiple personalities, which can become part of a serious condition called dissociative identity disorder. (This is the condition that was once called multiple personality disorder.)

If you have periods of severe dissociation, you may actually lose awareness of yourself while another dissociated part of you takes over. This leads to even greater problems, because you may do and say things you wouldn't ordinarily do, and you may not even remember. This is sometimes called *losing time*.

You may have some vague, dreamlike recollection of yourself during these periods or you may remember nothing. Beau sometimes left work in a completely dissociated state when his terror got triggered by the adolescent boys who reminded him of his teenage rapists. He had no memory of traveling to a distant part of the city. He suddenly "came to" with no idea about what had brought him into a strange neighborhood.

You may even develop creative explanations for lost time. One of the characters in Scott Heim's novel *Mysterious Skin* does this. Molested twice by his baseball coach at age eight, he doesn't remember those experiences. Yet he's bothered by a missing part in his life story. As he grows older, he comes to believe that he was abducted by aliens during the lost time. This allows him to think of himself as a perfectly normal person who happened to have had a unique experience. For years, he reads everything he can about UFOs and claims of alien sightings and abductions. Then, during his late adolescence, the real memories begin to float into his awareness, and he realizes what happened ten years earlier.

Using Dissociation to Deal with Everyday Stress

Healthy people develop diverse ways to handle the anxiety that everyone experiences. But if at a young age you learned to dissociate to escape from your trauma, maybe you still dissociate as your primary way of handling stress. You may dissociate to avoid anticipated anxiety, or to remove disturbing parts of your life story, or to calm yourself.

Sometimes men deliberately try to induce dissociation. An easy way to create a dissociated state is to abuse drugs or alcohol. When you're high, you usually don't care much about your anxieties.

PATRICK: Finding Solace in a Trance

Patrick engaged in compulsive behaviors such as alcoholism, incessant masturbation, and anonymous, unpleasurable sexual activity. These were ways to hypnotize himself so that he could return to a dissociated state rather than feel everyday anxieties. These behaviors helped him enter a trance where he felt protected.

"Right after family holidays," he told me, "I'd go to gay bars and give blow jobs to men in the back rooms." He'd concentrate on the other man's penis, just as he'd concentrated on the yellow roses of the wallpaper in his living room as a child. His intense sexual activity protected him from experiencing the full weight of his conflicts about being with his family. After a night of unsatisfying anonymous sex, Patrick was numb, exhausted, and could barely remember what happened either at his family's home or the bars to which he'd fled.

Patrick's tendency to dissociate was so well ingrained that it also took over in less perilous situations. He hadn't developed other ways to cope with anxiety. He couldn't detect the difference between minor stress and intense anxiety. He went through life on automatic pilot. When his unconscious radar signaled him that danger might be near, he began to dissociate. This happened even when there was really no danger at all.

"Last week," he told once me, "I was having lunch at a restaurant. The waiter was very friendly. I thought that he was too interested in me, and I got scared. The next thing I knew, I was out on the sidewalk. I don't remember leaving. But now that I look back at it, I think maybe the waiter was just doing his job. Maybe he reminded me of someone else. But it just got too intense."

Other ordinary events also triggered dissociation. Patrick had recurring night terrors about a stranger breaking into his room while he slept. Danger was signaled by the simple act of going to bed. In his early childhood, going to bed meant a "monster" might come into his dark room to molest him. Sometimes he could fend off his anxiety. At other times, he experienced a terror similar to what he must have felt as a small boy. In these states, he couldn't sleep and constantly checked the locks on his doors and windows to assure himself that he was safe.

What Helped Then May Hurt Now

You can't change what happened to you as a child. If you were sexually abused, it will always be part of your life story. But it's possible to stop the self-destructive, self-defeating things you do to yourself and others as a result of your traumatic past.

This isn't easy. You may have large portions of your emotional life unavailable to you. You may not remember all the facts. It may be hard to see the world realistically, to sort out what matters, what doesn't, what's threatening, what isn't, what people really mean when they pay you a compliment or get angry at you for little things.

As you dissociate to avoid anxiety, you may even dissociate the warning signs that tell you to safeguard yourself. So paradoxically you may not be aware of abuse when it happens now. The method you once used to protect yourself from pain may now leave you vulnerable to more abuse. Sometimes dissociation takes over your life so completely that you seem to have no feelings at all.

ANDREAS: In Pieces

Shortly after his own son was born, Andreas began to recall his sexual abuse by a group of men who took him off the street and abused him repeatedly over the course of many months. He also remembered his mother taking him to the hospital when he was bleeding after an anal assault. He wasn't sure whether to believe his memories, but they were confirmed when he searched hospital records and discovered his rectum had been surgically rebuilt during his childhood.

Andreas's remarkable ability to dissociate helped him get far in life. Despite a total lack of support from his family, he graduated from college, married, raised a large family, and was a pillar in his church. At work, he held a well-paid position with considerable authority over other workers.

But his thoughts were utterly separated from his feelings. He constantly and consciously tried to keep it that way. The only emotion he allowed himself was anger. He was afraid that if he felt anything else, it would be too extreme: He didn't know how to feel a *little* sad, *somewhat* frightened, or *moderately* happy. He didn't want to risk being overwhelmed by feelings, so he made sure he felt nothing. He called this "living topside," meaning living solely in his head.

On the rare occasions when emotion slipped through, Andreas fell apart. If he allowed himself to feel, he made himself focus on the occasion of his first molestation. He'd get flooded, crying incessantly. Then he ruthlessly made himself furious at everything in his life: "After four or five days of being enraged, I'm back in control."

It was as if two very different people lived inside him. Since they were separate, he felt no need to resolve their differences or find middle ground between these two opposing forces.

Andreas joined a group for men sexually betrayed as boys. He didn't like "exposing" himself and his emotional states to the other men, and he remained detached from them. His first crisis came when a new man, Seth, entered the group. Enormously apprehensive about a new man joining the group before ever meeting Seth, Andreas called me five days afterward and asked to see me alone.

He was gray and glassy-eyed. His terror had broken through, and it was right there, fully in his consciousness. He told me that he'd been unable to sleep since the night Seth entered the group because he was sure that Seth was an abuser. He asked me whether I knew if Seth had molested anyone. I reiterated my policy of not allowing men in the group who'd been abusers as adults, so obviously to the best of my knowledge Seth wasn't a victimizer. But I thought it was important to explore why Andreas was so sure that Seth was an abuser.

Eventually, Andreas figured out that his terror arose from thinking that Seth's hands were like the hands of one of the men who abused him. Seeing Seth's hands plunged Andreas back into the panic state he'd endured as a boy. Not having allowed this panic into awareness before, he was now terrified exactly as he'd been at age eight.

Being able to tell this to me helped Andreas integrate his dissociated terror into his life story. It was like finding a missing paragraph in a book; suddenly more things made sense. He could now return to the group and tell the other members, including Seth, about his panic reaction. He could do this on a more human level, without feeling as distant from them as before. He let himself experience emotions and connect them to his past and current life. He began to see how his perception of the world had been distorted.

Sexual Compulsions

Sexual compulsions are overpowering, insatiable urges to engage repeatedly in specific sexual acts. If you're sexually compulsive, you continue to engage in these sex acts even if they cause you great difficulty. You experience enormous anxiety without them.

It may seem strange that a sexually abused man would spend an inordinate amount of time and energy doing a version of the very behavior that caused him so much pain as a child. If you're sexually compulsive, there are, however, reasons for your behaviors.

First, you may be "replaying" the abuse, trying to master it. The more you feel in charge of sex, the less anxiety you feel about what you couldn't control as a child. It's a paradox that someone with a compulsion feels he's in charge of what he's doing, but this may be the only time in his life when he feels in control.

Second, the compulsive behavior tranquilizes you. You soothe your anxiety even if you don't understand where it comes from or why compulsive sex will soothe you. Why is this? The human body secretes certain hormones called opioids during stress. Opioids are related to opium and have a tranquilizing effect on the body. During sexual abuse, the body releases these opioids to allow it to get through trauma. But they're addictive, so the body continues desiring them.

The natural way to produce opioids is through stress. So a cycle begins: You feel anxiety. You seek out a way to relieve the anxiety. Your body knows that secreting these stress-reducing hormones will accomplish this. So it tells you to look for situations that will make it release opioids. And what better way to look for stress than sexual behavior, which first got your body to produce opioids?

Not that you consciously think, "I'm feeling stress. I'll dissociate so that I'll feel better." For most men with sexual compulsions, these thoughts don't have to occur. The cycle is automatic.

Sometimes compulsive behaviors control other more powerful and dangerous impulses. For example, if you have impulses to hurt yourself or others, you may control these urges by engaging in compulsive sexual activity. You're soothed and distracted by the compulsive sex so that you don't act on your impulses.

There are many problems, of course, with sexual compulsions. They control your life, wasting your time and energy. Because of the trance state they induce, your judgment may become impaired, leading you to expose yourself unnecessarily to danger. Recall how Patrick went to back rooms in bars when he was anxious, compulsively engaging in dangerous anonymous sex.

Multiple Compulsions

Sexual compulsions are just one form of compulsive behavior that aids dissociation. Devin was nearly destroyed by his multiple compulsions.

DEVIN: Driven without Pleasure

Devin came to me in serious legal trouble. He faced going to prison for behavior involving compulsive sexuality, but his numerous other compulsions further kept him from having a life.

Devin began his adult life drinking, chain-smoking, and doing drugs. He managed to break those cycles, but then he switched to other compulsions: gambling, looking at pornography, overeating sweets, and maniacally collecting baseball cards. He followed sports scores doggedly, laboriously making endless lists that duplicated information he could otherwise have obtained easily and instantly in computerized form. He spent many hours in sex-oriented Internet chat rooms and ran up immense phone bills on phone-sex lines. He shopped far beyond his means, incurring huge charge bills for items he never used. "When I have to buy something, I don't care about anything except the high I feel when I'm getting it. I have to have it! Then I get home, and I feel dirty and foolish. It's never stuff I really need, and I get embarrassed about buying it, so I never use it. It just sits there in my house—I'd feel too embarrassed to take it back to the store."

Devin's major solace was his incessant viewing of online pornography, which he downloaded and collected as compulsively as he'd tracked sports scores. He also went to peep shows, allowing men to fellate him there, sometimes vomiting afterward because of his conflicts about participating in homosexual acts. He claimed that if he had the money he'd compulsively go to female prostitutes instead.

Even when building a closet shelf, Devin spent hours on exhaustive measurements and calculations, not resting until every closet in his house had shelves. "I didn't eat until it was done. I stayed home from work to do it. And I hate doing home repairs! I don't really know what I'm doing. But once I decided to make a shelf, it was like someone else was in my body, making shelf after shelf after shelf."

As a younger man, Devin had severe alcohol and cocaine addictions. His driver's license was revoked for repeated drunken driving offenses. When I first saw him, he'd been alcohol- and drug-free for over two years following four previous attempts at rehab programs, and he attended AA meetings daily. But his life remained chaotic, pulled together loosely by his compulsions and his ability to continue functioning at his job.

Devin's father began to abuse him when he was about five years old. At first, his father fondled him in the bath, but soon he was coming to Devin's room at night, groping and fellating Devin and asking him to touch and squeeze the father's penis. Later, his father took Devin on business trips where the sex sessions were more extensive. The father also took photographs of Devin in explicit pornographic poses. The abuse ended when Devin was about fourteen.

Devin dissociated his feelings about his father. He said, "I know I should feel rage, but I don't. I don't actually miss him, but I also don't hate him—I'm emotionless. I guess I make sure I have no feelings about him."

Devin married in his early twenties but began having affairs soon afterward. He had difficulty maintaining an erection with his wife and avoided sex with her whenever he could. They divorced, but his sexual difficulties continued with other women. He could only function with pickups or prostitutes, since he wasn't emotionally involved with them.

Devin's problems devastated his life. He gradually began to recognize his anxieties, however. As he put his life story back together, he found some ways to relieve those anxieties and begin to take charge of his behaviors. Eventually, he learned that sometimes he could experience emotions without instantly dissociating them through sexual or other compulsions.

Emotional Extremes

When dissociated emotions come into awareness, you may have difficulty managing them. You may find yourself always feeling emotional extremes. This may lead you to be *hypervigilant*—to be extremely sensitive to possible danger signals like noise or sudden movements. When you perceive these danger signals, you may shift into a state of *hyperarousal*, a sort of superreadiness to fight, run, or protect yourself. It's hard to control these states. Your emotions seem to go off the scale, overwhelming your ability to think rationally. This is especially likely if you were traumatized at a very early age, because you hadn't yet learned to handle strong emotions. Returning to that child self, you may fall apart.

If this has happened to you, maybe you've taught yourself to avoid situations where you might have intense feelings. You might even be afraid of all emotions.

Keith summed up his need not to feel: "When I feel emotion, I'm all consumed and lost and hurt—that's what it was like when I lived with my mother—I was either alone or consumed with her and by her. I was so emotional as a teenager, so sad, so unhappy. I had to do drugs to numb it out, but they can't numb it out completely. I equate emotion with pain—I'd like to feel emotion without all that pain, but I'm not sure it's possible." No wonder men abused as children find ways to avoid feeling intense emotions!

To make matters worse, as an adult you're more powerful than you were as a child. With your child rage in your adult body and mind, it's terrifying, exhausting, and disorienting to have to keep these feelings in check. A child usually doesn't know how to kill people, but an adult does. It can feel impossible to handle these feelings while inhabiting a powerful adult male body.

It isn't easy to recompose yourself after experiencing these states. Strategies that ordinarily work to relieve anxiety, like taking deep breaths, may not help much at these times. So abused men often alleviate stress by resorting to self-destructive behaviors like substance abuse, overeating, self-mutilation, gambling, and compulsive sex.

As they recover emotions, some men experience new and confusing symptoms, such as physical aches and pains, headaches, dizziness, or fatigue. Others, like Andreas and Willem, whom we will meet later, deliberately avoid situations where they may feel any emotion at all.

Multiple Selves

While dissociative identity disorder is rare, everyone has multiple aspects to his personality. As you go through life, you shift and adapt yourself to situations. A new daddy, for example, playfully cooing at his baby, is one self with that baby, but when the phone rings and his boss is calling, the man's self can quickly shift into a businesslike, adult mode. As his wife comes into the room, he may shift into yet another self as he signals her to watch the baby while pointing to the phone and mouthing the word *boss* so that she'll understand who's calling.

As he rapidly shifts his self during this brief period, everything fits effortlessly into his life story. It all makes sense. While there may be momentary conflicts between his need to look after his baby and his need to be a good employee, he can remain who he is. He doesn't have to deny or forget he's a father with a baby when he's talking to his boss about a business problem. Presenting a particular self prominently is how he faces the world at a given moment, including the role he's playing and with whom. He's learned to play many parts, and he plays them as well as he can based on what he's learned in his life and what his life story is about.

But men who dissociate when it's unnecessary may have difficulty flowing from one moment to the next. It becomes impossible to make connections between one self and another. Sometimes they may even deny the other self exists.

WALTER: Running on Two Separate Tracks

It's also possible to remember an event without remembering how you behaved. In Walter de Milly's book, *In My Father's Arms: A True Story of Incest*, he illustrates this in a conversation with his minister, Steve, whom he'd approached for counseling. They talked about a banquet both had attended several days earlier:

Steve asked me if I had been attracted to the man who sat next to me.

"No one sat next to me," I said.

"Yes, Walt," Steve told me. "There was a nice-looking man sitting next to you."

"I don't remember anyone."

"You were flirting with him."

"No, I wasn't."

"Walt," Steve said, "you spent half your time talking to the guy. I saw you, and you were flirting with him. Please don't think I disapprove, I'm just asking if you liked him."

"Are you sure? I don't even remember anyone," I said.

"He was there, Walt. He was wearing a white polo shirt, and he sat a foot away from you, and you were flirting with him, flashing your eyes, giggling."

"I'm sorry, I guess I just don't remember."

"I wonder if you were a different person," Steve said, touching his fingers to his desk. "Do you think so?"

"You mean like a different personality?" I asked.

"Yes. Maybe."

"But I remember the lecture," I said. "I remember being there. I remember seeing you and giving you a smile."

At the banquet, Walter dissociated two of his "selves," disconnecting two roles he was playing. He was unable to link his "flirtatious self" to his "citizen self." They operated independently, without even knowing about each other.

Healing for anyone who experiences this disconnect involves creating associations between different roles we play in life, building bridges over the empty spaces between our different selves. It's a matter of moving fluidly from one form of self to another. Learning to do this isn't easy. It requires resolve, as Ted demonstrates.

TEO AND TED: The Betrayed Boy Speaks

Ted worked his way out of the gang-ridden streets where he grew up to become a family man and globe-trotting entrepreneur whose skills and abilities kept him in demand. But he needed to face the demons from childhood sexual abuse by his godfather, Arnie. The specifics of this abuse were vague, but he knew Arnie molested him for a period of time when he was about seven.

In his late forties, Ted sought therapy to confront the effects of Arnie's abuse. He had to temporarily undo in therapy what he'd achieved as Ted, the accomplished executive businessman, in order to again find the frightened child, Teo, whom he'd silenced four decades earlier. As part of his therapy, Ted joined a group, asking to be called Teo.

Teo was devoted to the group. When he spoke, he offered support to other group members. If he talked about himself, it was usually about how tired he was of being capable Ted in the business world, or about family problems he might be having, or eventually about his rage toward his godfather and toward the parents who didn't protect him from molestation.

With time, Ted rearranged his business and stayed home to allow Teo time to recover. Teo became even quieter than before, retreating to a place inside himself that none of us could see or know. After months of near-total silence in the group, he began to emerge from his cocoon. He talked more openly about his abuse, even with business clients. He gave voice to his corrosive, alienated anger and cynicism, telling the group how he'd bitterly divided the world into victims and victimizers: "The world is full of either victims or Arnies—or, at best, victims-in-training or Arnies-in-training."

A few months later, Teo felt ready to leave the group, immensely grateful to the members and his therapists. As he put it, "What made me better was that through individual therapy and my group, I was able not to keep this abuse a secret anymore—the more I could tell people, the better I got. It seems so simple, but I would never have believed it on my own."

Ted put his childhood experience into words, then placed those words into his life story. He learned to describe how he'd coped with his world and the price he'd paid. He began to move effortlessly from one self to the other, to be glib when necessary in the business mode, to be sensitive and compassionate in his relationships. "Before, I could handle any situation by hiding while my mouth talked. It was only by learning that it was okay to be quiet—not to be on top of everything—that I found my voice. That was the paradox—I had to be quiet to find my voice."

The Need for a Confidant

Some sexually abused boys grow up with more psychological and criminal problems than others. Why is there such disparity? Ted's need to find a voice helps explain it.

It seems to make a big difference if an abused boy has a childhood confidant, especially an older boy or man. Boys with someone to talk to—even if they don't talk to their confidant about their abuse—grow up with fewer problems than boys forced to keep secrets. Those without a confidant are, for example, far more likely to become rapists, molesters of children, or violent criminals.

Sadly, the people most likely to be good confidants—teachers, relatives, coaches, ministers, guidance counselors—can be in the same position in relation to a boy as adults who become abusers. It's important to remember that the vast majority of these mentoring adults are constructive, positive influences on children.

There is power in naming and describing traumatic experiences. Boys with confidants learn to put emotional experiences into words, so they can include their abuse in their life story. Putting an experience into your life story gains you mastery over it. You achieve control over the memory and learn how it fits into your world. You make sense of your own experience. In so doing, you progress toward mental health.

As you recover from childhood sexual betrayal, you'll need to find ways to express what happened. Being able to articulate your experience—whether through speaking about it, through journal or poetry writing, or even through art or some other nonverbal form of expression—is a powerful tool in recovery. In doing so, you take dissociated pieces of your story and give them their proper places and names. In the second part of this book, we'll talk about ways to help you accomplish this.

Putting Your Story Together

Every man has his own way of recovering. But being aware of self-destructive behaviors and preparing yourself for times when you're hyperaroused will help you recover more quickly.

Denying parts of the past—refusing to allow traumatic experiences into your life story—leaves you debilitated, incomplete, and far less competent to deal with the world. Ultimately, we're all responsible for our behavior, even behavior during dissociated states, so it's important to overcome incapacitating dissociation.

Prevailing over dissociation requires patience, courage, and trust. There are always setbacks, and there's always the dread of encountering something you can't handle. But this dread isn't rational and needn't last. Your need to develop and grow gives you strength as you prepare to move to the next stage. This strength may not arrive when you want it to. Instead, it will probably emerge slowly. You'll eventually make the associations you need. As this happens, you'll begin to reclaim the life you were given, the life you deserve.

5

Betrayal in Families

More than Mistreatment

Abuse doesn't mean just mistreating somebody. At times, everyone loses his temper, neglects a loved one, or ignores another person's opinion. This is true between husbands and wives, parents and children, employers and employees. It's true in sports, in spiritual houses, and in friendships. Entire groups of people feel poorly treated or even harmed in everyday affairs. And, of course, any mistreatment of another person is wrong, and chronic mistreatment within a family can become abusive.

One difference between everyday mistreatment and abuse is that abuse occurs in a relationship in which one person has power over another. An abuser uses that power to satisfy his or her own needs without thinking about the needs of the person being abused. This is very different from the everyday kind of mistreatment we all may sometimes engage in when irritable, distracted, or otherwise unattuned to the needs of others.

From a moral point of view, abuse is always wrong. But the trauma it causes isn't always the same from one person to the next, or even from one occasion to the next. And people may differ in their perceptions of abuse, even when the behavior is the same. What matters is not how serious the abuse may seem to someone else but how it has affected you.

If the abuse you suffered involved physical assault, sexual aggression, or mental persecution by someone you knew and trusted—

especially if the abuser was a family member—something fundamental went awry in your world. You were abused, but also betrayed. That betrayal affected how you see yourself and how you relate to others. It changed how you experience life with your family, your school, and your culture. Your private attempts to recover from the pain and confusion may even touch those in your life who have no way of knowing what happened to you. It's important to understand how your family affected your reactions to abuse even if your abuser was not a family member.

Family Environments and Abuse

When people important to you find out about your boyhood sexual betrayal, their reactions to your experience—supportive or not—influence your attempts to recover from it. This is true whether they find out when you're still a boy or years later after you've grown up.

Some families set the stage for abuse to occur, even abuse by an outsider. Others create a sense of safety that enables a boy to weather abusive or potentially abusive situations. Your family may have been supportive and capable of protecting you from further abuse, or they may have ignored, shamed, or blamed you. See if any of the following characteristics describe the family you grew up in:

- Your parents didn't communicate well, either with one another or with you and your siblings.

- There was a failure to respect family members' personal boundaries and identities (for example, your parent read your diary).

- Discussion of sexuality was avoided altogether.

- At the other extreme, sexuality was ever-present, with stimulating and suggestive overtones.

If you were abused, you needed to share your experience. If your family was loving, supportive, and understanding, then this helped your recovery.

In too many families, however, there's no support. If your family was secretive, punishing, uncaring, or denied what you had to say, then you learned that relationships are fundamentally dishonest, dangerous, and mystifying. Cory expressed his anguish about this dishonesty by saying, "Our family motto was always, 'If you can't say anything nice, don't say anything at all.' But for me the best family motto would be 'If you can't say anything honest, say nothing.'"

What follows are seven family profiles. None of them is likely to fit your own family environment exactly, but chances are you'll see some familiar patterns.

Ideal Families

The perfect family doesn't and never will exist. Generally, however, in a healthy family the parents communicate well enough with each other and their children. Family members respect personal boundaries. When questions of human sexuality arise, they're discussed in age-appropriate, factual ways, without avoiding them but also without suggestiveness, overstimulation, or erotic overtones.

Healthy, nurturing parents make it easy for their children to approach them with problems. They offer alternative ways for their children to obtain the information they need (for example, through professionals or libraries). They're supportive of their children, provide for their needs, and protect them from exposure to inappropriate sexuality.

Evasive Families

When parents are evasive in discussions about sexuality, the family can easily develop sexual secrets, since no one is willing to talk openly about sexual matters. In these families, parents may provide little or no accurate sexual information, leading the children to develop false and harmful beliefs. Parents' anxiety about sexuality may lead them to communicate through such fables as "the stork brought the baby." Children growing up in this type of family don't know how to talk clearly about sexuality, and, in any case, they learn that this kind of talk isn't acceptable.

Silent Families

Some families go further by offering no information about sex. This may be done in the guise of protecting children. These environments veil sexuality in secrecy. Children learn that it's forbidden to bring up sexuality. If a child feels it's unsafe to talk about sexual betrayal, then he won't.

If there's a family taboo about sexuality, children stay overly innocent. They're unprepared for their sexual feelings. They're vulnerable
to sexual molestation. If it occurs, their shock, shame, and trauma may
be crushing.

Judgmental Families

Some families are overly judgmental about sexuality. This leads to a negative environment. Sexuality is considered bad. The child is told in
countless ways that sex is harmful, evil, and a sign of weakness. Little
sexual information is provided, and a child's attempts to find out about
sex may be blocked, ridiculed, or punished.

Permissive Families

By contrast, in an overly permissive environment, adults allow children
free exposure to sexuality. Parents may walk around scantily clad at all
hours. Or they may give children free access to pornography at an early
age, saying this will make the children less prudish and anxious about
sex. While this *may* arise from well-meaning motives, often its effect is
to overstimulate and overwhelm a child with material he doesn't have
the capacity to understand or process.

Seductive Families

In a seductive environment, things go even further. One or more adults
directly communicate a sexual interest to a child either verbally or behav-
iorally. While overt abuse may not result, the child is constantly aware
of his attractiveness to the adult, who may do such things as "inadvertently" expose him- or herself to the child. Or an adult may tell a child
far too many details about the adult's sex life. This titillating atmosphere
also surrounds any sexual education a child in this kind of family
receives. This is the sexual *misuse* of a child.

Overtly Sexual Families

The overtly sexual environment often includes sexual abuse and misuse
of children. In this environment, sexuality is openly or covertly present
in all interactions. There is often overt sexual contact between the child

and one or more adults. Sexual information is communicated for exploitative purposes. For example, a child may be shown pornographic material in the guise of sex education. In addition, adults may covertly or even openly encourage sexual contact between children.

Understanding Your Family Environment

Sexual misuse or abuse of children may occur in any of these environments. But some encourage inappropriate sexual expression more than others do. Understanding these different environments can clarify what happened in your own family.

Seth's family exemplifies how a family can set the stage for abuse without itself being abusive.

Seth: Well-Meaning, Silent Parents and Abused, Silent Sons

Seth never revealed his story to anyone until he began therapy in his late thirties. It never occurred to him to do so—he'd learned not to talk about emotionally loaded topics.

Seth's molestation might seem minor to someone who'd been chronically abused, although he felt deeply ashamed of his one-time molestation by an adult family friend. He hesitated to join a group of sexually abused men because he thought his experience, while devastating to him, couldn't compare to the abuse he was likely to hear about from other survivors. He was afraid that if he spoke about his experiences, he'd be humiliated for complaining about something so minor to people who'd lived through far worse.

"The morning after this man molested me," Seth told me, "I pretended to him I had no idea anything had happened." Seth's refusal to acknowledge his abuse was in keeping with what he had learned from his family: don't talk about sexuality, feelings, or conflicts between people. The way to maintain peace is through silence and looking the other way.

Seth grew up in a small town, one of many brothers in a middle-class Catholic family. He went to parochial schools and attended church regularly. He learned in his family that obedience to authorities should be immediate and unquestioned. His church and school further enforced this attitude. In addition, he said, there was little tolerance in his family for discussing your inner life.

"I would entertain myself," he said, "by painting and drawing pictures. No one in my family discouraged me. In fact, they rarely mentioned my art at all, just like they never talked about anything else that was important. Still, I think they thought all my artistic interests were odd. I'm sure they would have preferred that I just go play ball like my brothers did."

When Seth was about ten, Billy, a man in his thirties who served as handyman and assistant to a priest in another part of town, somehow attached himself to Seth's family. Seth doesn't recall how Billy first entered the family circle, but Billy quickly became a fixture there, coming to Sunday dinner after church, doing favors for the parents, babysitting and generally making himself useful. Billy lived alone and was viewed as limited in intelligence but harmless and pleasant.

"Sometimes Billy would come in when I was playing or drawing, and he'd put his hand on my shoulder and leave it there. As I think about it now, he was a creepy presence in my life. But I am not positive that I felt that way about him until after he molested me."

When Seth was twelve, Billy offered to take him to New York City for his birthday, where they would see Seth's first Broadway show, go to museums, and stay overnight in a hotel. "I was very excited about the trip," he said. His parents assumed he'd be safe with Billy.

All went smoothly until Seth and Billy were alone in the hotel room after the show. Billy began to massage Seth's back "to ease the exhaustion of the busy day," slowly undressing him and making the interaction more and more explicitly sexual. Seth cannot recall precisely what happened, but he knows there was mutual touching of genitals. In the morning, Billy said to Seth, "I'm sorry about what happened last night."

Seth interrupted him and professed ignorance, saying, "What do you mean? What happened?" Billy then said, "So you won't tell anyone about what happened last night?" Seth firmly answered, "Last night never happened!" Neither he nor Billy ever brought up the molestation again.

After they returned home, Seth avoided being alone with Billy but didn't tell anyone what happened. As an adult, Seth went over and over this fact, not forgiving himself for maintaining his silence. Yet he also believed that talking about unpleasant sexual and aggressive feelings rather than denying them would be breaking a central taboo in his family. As a boy, he never considered acting so contrary to the family's unwritten laws.

Billy maintained his relationship with Seth's family until his death twenty years later. Only then did Seth break his silence and enter therapy to talk about feelings regarding both his molestation and the silence that over the years had grown within him like a cancer.

In his mid-forties, Seth discovered that Billy or other men had molested all his brothers except one. None of them had ever talked about their abuse as boys. Each had considered his own abuse a guilty secret that he carried with shame and suppressed rage. Each also now felt guiltily responsible for the abuse his younger brothers suffered, feeling that had he spoken up, the younger ones wouldn't have been molested.

Characteristically, Seth's older brother said, "Of course, Mom and Dad must never know about this." A sense of secrecy and shame continued to rule how the brothers dealt with their abuse, as they continued to feel that they must protect their parents from knowledge of bad things.

When Seth told me about these revelations, I observed that each brother had lived in a private hell. He responded that his father had been severely traumatized during World War II but had always refused to talk about his many battle experiences. I said quietly that he and his brothers had had a model for men living in private hells rather than revealing emotional anguish. He nodded, his eyes filling with tears.

The history of this family pattern was clear, but it had already begun to change. The brothers were talking to one another, each opening up about his guilt, shame, and despair. This enlivened the emotional connections among them, which had been deadened over the years. With joy, Seth said, "For the first time in thirty years, I really have brothers again!"

Relating to the World

An Untrustworthy World

If you were sexually abused by someone close to you, the dishonesty in that relationship may have become a model for all your relationships. Expecting dishonesty in every relationship may protect you from further abuse, but it also isolates you from the world. After all, most people don't try to abuse others.

People usually expect some difficulties and doubts in their relationships. If you were betrayed, however, any sort of setback might easily send you into periods of self-questioning, self-recrimination, cynicism, depression, and isolation.

Julian, whom we'll discuss later, explains it this way: "We have a double whammy. We're vulnerable in two ways. First, we have families that make us yearn for contact, so we're vulnerable to sexual predators.

Then we get abused by them, and we have nowhere to go back to for help, because we have those same families that can't give it."

Boys like Julian are likely to develop profound difficulties as they try to establish healthy relationships with the important people in their lives. Whether they're relating to romantic partners, friends, coworkers, bosses, or others, these boys often develop the idea that sooner or later they'll again be victimized by people who weren't really who they appeared to be.

An Idealized World

While some betrayed boys grow up to view the world through skeptical, distrusting eyes, others have a need to deny how much the world hurt them. If you're in denial, you may see the world in an idealized way, as a place filled with benevolent people.

Perhaps you even idealized your abuser and found it impossible to feel anger or hatred because of all the good things the victimizer did for you. Idealizing your abuser may have been crucial to your health, especially if he took care of you and guided you through life, someone like a parent, sibling, counselor, teacher, clergyman, scoutmaster, or coach.

Perhaps you also idealized other adults who were present and should have known what was going on. It can be just as traumatic to have your hurt ignored by those you love as to be hurt in the first place. After all, it's hard to imagine that someone you love, trust, and respect can also be unseeing, uncaring, and unable to acknowledge your suffering.

If you're prone to idealization, you may not recognize victimizers until it's too late. You may enter into victim–victimizer relationships again and again, unable to learn from these relationships because you can't incorporate bad experiences into your understanding of the world. In chapters 2 and 8 we see how Isaac had twelve different abusers from age six to age seventeen, in part because he kept himself trusting and naive.

The Need to Communicate

Denying Reality

If you spoke up about your abuse, or tried to, the reactions you got (or didn't get) may affect how you see the world today. Perhaps you knew you wouldn't be believed. Perhaps you lived in a world that seemed ordinary or even quite wonderful except for one horrible secret you knew but no one else acknowledged. Maybe you tried to tell, only to be dismissed, accused of lying, punished, or told you were sick.

If you lived in an environment unfriendly to the truth, your reality was denied. You were forced to relate to people who were not honest about themselves or about their relationships with you. You may as well have been told, "What matters is pretending. Real things don't matter. You don't matter."

As one man put it, "Denial was our survival mechanism. My family lived on denial—air, water, and denial. That's how we got through." With gallows humor but real wit, he went on to say, "The cast had already died by the time I was born. My family was already dead, and the die was cast for my abuse."

Imagine yourself speaking up at a meeting or in a group of friends, or saying something important to your physician, partner, parents, or siblings. Instead of being listened to, you're ignored. Your hand is patted and your listener smiles blankly, but nothing else happens. It's like being told you don't exist. This is devastating. In the movie *Spanking the Monkey*, a boy's mother denies having committed incest with him after he tells his father about it. The father believes her denial. Betrayed twice, the boy tries to commit suicide.

Maybe you were warned not to talk. Children know adults can hurt them. Even without a specific warning, most children know that if they talk about a dangerous topic, the consequences for them or people they love could be disastrous.

Speaking Up

It's no wonder sexually betrayed men find power in telling their stories. Brooke Hopkins says, "Maybe the most damaging form of abuse . . . is silence and the denial that is implicit in it. I mean the denial not only of what happened but of the person it happened to." Brooke describes his need to confront and undo this silence: "I am writing this in order to break that silence, because the denial represented by it strikes me as something like a disease, a disease for which the only hope of a cure is in speaking, in making public what has been hidden for so long."

Humans have certain fundamental needs: food, air, water, and shelter. But we also need to communicate. We're injured when we can't. In the movie *Castaway*, Tom Hanks spends years alone on a deserted island with no one to talk to, no ability to send letters, and no television, radio, or e-mail. Eventually, he creates another person in the form of a volleyball on which he paints a face. He talks to the volleyball and begins to take it with him wherever he goes. Paradoxically, this "insane" behavior is how he keeps his sanity on the island.

The impulse to share your thoughts is natural and normal. If no one allowed you to tell the truth, you were injured. You were expected to stuff an explosive reality into yourself for years, even decades. No one can do that without cost. Often, the cost is enormous.

The answer is to tell your story. You can find healthy and safe ways to say what you couldn't as a boy. In doing this, you will find power. We'll discuss these ways in part two of this book.

Families and Authority

If you were taught never to question your elders and always to obey adults, you were at particular risk for abuse. Families with authoritarian rules and structures tend to have children who don't know how to question someone in power. If you were raised like this, you may have been abused because you felt that you had no choice.

Compliance with Authority

Bruno, whom you'll read about in chapter 6, was punished frequently as a boy, often for little reason and seemingly at random. He'd been taught that punishment is part of life. He'd also been cautioned by his family to accept the derisive reactions to his dyslexia by the nuns who were his teachers. So it's not surprising that he also accepted molestations by his family doctor. Actually, it's remarkable that he protested when the family complied with the doctor's instructions to bring him back for weekly appointments.

If you grew up in an authoritarian family, maybe you learned to covertly outmaneuver and manipulate authority figures, since you knew it would be useless to openly defy them. If you figured out how to manipulate and disobey authority figures, you may have felt encouraged to take legal risks or even to become more like your abuser.

But maybe you secretly kept your contempt for authorities inside, allowing it to fester and get in the way of your relationships. If you were afraid to defy authorities as a child, you may continue to feel you're not allowed to express your feelings and opinions as an adult.

Even though it will probably be hard at first, you'll do better if you express yourself, setting limits and telling others what you will and won't accept. You may be surprised at the new respect you're given. Maybe you were punished as a boy for standing your ground, but this is less likely to happen now that you're an adult.

Abuse and Religious Authority

Religious families often consider members of the clergy to be family members. If a clergy member betrayed you, this could be as devastating as incest, especially because of damage to your spiritual beliefs. Widely publicized scandals about abuse by Catholic priests have boiled over in the earliest years of the twenty-first century. They have shown how widespread this devastation can be and how organized religions may try to cover up these abuses for their own protection.

If your family was deeply religious, maybe you were taught to obey religious authorities. Maybe you were an altar boy or choirboy, or had some other role in religious life. Maybe you developed an idealized view of your spiritual mentor. If you came from a troubled family, you may have sought out parental figures in your church environment to act as role models and provide structure that was lacking in your family.

When a member of the clergy or other spiritual authority molested you, you may have felt a representative of God misused you. Maybe you felt God neither loved you nor protected you. Or you may have felt you were betraying God either by participating in the sexual acts or by feeling angry at your abuser. If your victimizer took a vow of chastity, as Catholic priests and nuns do, maybe you even felt that somehow you instigated things. If your abuser told you that you were special or beautiful, you may believe you tempted your abuser to break that vow.

All this can leave you feeling isolated, confused, and spiritually devastated. Maybe you concluded that the belief system you were taught to accept was inherently defective or even dangerous. You might feel there's nothing in the world you can trust or believe.

Dr. X: Destruction of Spirituality

A colleague of mine whom I'll call Dr. X was raised in a rural area of the American heartland as a pious, literal believer in Catholic doctrine. He absolutely believed priests are God's representatives on earth.

His mother was, he said, "a praying, God-fearing woman. She was the ultimate Catholic, and she wanted me to be one, too." His father was unpredictable, a workaholic, sometimes dangerous, demeaning, and physically abusive, and at other times strong and capable.

Dr. X's self-esteem depended largely on the family's worldly parish priest. He visited the family frequently, often staying the night even though he lived only three blocks away. He slept on a couch outside Dr. X's room. Starting when Dr. X was five years old, the priest would take the boy out of his bed, bring him onto the couch, and reach organsm by rubbing the boy against his body.

After he moved to another parish, he'd visit every few months and take Dr. X away for the weekend to a house some priests apparently kept for encounters with young boys. Other priests also brought boys to these weekends. There were multiple sexually abusive encounters until Dr. X was fifteen years old, one of them witnessed by his younger brother. "As I grew older, the guilt intensified. I sensed that things were off, but I felt it was only me, that I was not able to exercise self-control. I grew increasingly wary of his visits. I dreaded them but felt obliged to be good—a good Catholic, a good, compliant boy in both his eyes and my parents'. I couldn't disappoint him."

At one point, Dr. X's mother told him there were rumors that the priest was sexually involved with children. "I told her what he'd done to me, but amazingly she stayed in touch with him, and so did I! I didn't truly realize that I'd been abused. It was just something that happened." In retrospect, Dr. X believes his mother was in love with the priest, although from a worshipful distance.

Dr. X never considered telling anyone about his abuse. The priest said, "This is between you and me. God thinks it's okay. You don't have to tell your mommy and daddy." Dr. X felt sure all hell would break loose if he disclosed his abuse, and that he, not the priest, would be the loser. "He was awesome. He would not be blamed. He was God-like."

Dr. X now feels he was somehow seduced into thinking that participating in these acts was good and noble. "I remember once, at age six or so, laying there, expecting him to come in. I lay there in the form of a crucifix. I thought he'd see me as Jesus. I'd please him. I so wanted his attention!" His self-esteem depended on the priest's coming in and making him feel special. "I had a love affair with him in my heart, even at age five."

As a young adult, Dr. X began therapy and started to see his experience was abusive. He confronted the priest. "I told him, 'You abused me,' but he said, 'What I did was just love. It was good for you.' He never acknowledged any wrongdoing."

Only after years of therapy did Dr. X realize how enraged he'd been all his life. "My rage was always under the surface, and I knew that. But there was more, and I knew that, too. Only now do I affix it to him as well.

"The priest, in his God-like position and his misuse of it, soured me to ultimate authority. It left me hopeless, angry, rebellious, hostile, and running in circles. I survived. I did not live."

Dr. X had a painful crisis of faith because of the specific nature of his relationship to his abuser: "I felt it was God's representative on earth that opened my eyes to God's failing. The idea of a Supreme Being was shattered for me by this man. He introduced evidence to me that God failed, that God won't protect you or prevent bad things from happening to you. The fact that it was a priest was cataclysmic. It taught me that there is a lie in the world. I developed a slowly evolving cynicism. As I got older and gave up on my piety, I grew to hate the smells, sounds, feelings of the Church—the incense, the collars, the robes. My spirituality and ability to believe in a higher power were destroyed."

"Being a priest," Dr. X continued, "was his ticket to taking advantage. His tool. Like anyone who abuses a child. They all have some tool."

Hungry for Love

If you were neglected emotionally when you were a boy and didn't receive the love and attention you needed, you were particularly vulnerable to molestation. This may have made it nearly impossible for you to resist affection and tenderness when it was offered, no matter what the terms. If your parents left you emotionally starved, they may not have abused you, but they set the stage for abuse to occur, as happened to Xavier.

XAVIER: Love-Starved

There was little emotional nurturance in Xavier's large family, and almost none was left for the youngest children, including Xavier, the seventh of ten. Both his parents also grew up in huge families. Xavier adored his mother, who died when he was twenty. He excused her neglect by saying she was distracted and depressed because of her cold marriage and many years of childbearing. His father was hardworking but withdrawn and angry. He ridiculed his children's achievements and spent little time with them. The children, in turn, were contemptuous of one another, and there was little companionship among them.

A sensitive and lonely boy, Xavier was starved for affection. When he was six, his twelve-year-old brother invited him into a bedroom in an unusually tender way. Murmuring what a sweet boy Xavier was, his brother caressed and held him, fondling Xavier's genitals and directing him to do the same for the brother until the older boy reached orgasm. The sexual contact continued over time on an irregular basis, eventually including mutual fellatio and anal penetration by the brother. The brother's tone was always affectionate and tender during the molestations, but otherwise he remained brusque, derisive, and uncaring.

When Xavier was eight, a second brother approached him in a manner almost identical to that of the first molesting brother. At twelve, this brother was two years younger than the first brother. Seemingly loving, he also held and fondled Xavier. Sexual contact continued on a regular basis. Like the first brother, this brother was affectionate while molesting him but remained cold otherwise.

Xavier felt that what he and his brothers were doing was wrong and religiously immoral. He didn't even feel much physical pleasure. But he desperately needed those tender moments, even if the affection did not last beyond orgasm.

As a heterosexual adult, Xavier was sure the priesthood was his calling, rather than simply an escape from the legacy of his two brothers' sexual abuse. Still, becoming a priest also seemed to be an attempt to repair his childhood trauma by establishing safer loving relationships with new "brothers." Yet he was afraid of intense emotional relationships and felt anxious in the company of other priests. He loved the fellowship among them but knew there was a potential for him to feel overwhelming emotional neediness again and lose all sense of his own purpose.

In therapy, Xavier articulated feelings and memories that had silently eaten away at him for over twenty-five years. He was surprisingly compassionate about his abusing brothers, feeling their severe alcoholism and failed relationships were signs of how miserable their own childhoods had been. He believed that they'd also been abused and that there was probably a pattern of sexual abuse of emotionally needy young boys by older brothers or cousins throughout his enormous extended family.

Seeing this pattern helped him feel compassion for himself as a child and for all the deprived young men in his family.

The Influence of Culture

Every culture has its own rules about sexuality. What is abusive or shocking in one society may be acceptable in another. The meaning of sexuality, including childhood sexuality, same-sex sexuality, and sexuality between adults and children, changes from culture to culture. For example, there are groups in which it is normal and often ritualistic in nature for adults to engage in sexual activities with children. These are usually considered rites of passage into adulthood.

It's hard to argue that we should embrace the ideas of these groups. They may hold other views of what's acceptable behavior between people that most Western societies would consider primitive. Adult–child sex occurred alongside slavery, cannibalism, infanticide, enforced clitorectomies, and rituals totally unacceptable to most of us. For example, as part of a coming of age ritual for boys, the boys from the Sambia tribe in New Guinea were physically assaulted, and stiff, sharp grass reeds were thrust up their nose until a copious amount of blood flowed. These boys were also expected to perform fellatio on older boys and men.

Most people in Western society would be thankful that we don't practice these rituals (although other societies may find rituals common in the West—like male circumcision—repugnant). But with America's diverse makeup, families have varied religious, ethnic, and cultural customs and standards. Each family has its own way of treating conflicts and sexual issues. These differences affect how the child experiences sexual encounters with adults and how he thinks about them as he grows up.

How can we tell if behavior is abusive within a family's social context? A rule of thumb I use is that the more secretive a boy knows he must be about his sexual experiences with an adult, the more those experiences are deviant, taboo, and traumatizing within his culture. So a Sambian boy expected to fellate warriors as a male rite of passage would not be traumatized by the experience, which boys in his culture anticipate. But if that happened in the United States—say, as part of fraternity hazing—the victim could well be traumatized.

The more your abuser silenced you or the more your own sense of appropriateness shamed you about what your victimizer wanted you to do, the more likely it is that what you were doing wouldn't be acceptable if it were known to others. You may have been specifically warned by your abuser about dire consequences should you reveal what happened (for example, Andreas's molesters told him that if he talked about his abuse, his mother would be murdered). Or from the social norms you carried around inside your head, you may have known without being told what was acceptable to talk about and when you'd better stay silent. Having no means to disclose your sexual abuse only added to your trauma.

Victor: Between Two Cultures

Victor was culturally trapped between old and new ways, with no one to help him through. He was abused during two periods of his life and was traumatized both times. He understood that sex with his father was taboo and had to be kept secret. But open sexual overstimulation by his grandparents seemed acceptable within their culture, although Victor eventually realized it was abnormal in the American society where he was raised.

Born in the United States, Victor was completely assimilated to the American experience. His abuse and his reactions to it, though, were influenced by two cultures, spanning the globe to the war-torn Asian society from which his parents had fled.

Victor's mother came from a prominent upper-class family in her native land. Her father had been a high government official, and he had moved the family from place to place during her childhood to ensure its safety during periods of danger, unrest, and war. They lived lavishly until they went into exile in another Asian country.

"My mother moved to the United States when she was twenty. That's when she met my father. You could say that he was an Asian Ricky Ricardo." Victor laughed at the analogy. "He was a flashy dresser, a suave dancer. He swept my mother off her feet. He had American manners, and, to her, it seemed like he had an ability to make his way through American society."

While Victor's father was born in the same country as his wife-to-be, he came from a class at the other end of its economic spectrum. When he was only seven years old, his own father died, leaving the family in utter poverty. They moved to a large city where a relative reluctantly took them in. He didn't support them, however, and they were reduced to begging on the streets to sustain themselves.

Victor's father ran away at age sixteen, signed up as a sailor on a ship, and eventually came to the United States. He quickly constructed the Americanized public persona that so impressed Victor's mother when they met.

He made decent money in a service job, but he was nearly illiterate in both his native tongue and English. This wasn't completely apparent to his educated wife until they married following a short courtship. However, his illiteracy was often at the heart of the disputes that raged between them until they divorced when Victor was twenty, following an incident in which the father physically attacked the mother. Victor never saw his father again.

From the time Victor was nine until he was sixteen, his father regularly came to his bed at night, stroking Victor's torso, and, with time, his genitalia. Victor was confused by the combination of intense pleasure and revulsion that he felt about what his father was doing. We'll talk more about this in chapter 9.

By his late twenties, Victor was depressed. He hadn't been able to finish college and had few friends. Although he claimed to be comfortable with his gay sexual orientation, he'd been unable to form an enduring intimate relationship with another man. He decided to enter psychotherapy. Early in his work, he started to deal with his history of abuse by his father. Later, however, he also began to remember an earlier series of incidents.

These earlier incidents involved his maternal grandparents. They occurred during visits to his grandparents in their Asian home-in-exile for two years starting when he was four. The grandparents played a game with him called "Where Are the Eggs?" He would be naked, and they would chase him around the house looking for his testicles, which they playfully called eggs. When they caught him, they mercilessly tickled him as they touched his scrotum and stroked his testicles. The game was exciting, accompanied by hysterical whoops of laughter on all sides. Sometimes his mother was present during the game, although she didn't participate. But when Victor began school, the game suddenly stopped, and his grandparents refused to engage in it even when he begged them to. He remembered feeling hurt and even depressed at the loss of this exciting connection to them.

Victor's parents tried to put their childhoods behind them and never spoke about their early life experiences. He grew up with virtually no knowledge of their culture and an aversion to learning anything about the country his parents fled. He therefore didn't know whether "Where Are the Eggs?" was traditional there. Nevertheless, he was deeply uncomfortable remembering it.

So for Victor there were two periods of his life when he was sexually betrayed. The recurring nighttime visits by his father were both abusive and traumatic. Victor instinctively remained silent about them. Both he and his abuser knew an incest taboo was being broken.

But his grandparents seem to have felt their game was acceptable with a preschool child. We never discovered whether the game was common in their larger culture, but apparently it was appropriate within his maternal extended family. After all, the sexual play was openly acknowledged. So perhaps the game was normal in his grandparents' culture and initially only traumatized Victor because they stopped it suddenly. As Victor matured and looked back on what happened, however, it became traumatically shameful because he had acquired values from American culture, where such play isn't acceptable.

Fortunately, Victor was eventually able to see how distorted his relationships had been with his father and, to a lesser extent, with his grandparents. After several years of therapy, he finished college, developed a relationship with another man, started work in a profession he liked, and reconnected to his maternal extended family, feeling much more at ease.

6

Same-Sex Abuse and Sexual Orientation

If you were sexually abused by a man or another boy, you may have worried about why you were his victim or about your sexual orientation. You may have asked yourself these questions:

- Was it really abuse?

- Who started it?

- Why did he choose me?

- What if I liked all or part of it?

- If I was passive or didn't fight back, am I a sissy or a girl?

- If I felt physical pleasure, am I gay?

- Was I gay to begin with?

- Am I fooling myself by dating women now?

- I'm gay—did my abuser make me that way?

- If I recover from abuse, will my sexual orientation change?

- Was my abuser gay? Or a straight man taking advantage of me in a very specific situation? Or a pedophile?

- What does it all mean about who I really am?

Sexual Orientation

Sexual orientation is a predominating attraction—sexually, mentally, physically, and/or emotionally—to one sex or the other. In your lifetime, you may shift from being attracted to women to being attracted to men, or from men to women. You may even feel sexual attraction to both sexes simultaneously. This can be very confusing, but it's important to remember that almost no one is entirely heterosexual or homosexual. We don't know exactly what determines predominating sexual orientation, but there is evidence suggesting substantial biological origins.

Sexual *orientation* is not the same as sexual *behavior*. Having sex with men or women—even repeatedly—doesn't in itself mean that you're gay or straight. For example, if at twelve a boy is coerced to engage in sex with a thirty-five-year-old man, this doesn't necessarily mean he's homosexual in the sense that he is fundamentally attracted to men. He may be basically heterosexual yet so frightened or starved for affection that he has sex in order to get what he needs from an older man.

Homosexuality

Until 1973, mental health professionals were taught that homosexuality is a mental disorder. Times have changed, but even now there is controversy among some professionals about what causes homosexuality, whether homosexuality is deviant, and whether therapy can change a person's sexual orientation.

In evidence offered since the 1990s, scientists have found physical differences between the brains of heterosexual and homosexual men, suggesting that sexual orientation is at least partly biological in nature. This evidence isn't definitive, but it has relieved many gay men from anguished feelings that they have somehow chosen to be homosexual and are therefore responsible for hurting their families, or for what they may think of as their own degeneracy.

Sexual orientation is virtually never a conscious choice. Whatever its origins, there's no reason to think that sexual abuse is a major influence on it. Nor is an established predominant sexual orientation likely to change, despite the claims of proponents of so-called reparative therapy. We should concentrate less on why a man is gay or even *whether* he is gay and more on helping him improve his life and feel good about himself.

Who Are You Sexually?

We all have ideas about who we are, including who we are sexually. Your self-concept can be the most important factor in knowing whether you're predominantly gay or straight. For example, you know what your sexual fantasies are. Sexual orientation has more to do with what you *feel* and *think* than what you *do*. If you only have sex with women but your fantasies are usually about men, you may be predominantly homosexual, although this inner orientation diverges from your current sexual behavior.

In contrast, the twelve-year-old I just mentioned might be sexual with a thirty-five-year-old man but fantasize about girls when he's alone or even while having sex with the man. His fantasies are like those of most boys growing up straight, not those of boys growing up gay. Yet he may be confused about having had sex with a man, especially if he was physically aroused, and then torture himself about what it all meant. Similarly, a gay boy whose victimizer is female may be confused if he was aroused with her but still feels a far greater pull toward men.

Sexual Initiation or Sexual Exploitation?

You may think of early sexual experience as a wonderful sexual initiation, especially if your "partner" wasn't a parent but was the same sex you were attracted to as you grew up. So if you were headed for a heterosexual orientation, you might not consider molestation by a woman to be abusive. (We'll talk more about this in chapter 7.) But if you weren't sexually aroused by the woman, you might take this as a sign that you are really gay.

But if you were heterosexual and abused by a man, whether you were aroused or not you may see your molestation as some shameful sign of queerness or femininity. Maybe you're worried that you somehow invited abuse and that you're actually interested in men. Or you may wonder whether your being chosen by a man as a sexual target means you're truly homosexual. This situation gets especially complicated if you were physically aroused while being molested, even though this often happens when any adolescent boy is touched sexually.

In contrast, if as a boy you even partly knew you had a gay orientation, an experience with a male abuser might have seemed like an exciting sexual initiation by a man. Perhaps you were excited and happy that at last you found a man who also wanted a male partner. Still, it might have made you feel prematurely hurried into defining yourself as gay. And if your victimizer was female, you may have felt repulsed or frightened.

If you felt sexually initiated by your experience, did this blind you to any hurt or cruelty involved? Being exploited may set the stage for mistreatment in future intimate relationships.

Owen: Closeted, Self-hating, and Exploited

Owen struggled all his life about his homosexual orientation. He lived an outwardly conservative life, crippled by the beliefs of his culture that homosexuality is a despicable sin. He was sure that his interest in boys and men was a defect and that revealing it would mean rejection by his family. When he came to me at age sixty-eight, he had come partway out of the closet but still felt ashamed of his homosexuality and depressed that he'd never had a satisfying relationship with a man.

At age twelve, Owen became involved in what he called an affair with Calvin, a wealthy twenty-nine-year-old man. No one acknowledged the sexual nature of their "courtship." His family gladly turned a blind eye, even profiting from the liaison themselves. Calvin was a constant visitor in Owen's home, showering him and his family with gifts and favors. Owen's father used to ask Owen to get Calvin to lend the father his car. (This was during the Great Depression, when private cars were a rarity in their town.) Owen hated asking for the favors requested by his parents, but Calvin was always happy to give them what they wanted.

Owen's father once asked him if Calvin ever did anything with Owen that "he shouldn't." Owen quickly answered no, and the question was never brought up again, even when Calvin took the family on vacations at his own expense and shared a room and bed with Owen while the rest of the family shared another room.

Only sixty years later did Owen begin to think that his family had used him to get what they wanted from Calvin and that they would have lost out if they had stopped Owen from seeing this man. He began to wonder if his family had exploited him.

Owen acknowledged that if he heard about a relationship between a twelve-year-old boy and a twenty-nine-year-old man, he would feel it was inappropriate and exploitative. But he maintained that because he was interested in sex with men, Calvin couldn't have abused him. It was almost an afterthought that he never loved Calvin and was far more interested in boys his own age. He felt homely and unlovable, highly sexual but unattractive. Sexual responses from any man, starting with Calvin, made him feel loved and sexually fulfilled.

In his mid-twenties, after a series of affairs with other closeted gay men, Owen married a woman who accepted his lack of enthusiasm for sex with her. He became depressed, however, and started to see a psychiatrist who (with Owen's relieved permission) told Owen's wife that Owen was homosexual. She wanted to stay married, and, feeling that he couldn't bear to disappoint her further, Owen agreed. They divorced after twenty-five years when his wife fell in love with another man.

After his divorce, Owen began to live a relatively open homosexual life, although he never came out to any of his family. While he said his family must know he was gay, he couldn't bring himself to broach the subject. He had a few brief but serious affairs with men who were needy and dependent. Each time, Owen eventually felt used by the other man for money or other things, and the relationships all ended badly.

Although Owen's therapy with his psychiatrist was helpful, in the thirty years they worked together they never considered Owen's sexual abuse by Calvin. Instead, they set out to "cure" Owen of his homosexuality. The relationship with Calvin was only addressed as an example of Owen's early gay experience. Calvin's exploitation of Owen was overlooked, and Owen didn't make a connection between his "affair," his family's misuse of him, and his later relationships with men where he felt manipulated.

What Does All This Say about Me?

Was I Responsible?

Sexually abusive behavior is often more about power and aggression than sexuality. But it hardly matters what the abuser is thinking. Whether you're straight or gay, if you were molested by a man, you may believe you almost magically communicated a homosexual invitation—that it was your seductive powers that led to his sexual advances. You may feel even more responsible if you became erect or ejaculated during the abuse. While these are the normal physiological responses to stimulation of a boy's genitals, you might feel that they provide proof of your role as a gay seducer.

So as a boy and later as a man, you may have asked yourself, "Was I chosen because I seemed interested? Was I interested? Did he know I wasn't man enough to resist? Was he attracted to me because I'm feminine or a sissy?

Did I Consent?

Most of us can see that a very young child can't give informed consent to sex with a grown-up. But abusers, especially hebephiles—molesters who are specifically attracted to teenagers—may convince themselves that a boy is a willing sexual partner. Even the boy may believe he consented.

What about teenagers? They are swiftly becoming men. But their bodily changes don't mean they've developed the capacity to understand and consent to sexual behavior with an adult. How many thirteen-year-olds can even begin to understand the implications of having sex with a father, a teacher, a scoutmaster, or a priest?

Before dismissing these arguments because you agreed to sex with an adult, consider these questions: How primed were you to do what an authority told you to do? Did he make it seem like fun, or a game, or what all the guys do? Were you groomed in some way to consent to his desires? How prepared were you for whatever feelings you had afterward? How much did he care about you and how much about his own gratification? Even if you enjoyed yourself, did you learn to equate sex with exploitation? Have many of your intimate relationships since then been characterized in some way by exploitation?

I Had Sex with a Man

Even if you don't question your sexual orientation, you may have intense, disturbing feelings after same-sex abuse. If you're gay, you may feel ashamed, sometimes without connecting that shame to any particular thought or memory. The shame may be attached to all sexuality and the fact that you are gay, or even stretch so far that you feel generally ashamed of who you are. Maybe you're even scared you'll become a child molester. You may mix up being gay with being a pedophile.

If you're heterosexual, you may detest gay men. You may think they all want to molest boys or seduce you. Maybe you're afraid that any affection at all from another man is a homosexual advance and that this advance is being made because there's something gay about you. Or you may feel disturbing, surprising impulses to be sexual with other men, even if you feel no real sexual attraction to them. Like some abused gay men, you may worry that you'll become a child molester. Lastly, however, you may eventually feel more understanding and accepting of gay men if as an abused straight man you've always felt on the margins of society, just as many gay men do.

Your concerns may make you question your manhood. And you may be afraid that voicing your worry will lead you to a truth you're scared to hear.

RAMON: I Need Tenderness. Am I Gay? Am I a Man?

Ramon was deeply troubled about his sexual identity and the role he played in his abuse by a neighborhood puppeteer. He feared that if he told me about his inner thoughts, I'd conclude he was gay, bisexual, or at least unmanly and judge him for how he'd lived.

But Ramon eventually found the words to tell me that his neighbor had been tender and had known how to make him feel good. The sex had been sensuous and arousing, and even when Ramon had bled, he'd never felt pain. He said miserably, "It's never been so sweet, so nice with anyone again. What does that mean? Who am I?" I remarked that he had felt safe and cared for with this man. He'd clearly felt this was the one person who focused on him and was attentive to him when his world was coming apart.

Later in treatment, Ramon revealed ashamedly that when he thought about his experiences with the puppeteer, he felt an erotic tingling throughout his genital and rectal areas. He then talked about how during the period of abuse he woke up every morning waiting for the moment he could go visit the puppeteer and feel his tender lovemaking. He said, "I've been looking for that again ever since. I wish every day I could feel so good. But I don't think I'm gay—I never look that way at men on the street, and I like being with women. And if I tell anyone—my girlfriend, my friends—how I feel turned on when I think of being with him, they'll think I'm indecent—they won't take care of me anymore."

Here Ramon revealed his prime motivation for being sexual at all. He yearned to feel cared about, to be dependent, as if he were still a needy boy. The safety and nurturance that accompanied his abuse were more important than the sex of his abuser.

Male Abusers: Gay? Pedophiles? Both?

There's a myth that men who abuse boys, especially men who abuse large numbers of boys over time, are homosexual predators who want to turn their victims gay. While some child abusers may consider themselves gay, most pedophiles who abuse children consider themselves heterosexual. In fact, in a study of over three thousand incarcerated pedophile sex offenders, *not one* said he considered himself homosexual. Many of them were repulsed by the idea of homosexuality or expressed hatred of gay men. Many pedophiles are attracted to adult women as well as to young boys and girls, and they're often married with children.

If we define homosexuality as involving attraction to adults of the same sex, there seem to be virtually no true homosexual pedophiles. Remember, pedophiles who abuse boys consider themselves straight and say they're not attracted to adult men. So it's misleading to talk about homosexual child sexual abuse. I use the clearer term *same-sex abuse*.

Many pedophiles explain that they are attracted to a young boy's hairless body and relatively delicate features. These characteristics may remind them of a woman. Once a boy reaches puberty and develops male sexual characteristics like body hair and large musculature, he's no longer attractive to the pedophile.

Hebephiles are not as well studied, although they abuse many adolescent boys. We don't know how many hebephiles are also sexually attracted to adult men or women, but many of them seem to feel no older sexually than their teenage victims.

Doesn't Abuse Make You Gay?

Research shows that a greater percentage of homosexual than heterosexual men were abused as boys. This doesn't prove, however, that abuse causes homosexuality or that gay children cause their own abuse.

Consider how pedophiles select their victims. They look for quiet, vulnerable children, not loud, aggressive boys who might fight back or report them. The "different" boy, lonely and vulnerable—especially if he shows some interest in men—has the highest risk of being molested. Many of these boys are already headed for a gay orientation before being abused, although they may not have words to understand this.

This doesn't mean that a boy responsive to men caused his own abuse by revealing his interest in them. As they mature, all boys and girls are curious about men and women. They're especially playful with adults of the sex that interests them romantically. But a flirtatious little girl isn't asking a man to hurt and molest her. Nor is a little boy who gravitates toward a man asking him for adult sexuality. Grown-ups should know not to take advantage of children's explorations into their feelings about adults. If they do, they're child molesters, even if they believe the child willingly participated in sex.

If a man molests a boy, does this turn the boy homosexual? If the abuse lasts for a long period of time, would it increase the likelihood that the boy will be gay? Do adult gay men prey on little boys to recruit them into their lifestyle? The answer to these questions seems to be no.

While scientists don't agree about what causes sexual orientation, most researchers and psychologists believe it's established in early childhood before the age when boys are likely to be sexually abused. (The average age of a boy's first molestation is about nine.) Also, most abused gay men say they knew in some way that they were attracted to their own sex *before* they were ever abused. So there's evidence that a gay orientation is not fundamentally caused by sexual abuse.

But if you're gay, it's natural for you to ask the following questions:

- Did I ask for it?

- Was my interest in men so obvious?

- Did I really want it?

- If it excited me, was it molestation?

- Am I gay because I was abused?

Any boy growing up gay is likely to endure painful inner struggles as he tries to understand his sexual orientation and handle people's reactions to it. He often goes through a period of wondering about how he came to be homosexual. He will look everywhere for an answer to the question: Why am I gay? And if he's been sexually abused by a man, it's easy to blame his orientation on his abuse. This, of course, prolongs whatever pain he may feel as he tries to settle his sexual orientation issues.

If you believe molestation caused your sexual orientation, you may hate being homosexual. You may even think that if you feel good about being gay, you're allowing your abuser to win. This makes it extraordinarily hard to develop positive feelings about being a gay man—about being yourself.

I'm Straight, Aren't I?

Straight men who suffered same-sex abuse commonly have a period of sexual acting out with other men. At the same time, they may wonder if they are really gay, if they were always gay, or if the abuse turned them gay. Andreas, for example, at one point in his thirties experimented sexually with men because of the numbness he felt during sex with his wife. Eventually, he decided he had even less interest in sex with men than with women.

Other straight abused men are at times attracted to men and may compulsively act out sexual desires with them. This can be troubling and bewildering. Even more frightening is being sexual with men while feeling little or no desire for them. This compulsive behavior can be a way of repeating your boyhood abuse with a major difference—this time you have more power and control. Or it can be a way of soothing yourself by releasing chemicals that calmed you down when you were abused (see chapter 4).

Even so, sexual abuse doesn't seem to make predominantly straight men become predominantly gay, as the following men demonstrate:

- In his early teens, Julian had an ongoing relationship with a priest. Despite their close relationship, Julian is married and heterosexual.

- Abused by his grandfather from the time he was a preschooler, Quinn is straight as well.

- Teo was abused by his godfather for an extended time but is also heterosexual.

EZRA: Hungry for a Father, Hungry for Women

Ezra's father was chronically depressed, emotionally inaccessible, and even mean. He did little but go to work and do the bare necessities required of him. When provoked, he lashed out emotionally or physi-

cally at Ezra. Ezra was hungry for the attention of a male authority figure. When he was ten, he was easy prey for the neighborhood teenager
who enticed him into the woods and masturbated on his bare chest. Ezra
was embarrassed that this single episode had a profound deadening effect
on him. He became a shy young man who was unable to maintain relationships with women and felt painfully constricted when near them.
Still, he was avidly interested in women. He reported gleefully how he
would walk down the street looking at them, saying to himself, "There's
a babe! . . . Another babe! . . . There's another!"

In rare cases, however, sexual abuse stunts the ability to solidify any
sexual orientation at all.

BRUNO: Lonely and Sexually Confused

Bruno, a single man in his mid-sixties, suffered physical, verbal, and
sexual abuse from several people as a boy. He's one of the very few men
I've treated whose capacity for sexual orientation seemed fundamentally disordered by his reactions to same-sex abuse.

In late middle age, Bruno wanted to discover his sexual orientation
so that he could pursue either men or women with a vigor that had eluded
him all his life. The youngest in a large immigrant working-class family, he received severe beatings from his father. He considered this physical brutality acceptable, not unlike what happened in other families from
his culture. Having had a learning disability, however, he was furious at
the nuns in his parochial schools, who were critical, derisive, terrifying,
humiliating, and cruel.

When he was twelve, Bruno was taken to the family doctor for a
mild illness. The doctor manipulated Bruno into having mutual oral sex.
Afterward, the doctor told Bruno's parents to bring him back every
week. They brought him back weekly for over three years. Bruno
protested, but he didn't tell his parents about the abuse. They angrily
told him he was ungrateful for the doctor's interest in him. Not coinci-
dentally, the doctor didn't charge anyone in the family for medical attention during the years he was molesting Bruno. Finally, when Bruno was
fifteen, the doctor lost interest in him, and became similarly attached to
a younger boy.

Bruno enjoyed socializing with women, flirting mildly with them,
and escorting them to social events. In more intimate moments, however,

he was terrified they'd make sexual demands on him. He had some mild sexual interest in them but was sure he couldn't perform adequately and would be subject to ridicule from even the kindest women he knew.

He did try to attract other men. He often followed through and completed sexual acts with these men, but more from a wish to please them than from his own sexual attraction. He often walked away from other men once he felt their desire.

Bruno went through his entire adult life like this. He never had an intimate relationship and was uncertain about his sexual orientation. He sometimes thought of himself as a homosexual who didn't enjoy sex with men and at other times as a closet heterosexual who was afraid to have sex with women.

Initially, I thought Bruno was a closeted gay man with low self-esteem whose restrictive cultural background made it impossible for him to accept his homosexuality. It was crucial to distinguish his feelings about homosexuality from any homosexual wishes. Bruno certainly shared some of the antigay attitudes of the working-class Catholic family he grew up in during the 1920s and 1930s. But he said he'd reached a point where he was more afraid of staying confused about his sexuality than of discovering that he was gay.

Having declared this, Bruno proceeded to tell me that while he was enraged about the doctor's molestations, they'd provided him with the exhilarating experience of feeling attractive and desired. This was what he tried to repeat with men as an adult. He froze at the thought of getting close to a woman. "None of my affairs with men are really gratifying," he said, "but at least we have sex, something that never happens when I'm with women." Yet he wanted to be with women. "I wonder," he said, "if my doctor turned me into an unwilling homosexual."

Most men I've treated have eventually been able to discern at some fundamental level whether they are gay or straight. Most men predominantly have sexual fantasies about either women or men. But Bruno was different. He had no strong fantasies either way. His ability to relate to anyone sexually was very limited. In many ways, he'd never reached a level of maturity that could allow him to have any meaningful, intimate relationship. He was developmentally stuck at a very young age.

For a period of time, he seemed to lose interest in both sexes. Then he came in one day and told me he'd been fantasizing about having sex with a hermaphrodite. This ideal lover would have breasts and both male and female genitals. Young, feminine, naive, and virginal, her male genitals would calm his anxiety over being with a woman, while her virginity would ensure that she wouldn't criticize Bruno's sexual performance.

This fantasy frightened Bruno. He quickly left therapy before we ever got the answer to his original question: Was he gay or straight? Maybe he was fundamentally heterosexual and was right to say he was an unwilling homosexual. If so, his abuse did play a defining role in shaping his orientation. Or maybe he was basically gay but unable to acknowledge this because religious and cultural strictures against homosexuality, combined with his abuse, made it impossible. But I think he was so traumatized that his development froze—that he was not gay, straight, bisexual, or transgendered. Rather, he was so crippled emotionally that he was basically asexual, unable to relate with anyone in intimate situations.

Hatred of Gays

Sometimes boys who "look gay" are attacked by adolescent boys and even by grown men. This is called *gay bashing*. These attackers may feel threatened, fearing that if any boy or man is comfortable with homosexuality, then all straight men risk losing their masculinity and heterosexuality. In some cases, these attackers are even disturbed by some unacknowledged attraction they feel for the boy.

Afraid that their own masculinity or sexual orientation is at risk, they attack the boy, as if he caused their anxiety. This kind of behavior is especially likely among those who've never evolved beyond the simplistic views of homosexuality often held by adolescent boys without much confidence in their own masculinity. The virulence of gay bashing can lead to particularly ugly outcomes.

BEAU: Despised, Powerless, Raped

Beau is a gay man who suffered multiple abuses and rapes as a teenager. Before he ever had a conscious thought of being gay, his effeminacy left him open to a severe gay-bashing incident in early adolescence that eroded his already shaky sense of himself.

Introverted and small for his age, Beau grew up in a conservative small town whose population included many rednecks and members of the religious far right. Both parents were well educated, but his mother was vicious and verbally abusive while his father was fussy, fastidious, and withdrawn, passive with his wife and uninterested in his son. Teased for his effeminacy, Beau was nevertheless often groped or otherwise approached sexually by adult married men.

As a high school freshman, Beau was taken under the athletic field bleachers by three student athletes and anally raped. An assistant coach passed by, saw what was happening, said, "I want some of that, too," and also raped him. Beau already knew he was emotionally drawn to men but had only the vaguest sense of what physical sex acts involved. His rape was a profoundly traumatic introduction to sex.

School authorities never punished the assailants. (Indeed, the assistant coach was eventually made head coach!) When they called Beau's father to tell him about the assault—it's not clear that they conveyed that his son had actually been raped—he told them to send Beau back to class. When he got home, his mother called him a "little bitch" for having caused so much disruption.

Afterward, Beau became an object of rampant abuse and derision on a daily basis. Boys would force him to choose either to fellate them or give them payoff money to leave him alone. Girls knew about this and openly called him a faggot and a sissy. He was miserable, frightened, and endangered until he graduated from high school and went away to college, never to return to his hometown again except for brief visits to his parents.

In the Movies

If a boy has sex with an older woman in the movies, it's almost always portrayed as an exciting, pleasurable education for the boy (*Summer of '42*, *Murmur of the Heart*, *The Graduate*). In contrast, when men have sex with boys, the scene is often brutal and humiliating (*The Prince of Tides*, *Sleepers*, *The Boys of St. Vincents*). Other movies treat sex between boys and men as laughable (*My Life As a Dog*, *Porky's*).

Sex between boys and men is inevitably portrayed as shameful. The boys are depicted as believing they must never discuss what happened to them. This silence usually has disastrous effects on them (*The Prince of Tides*, *Sleepers*, *The Boys of St. Vincents*, *The Celebration*, *Mystic River*).

Boys abused by men are often portrayed as criminals in later life. This is indeed sometimes the case, but rarely do the movies show what is more likely to happen: an abused boy grows up to be sensitive and compassionate, although perhaps depressed, anxious, or agitated.

I don't know of any film where a young boy tells someone else what happened. Nor do the boys heal. And they are certainly unlikely to become heroes in boyhood for being brave enough to speak out.

A boy abused by a man can easily learn from movies to be silent and ashamed, and his silence may spread far beyond the betrayal situation, leading to devastating results. He learns that same-sex abuse causes ridicule or social ostracism if it's known. So he keeps quiet to avoid derision and humiliation.

Silence has terrible effects on the boys in these movies. But the only action filmmakers allow them is hypermasculine revenge, as when the boys in *Sleepers* who'd been raped by prison guards hunt them down one by one.

I'm not advocating censorship or limiting artistic freedom of expression in any way. I believe, however, that consciousness-raising about male sexual victimization is as appropriate for creative artists as for all other members of society.

In *Mysterious Skin*, a novel by Scott Heim, when two boys sexually abused by their Little League coach meet in early adulthood, they're finally able to put the experience into words. The trauma led one to believe he'd been taken away by aliens and the other to become a sexually compulsive hustler.

One of them says afterward, "If we were stars in the latest Hollywood blockbuster, then I would have embraced him, my hands patting his shoulder blades, violins and cellos billowing on the soundtrack as tears streamed down our faces. But Hollywood would never make a movie about us."

In the future, perhaps someone will.

7

When the Abuser Is Female

Funny or Criminal?

A 1997 *New Yorker* cartoon depicts a young boy's bedroom. The window shade is down. On the wall are pennants and a poster. On the bureau, a model airplane. Clothes spill sloppily out of the dresser drawers. A baseball bat leans against the wall. Scattered about the floor are board games, model cars, and a football. A boy of ten or eleven is sitting up in bed next to a young woman in her late teens or early twenties. A post-sex scene straight out of an old French movie: Both are naked. Both are smoking. The woman is a glassy-eyed blonde, exhaling clouds of smoke. The boy gestures grandly to her as he says in the caption, "I want you to know, Sheila, that you'll always be more than just another babysitter to me."

The gag is clear. The boy, barely into puberty, managed the sexual tryst with his much older babysitter. He's gently letting her down before he dumps her. Typical of boys his age, he'll no doubt soon be bragging to his friends about his conquest, one of many to come. It's a clever cartoon.

The cartoon represents the general view of our culture when it comes to sex between older women and boys or very young men. She's been generous to him. He's taken advantage of her. Certainly she's not a sexual abuser. She's the one who's been used.

To most Americans, this cartoon is amusing. But what if the sexes are reversed? What if the cartoon showed a ten-year-old girl naked in her bed with her twenty-year-old male babysitter? For most of us, the joke is suddenly no longer funny. We'd feel uncomfortable with the image and angry at the babysitter. In virtually every state, he'd be prosecuted for lewd and lascivious behavior, child molestation, and rape. Why, we would think, would the magazine publish such a tasteless cartoon?

The cartoon reveals the double standard about adult–child sexuality: When an older woman has sex with a boy, it's okay, but when an older man has sex with a girl, it's not only unacceptable but a serious crime.

We learn this double standard early. Boys should happily accept any woman's offer of sex as a treat that they can later brag about. A woman abusing a boy is far from our minds. If anything, sexual experiences between boys and older women are considered sexual initiations—rites of passage from boyhood to manhood. We're all familiar with coming-of-age stories and movies that reinforce these traditions. (Of course, it's required that the woman be attractive. If she's not, all the fun is gone.)

Myths about Sex with Women

The following myths make it hard to even think that women can be abusive:

- Sexual abuse requires physical force against an unwilling victim. Women aren't strong enough to force boys into submission. And boys wouldn't be unwilling anyway.

- Boys and men can protect themselves from the "weaker sex." If they don't want to be with a woman, they can easily escape. If they think they were assaulted, they're fools.

- Men and boys who don't enjoy sex with a woman must be gay.

- Men always enjoy aggressive sex.

- Men's orgasms and erections are always voluntary.

- A woman can't harm someone sexually because she has no penis.

We all learn about life from commonly held beliefs, so these stories and myths have a powerful effect. Even mental health researchers and professionals have difficulty seeing past these myths. As recently as

1988, one researcher said that the abuse of boys by women is "virtually nonexistent."

Having bought into these ideas, a boy molested by a woman has no internal guide for comprehending his experience as anything but good luck. No one will listen empathically and explain that, yes, women can hurt boys sexually just as men can.

He quickly figures out he's supposed to enjoy what happened, no matter what he actually felt. If he didn't like it, he concludes his friends won't understand and may think there's something wrong with him. So he keeps quiet or pretends it was great.

If a sexual encounter with a woman wasn't exhilarating for you, maybe you believed it meant there's something wrong with you. Maybe you felt ashamed of yourself. Maybe you sensed you'd be blamed for not enjoying it. Maybe you felt it was wrong to report the incident or talk about your anxiety.

For these reasons, we don't know how common woman–boy abuse really is. But we know it happens. Women are just as capable of betrayal as men are.

Is it Okay for Women to Be Boy-lovers?

If you were abused by a woman, you may never have found anyone who could relate to your trauma. Even other survivors of boyhood abuse may not understand your situation, especially if they were forcibly molested or feared violence by an older, stronger boy or man. Some survivors may not be able to understand that your molestation by a woman could scar you as deeply as theirs by a man. And you may agree with them, because you've learned the same myths.

If you tried to report your abuse to the authorities, you may have found little support. In those rare cases when a woman *is* reported for molesting a boy, the authorities often shrug it off, considering the incident a harmless tryst, perhaps insinuating that the woman is immature, love-starved, or oversexed.

Discussing a case of woman–boy rape, one prosecutor said, "The reaction in these cases is usually winking and nodding and saying boys will be boys and that this is all part of the learning experience. . . . It's very hard for boys to come forward because they feel ashamed at admitting they've been victimized."

MARY KAY LETOURNEAU

Most of us remember the case of Mary Kay Letourneau, a thirty-five-year-old Seattle schoolteacher, and her thirteen-year-old sixth-grade student, a boy she'd also taught in second grade.

As I write this, I see how even our language stops us from casting a woman as an abuser. The easiest way to describe what happened is to say "the boy impregnated her," or "she became pregnant by him." But this kind of language implies that *he* was the aggressor, the person in charge of what happened. See how thoroughly our culture considers women to be passive and submissive during sex? I don't think that's how it went, yet it's hard to find language that describes her as the active one in the relationship. The best I can do is to say that she *got herself* pregnant by having sex with him.

In any case, Letourneau, a married mother of four, gave birth to a baby girl. Convicted of two counts of child rape, she was sentenced to seven and a half years in prison. At her sentencing, she expressed remorse and pleaded for leniency: "I did something that I had no right to do, morally or legally. It was wrong and I am sorry. I give you my word that it will not happen again. Please help me."

Perhaps the judge pitied Letourneau or felt the boy wasn't hurt. The boy protested that Letourneau didn't deserve prosecution and that he was the sexual initiator. (Sound familiar?) So Letourneau was given parole for all but six months of her sentence. She was released after serving three months on the condition that she attend a program for sex offenders, take the medication prescribed for her bipolar disorder, and not see the boy again.

Within days of her release from prison, however, she stopped taking her medication and quit her required sex offender treatment. She was soon rearrested in a parked car with the boy. They seemed to be having sex and were apparently planning to leave the country. Her parole was revoked. But she wasn't prosecuted for this second offense, despite the fact that she was pregnant again.

Back in jail to serve out the term of her original sentence, she gave birth to a second daughter. Both girls are being raised by the boy's family. At that time, they were said to be accepting Letourneau as a member of their family.

Letourneau's behavior was recognized as sexually abusive and she was brought to trial, but she was penalized far more leniently than a man in her position might have been. Imagine again, as you did with the *New Yorker* cartoon, that the sexes were reversed. If a thirty-five-year-old married male teacher impregnated his thirteen-year-old student, how would he be treated? Would the girl's family welcome him into their family? Would he be let out on parole because he gave his word not to recontact the girl? The answers are obvious.

The boy insisted there was nothing wrong with the relationship and that he was the one who had made the first moves on his teacher. "All that matters," he declared to a reporter, "is that we loved each other."

But *is* that all that matters? Is any thirteen-year-old ready to make the life decisions this sixth-grader was encouraged to make by his teacher? Can he think through the consequences for himself and the babies he fathered? Thinking that love is all that matters in itself tells us that he wasn't ready to make such complex choices. This relationship involved a married woman committing adultery to get herself pregnant by a thirteen-year-old, betraying not only her husband but her own four children. A lot more than romantic love mattered.

The boy later changed his mind, deciding he'd indeed been exploited. Hoping to receive funds to help them raise the babies, he and his family sued the police and the school district for not protecting him. They didn't win the suit because it wasn't clear that the authorities had sufficient knowledge to prevent the relationship.

During this civil trial, the boy testified, according to ABC News, that he and his teacher first became involved when he needed help with history lessons. "I was supposed to do the test, and for every answer I got right on the test she would take [a] part of clothing off that she had on," he said. One night, as a reward for his improved work, Letourneau took him out to dinner, and they began to flirt.

"I asked her what she would do if I was to go over and kiss her," he testified. "She said only a coward would wait and a warrior would go over and do it." So he kissed her. Later, while on a three-day sleepover at her house with her husband and children at home, he proposed to her. He gave her a ring he claimed he found on the street. "She took off her husband's ring and put mine on," he said.

We can't say all the boy's future problems were due to the relationship with his teacher. Still, this boy, who Letourneau had originally said was exceptionally mature, described himself at age eighteen as an alcoholic with extensive psychiatric problems and perhaps a suicidal depression. He said he was no longer in love with Letourneau, was sick of the children, and was tired of being in the news. He'd also gotten in trouble with the law, pleading guilty, for example, to auto theft. Given that sexually molested boys are subject to these symptoms, is it a surprise that he had these difficulties?

When Letourneau was released from jail in 2004, the boy was twenty-one, and presumably they resumed their relationship and even planned to marry. Whatever the eventual outcome, the boy's life was inevitably changed by this betrayal.

The Letourneau case received great notoriety. Other boys react to sex with female teachers in equally complicated—though less public—ways.

IRA: A Boy's "Luck" Runs Out

Ira came to me in his early forties. He'd had difficulty being intimate with women and felt like a failure with them. He also had a sense of languishing in his career.

"When I was young, everyone predicted I'd become a creative success someday. But now, here I am at forty-three, and I simply haven't gone anywhere. My job is boring."

Since college, Ira had not had a relationship with a woman that lasted more than a few months. Recently, he hadn't even tried to meet a woman. He told himself there was no point in trying to establish a relationship while he was such a failure in his career. Yet he saw life slipping by. He was frightened that he'd grow old alone and never have the children he yearned for.

He mentioned that he'd left a prestigious university after his sophomore year following the breakup of a relationship with his girlfriend, who'd been a professor of his. He hastened to add that they hadn't begun to date until he was no longer her student. For two years after he left school, he'd made some false starts before enrolling at a far less prominent university close to his parents' homes. He told me he regretted never again seeing his friends from the first college and losing the sense of belonging he'd felt when he was there.

I asked what happened with the teacher. Ten years Ira's senior, she'd been his instructor in a grueling freshman course. She offered him special help with his work, as she did for other students. His grades rose under her guidance, and he received the highest grade among his classmates.

During the summer between high school and college, Ira's parents had announced they were getting divorced. This was disturbing news, although not a total surprise, since their relationship had deteriorated badly during his adolescence. His father had a younger girlfriend and told Ira far more about his sex life with her than Ira was comfortable hearing.

His mother was depressed, which was nothing new. "I'd always taken care of her throughout my childhood," Ira explained. "She was always needy. She criticized everything and everyone. She had a way of demanding attention from me, and I gave it to her."

When Ira started college, he also felt lonely and needy. His professor noticed him and provided him attention. Ira felt nourished and sustained, so he gravitated toward her.

When the course was over, they met once or twice informally, then she invited him for lunch in the faculty dining room, which was an unusual event at this school. Over lunch, she asked him to teach her some yoga exercises he knew and suggested he drop by her apartment that evening. When he arrived, they tried the exercises. She offered him something to drink and began to talk more personally to him.

She asked if he'd ever thought of her as a woman rather than a teacher. "When she said that, I kind of froze. I knew what she meant. I actually hadn't ever thought of her as a woman. I was too embarrassed to say that to her. She was a teacher I liked a lot. She helped me, and I was grateful for that and wanted it to continue. But part of me knew I was at a crossroads—if I turned her down, I knew that would be the end of our special relationship. So I hesitated, and then went along with her. I never put it into words this way at the time, but I was making some inner calculations. If I went to bed with her and made her my girlfriend, I wouldn't have to give up all this attention I craved—and, of course, I was young, and the idea of sex with a woman was exciting, so it didn't seem like so bad a deal. We saw each other all semester, always privately, never in public. But it wasn't working for me. I wasn't really attracted to her, and after a while I didn't even enjoy the sex. Eventually, I put an end to it, and the whole relationship went up in flames. I never quite said to myself that this was why I left school, but I guess it was."

Ira wondered if the relationship would be considered abusive if it happened today. He said he'd always thought he'd exploited her, using her for sex and nurturance. "But, as I thought about it this time, I began to remember that she was a professor. She was the experienced one. She was needy, too—she had recently broken up with a boyfriend—and she used me to satisfy her need for attention from a man. She had the upper hand."

Ira was shaken by this idea. He had never thought about how much pressure the relationship had put on him. At the time, the two friends he confided in about it thought he was "a very lucky guy." But as he considered his subsequent relationships with women, he said, unaware of the imagery he was using, "I decided not to thrust ahead anymore in life, especially with women. I'd gotten too banged up."

The stage was set for Ira's later sexual exploitation by his teacher when he was eleven and his fifteen-year-old sister often babysat him. "One time, we somehow wound up with all our clothes off. Then she started to kiss me, first on my body, then on my penis. I wasn't in puberty yet. I had no idea what was going on at first, but I got an erection and I had some kind of orgasm without ejaculating. It was our secret, and after that we did it a lot. I never really touched her—I wouldn't have wanted to—she always started it."

I asked how their clothes "somehow" were taken off. "I don't remember. But it must have been her idea, because I didn't think about those things yet. It was her need—she was overweight and unpopular—boys didn't like her and she wanted male attention. I enjoyed it, but I wouldn't have thought to do it. And somehow I knew I was making her feel better, too. We were very close and I felt sorry for her. I would never have turned her down for anything she really wanted."

But, Ira continued, "She was a juggernaut. There would have been no stopping her. For her, I was no longer Ira. I became Boy, a symbol of all the boys who rejected her. At the same time that I felt excited, I felt very lonely—even invisible."

Ira began to see a pattern in his life. Starting with his mother, then his sister, and then his college professor, his role with women had been to take care of them, meeting their needs but not his own. For him, women became exciting and fascinating on the one hand but dangerous and exploitative on the other.

Like many other boys and men who've made "conquests" of older women, Ira emerged from the relationship feeling not like a man but like a failure. His recognition of this helped him move on beyond the failed relationships with women that were rooted in his early relationships with his mother, sister, and professor.

Cultural influences make boys and girls learn to think differently about molestations by opposite-sex abusers. We learn at a young age that woman-boy sex is acceptable but man-girl sex is abuse.

ED AND DOREEN: Processing Opposite-Sex Abuse Differently

One day, I received a pressing request from a young woman named Doreen who was seeing another therapist. As a child, she'd been sexually abused by her brother, Ed. She had now asked him to come to New York so that she could confront him in person. He was to arrive later that day without having been told why it was urgent that he come. Not knowing how he would react to the confrontation, Doreen wanted to have a therapist "on standby" in case he felt he needed to talk to someone afterward. I told her I could be available. She mentioned in passing that she wondered if Ed had also been sexually abused as a child.

Ed wanted to see me, and we met the next day. An open-faced man in his late twenties, he was bright and articulate, although not particularly savvy about human psychology.

He was in shock from his meeting with Doreen. He didn't remember the events she described, although he didn't deny they'd occurred. Doreen said that when he was eight and she was five, he would tickle her while she was in bed. This went beyond the bounds she was comfortable with. He rubbed her chest where breasts would be and stroked her thighs and vagina. She protested, but he just laughed and continued.

At first, Ed was mainly interested in helping his sister. We talked about his upbringing, and Ed and Doreen seemed to have come from a basically happy, well-adjusted family.

Ed was amused that Doreen wondered if he'd also been sexually abused. But later he mentioned that when he was about seven, an eighteen-year-old female babysitter had encouraged him to touch her bare breasts under her sweater. Laughing, he joked, "I wish I'd been older when it happened because I would've enjoyed it. But I was dumb enough to tell my parents not to hire her anymore!"

I stopped him. "Why do you think it was dumb to have her fired?"

He was surprised by my question. "Because I'm sure it felt very nice to touch her breasts," he said, "and I'd love to do it now." Ed was obviously wondering why I needed this explained.

After we talked about it, however, he began to see that imagining the event as an adult might be different from experiencing it as a boy. As a boy, he apparently felt uneasy, uncomfortable, and even frightened about fondling his caretaker's breasts. "You certainly behaved like someone protecting himself from abuse when you asked your parents not to use her anymore," I said. His laughter vanished, and he nodded, obviously troubled. He'd never thought about it that way.

What he did to Doreen soon afterward began to make sense. When children are sexually molested, they can't understand the experience as an adult would. An adult can comprehend voluntary, pleasurable sexual experiences. But a child hasn't yet developed the psychological machinery to process these adult sensations. So a seven-year-old like Ed, not knowing what to do with his mental and sensory overload, might mimic the babysitter's behavior, trying to master his past experience through repeating it.

Ed became the powerful one with Doreen. He'd probably already been fairly rough in their play, and he'd already established power over her by being older and bigger. Molesting her helped him feel more in charge of his feelings of vulnerability and being overwhelmed by his overstimulation.

Female and more attuned to victimhood than most boys, Doreen was quicker to recognize molestation. She understood she'd been abused. Ed, however, was uncomfortable at the time but later thought he was dumb for not enjoying what "should" have been an exciting sexual awakening. Until he and I discussed it, he'd probably never read about, seen, or even considered the possibility that women can sexually traumatize boys. Like many men, over time he had revised a sexually abusive boyhood experience with a woman so that in retrospect it seemed normal and exciting.

If You're Gay and Had a Female Abuser

How you react to molestation may be influenced by your sexual orientation. If you're straight and your abuser was female, you may have considered it an initiation or rite of passage, even if you felt anxious about it.

But if you're gay and your abuser was female, you may have come away with entirely different feelings. Maybe you survived your experience harboring the following types of anger:

- Anger about being abused

- Anger about being abused by someone of the sex you're not interested in

- Anger about being expected to enjoy this abuse by someone of the sex you're not interested in

- Anger about being abused and having no one to affirm that it was abuse because our culture believes that women don't molest boys

Maybe you acted this anger out, as did Yale, a gay man abused by a nun when he was in the second grade. The experience affected his views of all human relationships, and he became a very angry man. When he could, he revenged himself on women, toward whom he felt scornful. Sometimes Yale combined this revenge on women with his anger at heterosexual boys, whom he felt mistreated him throughout his adolescence because he was gay. So in high school he seduced presumably straight boys as a way of demeaning them. He got sexual satisfaction, got even with them, and had the added bonus of knowing he was "stealing" these boys from their girlfriends.

When the Abuser Is Your Mother

It's difficult enough for boys to understand what has happened when a babysitter or other female caretaker involves them in sexual acts. Understanding sexual mistreatment by a mother is even more complicated. Mother–son incest is probably the most taboo incestuous relationship. In both professional and nonprofessional settings, I've often been greeted with blank stares of horror and disbelief when I bring up overt mother–son incest even as a theoretical possibility.

Yet we know it happens. It happens despite the cultural myths about motherhood, such as:

- Mothers love their children unselfishly.

- Mothers always have their children's best interests at heart.

- Mothers are altruistic and loving.

- Mothers are there to meet the needs of their husbands and children.

- A mother may be sexual as a spouse but is asexual as a mother.

- A mother is never sexually attracted to her children, and if she were, she'd quickly extinguish such thoughts.

- A mother would not even know how to molest her child.

Mother–son incest often masquerades as some aspect of caretaking, hygiene, or nurturing. For instance, a mother may give her son unneeded enemas or spend too much time washing his genitals.

KYLE: Incest Disguised

Kyle was lined up with his sisters for weekly anal examinations by his fanatically meticulous mother. She claimed to be checking for worms and probed each of them with metal instruments while the other children watched. Such situations are rarely recognized as either sexual or abusive. If Kyle's neighbors heard his mother examined her children's rectums for worms, they might have written her behavior off as harmlessly overcompulsive or perhaps as a sign of her overzealousness in her maternal role. And yet Kyle's adult fantasies focused on sadistic sex in which victims were tied down and bodily penetrated. Coincidence? I doubt it.

Mother–son incest can be hidden through covert sexuality, as vividly described by Dr. Kenneth Adams in his book *Silently Seduced*. Keith's seductive mother merged with him, allowing no boundaries. He was her companion in her alcoholic descent. To attain sobriety and build a life, he had to cut off contact with her.

KEITH: Emotional Orgies

Seemingly warm and friendly, Keith had a lifelong inability to commit in relationships. He didn't want to "lose himself" again to a woman. But Keith was actually holding on to his mother. Isolating himself kept him fixed in the push-pull of their "romance." Ironically, this kept them psychologically close.

In hindsight, he said, "I had an emotional orgy with my mother. I'd be exhausted by all this emotional give and take with her. I'd create situations with her—I'd act out; I'd get caught doing something awful by someone's parent and it would get back to her—then I'd be thrown back to her, and again we'd have this orgy of emotion. It was sexual in some way I didn't understand. We'd keep repeating that process over and over."

It can be cataclysmic for a boy to recognize that mother–son incest has occurred. Knowing he was excited by erotic contact with his mother can be unbearably disturbing. On the one hand, he may be proud in some way of his sexual prowess. This may even lead to a sense of overconfidence about his ability to seduce women. On the other hand, he may feel terribly confused, ashamed, and worried about his inability to really follow through and live up to a woman's expectations.

BROOKE: "Almost Unbearably Excited"

Brooke Hopkins wrote a moving account of his sexual victimization by his mother at age six. At the time, he understood the events to be wrong, yet powerfully inviting. He describes how he waited after bedtime for his mother to get into bed with him and spend the night. Lying in bed, he'd think it might be better if he were a girl. Then he wouldn't have to worry about "that thing of mine" and all the erotic urges he felt toward his mother:

> Somehow, I felt, it would have been easier with another kind of body, one more like hers, because what was happening was, I knew, not supposed to be happening, and very dangerous, even though I yearned for it every night, had become completely addicted to it, and could hardly have imagined myself living without it. But by the time she slipped into bed with me, her six-year-old son, all these thoughts vanished in the sheer pleasure of having her body next to mine.

He goes on:

> [I was] almost unbearably excited by being so intimately in bed with her, by exploring her body with my hands, . . . feeling her warmth and her smell. Sometimes my penis would be so stiff from rubbing against her that I was afraid it would break off, literally like a stick. . . . I could hardly contain myself with the desire to be touched as well. It was about this time that I began to anticipate my mother's coming down the hall with a combination of the most intense longing and an almost equally intense dread.

Brooke touched his mother's body everywhere, and, though seemingly not participating, she allowed this touching without ever openly acknowledging what was happening. The only exception was when he once tried to touch her vagina and she "said sleepily, 'No, I'm sorry. You can't touch me there. That place is saved for your father.'" Brooke then describes how his father put an end to the incest by suddenly coming into his room one night and violently pulling his mother out of his bed.

RICHARD: "A Hurricane Overtook My Small Boat"

The former president of American University in Washington, D.C., Richard Berendzen resigned in disgrace after it was discovered that he'd made multiple telephone calls suggesting he was committing child sexual abuse. After undergoing extensive treatment, he coauthored a book entitled *Come Here* in which he linked his bizarre behavior to severe sexual abuse by his mother. On one occasion, he had even been included in sexual intercourse with both parents. In the book he writes about his confusion:

> What happened . . . came in a dizzying blur, feelings of confusion, disgust, and terror slamming into each other, toppled by momentary convulsions of nausea, excitement, and shame. A hurricane overtook my small boat. I tied myself to the mast, closed my eyes, and tried to survive the storm. I felt a deep revulsion, a revulsion buried under my skin. My body knew a secret, hidden from the world. Yet within this awful revulsion, I experienced momentary pleasure ripples of tingling sensation. To experience pleasure and disgust for the same reason and almost simultaneously created overwhelming confusion and torment. If I knew I hated what happened between my mother and me, how could my body respond as it did? Arousal led to pleasure, which capsized instantly in shame and disgust. It sickened and bewildered me to hate my body for making me feel good.

In the Movies

Boys get a lot of their sexual education from movies as well as from books and television. A number of classic films (*Tea and Sympathy, Harold and Maude, The Last Picture Show, Summer of '42*) have portrayed positive sexual relationships between older women and younger men or boys. The boys never come away feeling discomfort or shame. On the contrary, these are coming-of-age stories. Experienced, caring, attractive older women tenderly initiate adolescents into manhood. In one film, *Murmur of the Heart*, a fourteen-year-old boy even has a positive sexual relationship with his own mother.

There's no sense in any of these movies that a boy might feel unhappy about a sexual relationship with an older woman. Although there is occasional, expected fumbling and embarrassment, the boys are often transformed magically into skilled lovers, reinforcing the idea that a relationship like this turns a boy into a "real man." Any long-term negative consequences for the boys (or the women's husbands and families) are ignored or minimized.

The women in these films are generally kind and nonmenacing, even noble and self-sacrificing. We may feel compassion for them when the boys eventually abandon them. These women are never seen as adults sexually molesting children. In fact, though, they are needy, with personal agendas that influence them to become sexually involved with boys. They may have shaky marriages, feel neglected or old, or be in mourning for a former lover.

Even though these movies may be entertaining, there's no model in them for boys to understand that woman–boy or –young man relationships can have long-term negative consequences. Almost without exception, the films suggest boys should welcome, enjoy, and take pleasure from sexual relationships with older women.

It's not that these films are bad films. What *is* bad is the failure of filmmakers to tell the *other* stories about older women who betray boys and who are selfish or pathologically needy.

Filmmakers also fail to tell the stories of young boys who feel undermined, anxious, or guilty after having sex with older women and are unable to be intimate with partners later in life because of this; they may even become sexually compulsive or afraid of sex altogether. Yet these stories are more common in life than the stories of boys who become magically transformed by their sexual experiences with a woman.

8

Relating to Others

Affection, Intimacy, and Betrayal

Being affectionate means having warm feelings for someone and being tender and caring. Most of us can give and receive affection, although sometimes we don't get it when we need it, sometimes we don't want it when it's offered, and sometimes it's impossible for us to give it.

Intimacy is different. You can be affectionate with someone without risking much, but being intimate means exposing yourself to others. The word *intimacy* comes from the Latin for "inmost, deepest, profound, or close in friendship." So being intimate means allowing another person to know your innermost nature. It means relinquishing caution, defensiveness, and self-concern, and being openly honest with your thoughts and feelings.

In romantic intimacy, two people seem to meld their souls together in love. But being sexual isn't necessarily being intimate. In fact, for some people, it's easier to go to bed with a near-stranger and enjoy hours of unbridled passion than it is to express or appreciate affection in more intimate relationships, romantic or not.

Being intimate is a complex challenge if you were sexually betrayed as a child. The prospect of intimacy may be unendurable, even if it's offered from someone you like and trust. If you're unable to be intimate, you're apt to feel isolated. The more isolated you feel, the more you may despair.

If you are betrayed as an adult, you most likely feel hurt and angry. Even so, you probably understand that you were betrayed by one

121

individual, not the whole world. Being an adult, you can do something about it. You can change the relationship. You can decide how to behave toward your betrayer in the future, and you have many choices. If you want to maintain your relationship, you can forgive and move on. You also have the capacity to put an end to it.

But what can a child do? He's dependent on adults to survive. He doesn't have the intellectual ability, the power, or the emotional maturity to change or escape the relationship. He can't independently choose how to react to betrayal.

If spouses mistreat one another, whether physically or verbally, each has the option to say, "Our relationship is over. I'm getting a divorce!" But a child can't divorce his parents or his caretakers. Children usually have to endure their treatment, no matter what it is, how long it lasts, or how often it happens. You know how catastrophic the results can be.

Children learn about all relationships from their own early relationships. Their entire interpersonal world is limited to those experiences. If your abuser was a caregiver who otherwise treated you with affection, you may have developed a distorted idea of what affection really means, since in your personal knowledge it is accompanied by abuse.

Abused Boys Become Distrustful Men

If you were betrayed by an adult you depended on for care, love, and attention, maybe you believe that all loving relationships involve hurt and betrayal. Maybe you learned that truth is never spoken in a family and that all relationships are just pretend. Maybe you believe affection means giving up your body to someone else's desire, that affection can't exist on its own without sex, and that you can't feel loved unless you have sex with someone.

Additional betrayals may have solidified what you already believed: relationships mean pain, anger, hurt, confusion, mystery, loss, and despair. These were logical conclusions based on what seemed like scientific evidence from your past. So how can you develop healthy relationships as an adult? Relationships involving trust, sexuality, intimacy, nurturance, power, affection, or authority are challenging unless you allow yourself to believe new "evidence" from your present life.

It's natural for boys to seek attention from older boys or men. This is how they learn to be male. If a man previously betrayed you, however, maybe you grew up needing attention from men but feeling afraid of it. So you either didn't get it at all or got it at the expense of inner peace and wholeness. Your fears would stop you from feeling close to others.

You may anticipate betrayal in many ways. Maybe you feel a general anxiety or an inexplicable fear about certain relationships, or play out inner scenarios where someone betrays you in some way or makes inappropriate sexual advances.

For example, at one time my office was located in a hotel. When Seth, whose story appears in chapters 2 and 5, first saw me, he was overwhelmed with anxiety because he was reminded that he was molested by a family friend in a hotel room. My office contained a couch that in his mind could serve as a bed, adding to his fears. He could hardly talk to me, much less form a relationship so we could work together. With time and effort, though, he overcame his distrust, and we very gradually developed a good relationship that lasted many years.

Group therapy may provoke similar feelings. You may feel anxious and distrustful about joining a group, especially if it's all male. You may fear that the group members will overpower and control you. Also, the group will probably talk about sex, which may trigger anxiety-ridden memories. Trust your ability to handle feelings you couldn't as a boy so that you can use the group experience to heal.

Ambivalent Relationships

If you had both positive and negative feelings about your victimizer, you felt ambivalent about him or her. Maybe you're ambivalent now if a new relationship reminds you in some way of what happened then.

If your abuse occurred in an otherwise loving relationship, your ambivalence may stop you from being able to live in openhearted intimate relationships now. All your adult relationships, sexual or not, may be confusing, filled with suspicion and fluctuating feelings ranging from intense love to intense hate.

If you were abused by one parent, you may have confusing feelings about the other parent. Your ambivalence arises from knowing that your nonabusing parent may have loved you but failed to protect you.

Victor, who you read about in chapter 5, described how his father's abuse affected Victor's relationship with his mother. He hated the mixed anger and love he felt for her. She was his more stable parent, but she had a passive role in his abuse: "I don't know how to feel about my mother. She should have protected me. But I'm a hypocrite. I still want to go home to have her dinners and get her approval."

It's especially hard to resolve ambivalence about an abuser who was also protective and loving. Julian remained grateful for what his victimizer gave him, even while feeling furious.

JULIAN: "The Best Mentor a Boy Could Ever Have . . . Except for the Sex"

At age twelve, Julian was unhappy. Physically abused and emotionally starved at home, he welcomed Father Scott's attention when the priest required that he come for special counseling sessions before being confirmed.

Father Scott taught Julian about language and music. He told him about the ancient Greeks, emphasizing the special relationships of that era between men and boys. Father Scott said that he and Julian had a similar relationship of intellectual mentoring, meaningful commitment, and intimacy.

A few months later, Father Scott began to encourage Julian to talk about the pain he felt about being abused and neglected at home. Afterward, he'd hug Julian. For Julian, the hugs felt precious. He was hungry for physical affection, or any kind of positive feelings from an adult.

But the hugs got longer, and then one day Father Scott gave Julian a long, passionate kiss. Julian was startled and confused, unsure of what was happening and what it meant. Then Father Scott said with a meaningful look, "I know you want more, but that's all for now." Julian pointed out, "So right from the beginning he made it that the abuse was my idea, so I felt responsible and guilty that it was happening even though I had no concept of men kissing at the time and certainly no interest in it."

For two years, Julian and Father Scott had regular sexual encounters that included anal sex and mutual masturbation. The priest maintained that their relationship existed on the highest plane possible for two human beings. They'd attained the ideal glorified by the greatest poets and philosophers of the ancient world and experienced all forms of love together: love of beauty, thought, logic, and art, and love of one another that was intellectual, sensual, and emotional.

Julian did love Father Scott. He craved the companionship and concentrated interest the priest offered him but was confused and conflicted about the sex. "He did so much for me! Anyone would think he was the best mentor a boy could ever have, and, except for the sex, he was." Julian said the activity with Father Scott was never what he really wanted sexually, but he shamefacedly acknowledged that it was satisfying in some ways as well.

After Julian started dating, he'd often sneak out of his house after dates and go to Father Scott's rooms for physical release of the sexual arousal he felt with his girlfriends. Likewise, when beaten by his parents for flunking out of school, he went to Father Scott for comfort. He only realized years later that the relationship with the priest had contributed to his depression, anger, and inability to concentrate on his studies.

At age fifteen, Julian put a stop to the sex and entered a new school, where he did well. His family moved away from Father Scott's parish, and Julian rarely returned to his old neighborhood. He excelled academically and eventually married, but he continued to be ashamed, conflicted, and secretive about his relationship with the priest.

Julian was grateful for the intellectual and emotional expansion that he got from Father Scott. Just below his awareness, however, churned a rage about the priest's abuse of their relationship and how it still distorted and confused his sexual thoughts, feelings, and behavior. He was a compulsive masturbator driven to furtively view peep shows, and consumed by female pornography when he was anxious. He'd spend all night on the Internet staring at images of naked women while supposedly working overtime. He felt out of control, in the grip of the sexual impulses that flooded him.

At age thirty, Julian attended a funeral in his old neighborhood. He was stunned when Father Scott approached him with nonchalance, introducing himself to Julian's wife as though he were simply an old friend. Wanting to shame and hurt Father Scott, he was barely able to speak to him. The priest drew him aside and whispered, "You may feel better than the rest of us now, but you and I know that all I have to do is rub your belly and you'll squeal like a puppy!"

Helpless and humiliated again, Julian finally was enraged at his betrayal. Feeling what he'd held inside so long, he finally progressed in reclaiming his whole self. It took a long time, but he gradually gave up his Internet compulsions and took more control of his trips to peep shows. Equally important, he started to open up to his wife, making that relationship more meaningful and satisfying to them both.

If your abusive relationship also provided love or comfort, you may deny one side or the other. You may feel it was either loving *or* abusive, not partly one and partly the other. You may even swing abruptly from love to hate of your abuser.

QUINN: "I Really Felt Good When Grandpa Held Me"

Quinn was ambivalent about a grandfather who, while abusing him, offered him the affection he desperately longed for from his father. Needing to love his grandfather, he used dissociation to postpone experiencing his rage until adulthood.

The molestations took place weekly in his grandfather's basement workshop, starting when Quinn was four. His grandfather fondled him, made him perform mutual fellatio, and penetrated him anally with fingers and at times his penis. Sometimes he took photos of Quinn. All the while, he'd tell Quinn he was doing this "because I love you so much."

Quinn instinctively knew to keep quiet about his molestations. He had an unsatisfying relationship with both parents. His father was harsh and dismissive, while his mother, although more nurturing, stayed in the background, having little idea how to relate to a son. Until he refused to wear them, she made Quinn elaborate Little Lord Fauntleroy clothes to wear to school, where he was subjected to taunts by his classmates.

Growing up, Quinn seemed to forget the events in his grandfather's basement. But at age twenty he saw a television show about sexual abuse and his memories rushed back with horribly overwhelming clarity. Still, he said nothing until his grandfather died. Then he became so depressed and moody that his sister convinced him to start therapy, where his story emerged.

Quinn then disclosed the abuse to his family. No one doubted his revelation, but his mother was unnerved and defensively said she hadn't known her father was capable of such acts, while his father minimized what happened. Quinn's sisters were supportive, recalling their grandfather showing them Quinn's photos and exclaiming about Quinn's great beauty.

By his late twenties, Quinn was in a constant fury. Overweight and at odds with his girlfriend, he was barely able to talk about anything except his outrage. He proclaimed he was now a survivor rather than a victim, but this didn't ring true. He got incensed if anyone suggested that he let go of his anger.

While continually expressing his rage in therapy, however, Quinn started a business. After many fits and starts, he became moderately successful. He related better to his girlfriend, although they eventually parted ways. His relationship with his father slowly improved. Seeing the difference between his former belittling father and the sickly old man who now wanted Quinn's love, he was better able to love him in return.

Three years after I met Quinn, he referred to his abuser for the first time as "Grandpa" rather than "my grandfather." When I noticed this, he reminisced about Grandpa adoring him when his father was hostile and unloving. Shyly, he said, "I really felt good when Grandpa held me. I felt loved. I must sound crazy for saying that. I don't want you to come down on me for saying that I love the man who abused me." He reminded himself that he'd never liked the sexuality with Grandpa. "But maybe it was a small price to pay. I really needed affection, and he was the only one who gave it to me."

Quinn connected to himself as a child—not just a little boy abused by his grandfather but a little boy starved for love and affection. Becoming more compassionate about himself as a boy allowed Quinn to be more caring about himself in adulthood. His rage didn't dissolve, but it subsided enough for him to reach inside for the hurt his fury covered. He wept as he murmured, "Why didn't they help me? Why didn't they help me?"

Getting in touch with his boyhood needs for tenderness and love freed Quinn. He then put together a life in which his sexual abuse remained an important influence but was no longer the center of his daily experience.

Like Quinn, victims of sexual predators are often needy. Victimizers look for children who are hungry for attention and affection. They're easy prey, unable to discern that the seemingly loving attention they're getting grooms them for abuse.

ISAAC: Ambivalence about a Needed Hero

Throughout his boyhood, Isaac had many abusers. Sent to boarding school at age six after his parents divorced, he was raped twice by older boys. Afterward, he continued to be sexually victimized. On ten additional separate occasions between the ages of eight and seventeen, he was approached sexually by older boys or men in circumstances that seemed innocent but turned intimidating, abusive, or dangerous. These ranged from being groped on a train by a stranger to being lured to a lonely cabin in the woods by two military veterans who nearly raped him before they stopped because of his terrified pleading.

A lonely, naive boy, Isaac lacked male role models and sought them out. At seventeen, he grew close to Ned, a man in his thirties who worked for Isaac's stepfather. Isaac idealized Ned as a mentor and older brother figure. Ned took an interest in Isaac's sports activities, taught him things, and flatteringly talked to him like an adult. Isaac had found his hero.

One evening when they were alone, Ned offered to give Isaac a haircut. Isaac stripped to the waist and Ned cut his hair. Then Ned offered Isaac a back massage. Working his way down to the top of Isaac's cut-offs, he jokingly asked about going further. Isaac uneasily said Ned shouldn't go too far down. They sat up and Ned began to stroke Isaac's belly. Isaac says he froze at that point, finally realizing that this was a sexual approach.

As Ned proceeded to stroke Isaac's genitals, first through the jeans, then opening Isaac's zipper, Isaac experienced a dissociative episode. He felt an enormous physical distance between his brain, which was repulsed by what was happening, and his pelvic area, which was excited. "I seemed to be watching my genitals through the wrong end of a telescope. I felt aroused, but my excitement seemed far away."

He started to shake uncontrollably, and Ned asked what was wrong. Suddenly, Isaac wrenched himself out of his passivity and yelled, "Hey man, I ain't no homo!"

Ned stopped, seemed deflated, and told Isaac he could go. Isaac felt he'd let Ned down. "I wonder why I spoke that way? Like a child might. I was old enough and smart enough to speak in a more grown-up way about homosexuality."

I suggested that it was out of strength that Isaac resorted to the language of the streets. It was an effective way to stop Ned. He responded sadly, "I guess so, but it made me lose him, too." And Isaac started to mourn the relationship with Ned, the hero he'd loved and needed.

Soon after this incident, Isaac visited his biological father and his new family in another state. He quickly decided to move in with them and never saw Ned again.

In college, Isaac's life revolved around smoking pot, and he quickly flunked out. He moved to New York City, where he remained underemployed for many years in a low-level service industry job. He attended

college sporadically. A few years after starting therapy, he finally graduated at the age of forty-one.

Power in Relationships

Your abuser exerted power and control over you. It wasn't necessary for
this person to use violence or physical coercion. Once a child senses that
an adult has the capacity and will to hurt him, the cycle of abuse has
begun. Even *fearing* harm might make you give up control.

Your abuser may have helped you somehow. The help may even
have been accompanied by affection and attention. But this person had
considerable power. Adults were your source of nurturance. You knew
this nurturance could be turned off if you angered this grown-up. This
may be how your abuser was able to control you, and it may be what
you still expect.

You may have learned to associate all intimate relationships with
power and control rather than trust and equality. Power and control are
at work when

- The relationship becomes a contest over who is in charge.

- Threats and violence are used to restrict your independence.

- You have to answer for everything you do.

- Arguments end with sex, not discussions and compromises.

- There's no shared decision making or negotiating as equals.

Having learned that power rules, you may feel a keen need to be in
control of intimate relationships.

LEWIS: Controlling Relationships at All Costs

Lewis was physically and sexually abused by his babysitter's family
from ages three to six. An attractive gay man, Lewis was a recovering
alcoholic who shaved his head and grew a big mustache in order to look
fierce and unapproachable. He was unable to be physically vulnerable
in intimate situations, even with men he knew well and seemed to trust.
If he even momentarily felt his partner was taking charge physically
during lovemaking, he panicked. In his fright, he had on occasion thrown
lovers across the room.

In contrast, you may revert to a people-pleasing manner that you used to get through your abuse.

ABE: Reverting to People-Pleasing

Abe's father told him his job in life was taking care of his needy, demanding mother. Abe both adored and hated her. He tried to please her but usually failed. Then she'd blast him. When his father came home and faced the mother's viciousness, he'd punish Abe for making him have to deal with her.

Abe expressed his anger by getting into trouble outside the home. Then he'd be afraid his behavior would infuriate his mother. He recalled once bringing home a report card that listed excellent academic grades but contained highly negative comments about his behavior with others. He wrote his mother an elaborate and distraught letter of apology, which he placed next to the report card, strewing the table around them with rose petals in a futile attempt to appease her.

Abe, an engaging, humorous forty-five-year-old gay man who worked in the creative arts, continued this pattern as an adult, anxiously giving presents to people who he felt he'd displeased or who were abusive to him. Feeling powerless and vulnerable around these people, he hoped his presents would placate them and keep them from attacking him. It never occurred to him that he could confront people and not only survive their disapproval but even emerge from these situations having earned their respect.

Avoiding Intimacy

Any relationship may produce anxiety for you if you were sexually betrayed as a boy. Maybe you try to avoid anxiety by keeping all relationships as distant, formal, and emotionless as possible. But this creates problems, too.

KEITH: Popular But Friendless

A recovering alcoholic, Keith married his wife at a time when she suffered from a very serious illness that seemed likely to cause her early death. Universally admired by their friends for his loyalty to her, he privately believed that their marriage would soon end with her death. He made a commitment to her, but he thought it would be short term.

She didn't die, however. While Keith loved her and was happy she survived, he was pessimistic about their relationship lasting since he didn't believe marriages can endure. Both his parents had poor relationships with one another and with subsequent spouses. To protect himself from the pain of an inevitable breakup, he removed himself from her emotionally.

Although there was no overt sexuality between Keith and his mother, they had an overstimulating, highly eroticized relationship. She was covertly seductive with him, relating to him as if he were a potential lover rather than her son. He'd learned to detach from his feelings toward her to keep from being overwhelmed by them. He froze them and numbed himself.

Keith had never learned what it means to feel safe while emotionally intimate. This was evident in his sexual relationship with his wife. "She isn't satisfied with her sex life," he told me. "She says she wants to be 'engulfed by my masculinity.' But I don't want to engulf her or merge with her like I did with my mother." Instead, Keith held back from her both emotionally and sexually, despite the longing for greater intimacy they both felt at times.

Keith had considerable charm and sweetness, and in general was popular and well liked. Yet he had no close friends except his wife, and of course he often felt walled off from her, too. He had strong interpersonal work relationships but didn't consider his colleagues as friends. As soon as they asked personal questions or revealed anything personal about themselves, he withdrew.

Successful in his work, Keith dealt intensively with groups of people for a concentrated period of time, then moved on to other, similar groups. While involved with these people, he had dinner with them every night, creating a little family, talking intensely about their work. Once he moved on, he rarely saw them again.

This pattern was very comfortable for him, because it had the side benefit of allowing him to keep his distance from his wife. He was often invited to industry parties, where, because he no longer drank, he had little to do. Once there, he networked as necessary, then withdrew into a corner, surveying the others and waiting until it was late enough to leave. He remained a stranger while surrounded by illusory friends whom he could not allow into his private space.

WILLEM: Detached and Suicidal

Willem grew up in Europe, the son of an alcoholic mother with a series of husbands, boyfriends, and one-night sex partners. Although Willem's memories were vague, he believed he sometimes witnessed their sexual relations and was certain that some of the men abused him. His own father left the family when he was three. Willem had no memories of him except for a feeling of danger when his name was mentioned. The one time he visited his paternal grandparents, they also frightened him. When we first met, he didn't know if his father was still alive.

Willem was rootless as a child. His mother's unstable relationships prevented any sense of their having a real home. After her last husband divorced her, his mother suddenly died. He wasn't told the cause of death. Willem was twelve and went with his ten-year-old sister to live with his maternal grandparents. This household was gloomy, grim, and filled with bickering. He was glad to be sent away to boarding school after a year and a half. But before he went, he sexually abused his sister, for which he felt tremendously guilty. I say more about these molestations in chapter 9.

Willem had great success in a career requiring intellectual prowess and analytic ability. He said he had no feelings, however. His emotional life was sparse, barren, and brittle. He had acquaintances but no friends. He had little capacity to connect to others. He married in his mid-twenties, but his wife divorced him five years later. He then abruptly tried to commit suicide and nearly succeeded.

Willem's life was saved, and he entered a psychiatric facility. When he was released, he'd begun to change. He was relatively more open, vulnerable, and needy.

He'd been urged to start outpatient psychotherapy, but this wasn't easy for him. Especially leery of working with a male therapist, he eventually faced his fear enough to start seeing me. When we went over his past and saw how little he knew about his early life or family origins, he decided to try to find out about his mother's death. He made international calls, wrote to appropriate authorities, and eventually received copies of his mother's death certificate. He was not totally surprised to discover that she'd committed suicide.

Willem didn't know much about his mother's depression and alcoholism. But when he combined what he did know with his memories and impressions of his grandparents and his father, he began to see his childhood with greater understanding and compassion. Reflecting on his mother's death, he began to believe that he'd always unconsciously known about her suicide and that this knowledge was behind his own attempt to kill himself.

He also began to understand his need not to rely on or create bonds with others. His feelings changed. He wanted to live, to accomplish something important. He decided to pursue a career in which he could advocate for abuse victims.

Eventually, Willem contacted the sister who he'd abused. She was very glad to hear from him. She told him that he had an uncle who was interested in seeing him. Also, their father had resurfaced, and his stories about the parents' marriage made him a far more sympathetic figure than he'd seemed during their childhood.

Finally, Willem was able to understand with compassion that his pattern in adult life of moving from city to city, job to job, and girlfriend to girlfriend had been a result of his devastating incapacity to connect to others.

Being Responsible

Being responsible for something, for someone, for an event, even for yourself can be an emotionally powerful feeling. In our culture, people—especially men—are expected to be responsible for their own fate. This crucial but (usually) unspoken rule is at the heart of the masculine ideal we discussed in chapter 2.

Boys usually feel they're responsible for themselves or that they ought to be. So it's not surprising that boys often feel responsible for their abuse. Maybe you feel you were to blame because you were interested in sex, or were vulnerable to predators, or were deficient in some important way.

Maybe your abuser said things to reinforce your belief that you were at fault. Victimizers may have said, "I'm doing this because you're so handsome," or "This is because I love you," or "I know this is what you really want—every boy wants it," or "I can see you really want it—look how hard you are!" If this happened, you were manipulated into believing there's something about you—some innate quality or fault or behavior—that caused your abuse and makes *you* responsible for it.

Your abuser may have coerced you by convincing you that you're responsible for your family's well-being, or for the mental health of one of your parents, or even for the the abuser's welfare. It's easy for an abused boy to believe that he must answer for how other people feel.

VICTOR: Always Responsible, Always to Blame

Whenever Victor's bosses seemed stressed, he believed it was his fault. To please them and assuage his sense of responsibility, he'd work harder. "When I feel tension in the air," he told me, "I assume it's about me. I submit to whatever is demanded, whether at work or with my family or with my lover." He paid another price for trying to please everybody, however: whenever he gave in to people, he got angry, creating scenarios in his mind in which they didn't care about him. This cycle was very frustrating.

As we talked about it in therapy, Victor began to see a pattern that started when his father told Victor that he was molesting him because Victor was so handsome and because he loved him. Victor felt he somehow caused the incest.

He also felt responsible in another way: he believed his nightly abuse calmed his father down and kept the family more peaceful than it would have been otherwise. He remembered how anxious he felt when his father got tense or angry, how he felt he had to do anything to calm his father down. His father would cry out, "If it weren't for all of you, I wouldn't have to be here—I'd be free!" Victor accepted the blame for his father's moods and felt guilty and bewildered.

He added, however, that his feelings of being responsible for others were also colored by his history with his mother. She'd tell Victor he was perfect and worth all the sacrifices she made: the job she hated, the marriage in which she was stuck.

Feeling responsible for both his mother's disappointments and his father's rages, Victor was chronically anxious. He felt trapped, just as each of his parents felt in their marriage.

Having identified these childhood patterns, Victor was able to make sense of the cycles that upset him now: the belief that he caused other people's tension, the attempt to soothe that tension by giving in to demands and expectations, the resentment for having done so, and the belief that no one cared.

9

Sexuality and Intimacy

Sexual Anxieties

If you were sexually abused as a child, you may be wary about your own sexual desire and sexual approaches from others. See if you can relate to any of these problems:

- Sexual thoughts triggering overwhelming feelings and memories
- Dissociating in order to have sex
- Getting high before sex
- Losing interest in sex
- Obsessing about sex
- Compulsively seeking sexual release
- Having difficulty with erections and orgasms
- Craving pornography, massage parlors, gay bathhouses, or prostitutes
- Being disturbed but aroused by fantasies involving acts that disgust you

Sex and sexual intimacy can be a challenge for any man whose early sexual experience was loaded with secrecy, betrayal, guilt, shame, overstimulation, or any other terrible baggage. So it's logical that you'd feel anxiety or even paralysis about sex. Perhaps it's easier for you to have sex with strangers than with someone you love. Maybe you think about sex all the time, or pursue pornography and casual sex more than you want to. Maybe you can't reliably get or keep an erection, or you ejaculate too quickly, or you can't ejaculate at all. Maybe your sexual relationships parallel those you had with your abuser in some significant way, and you find yourself being victimized subtly or even being a victimizer. These reactions are understandable and often can be helped.

Some sexually abused men avoid sexual relationships altogether. Others attempt to manage sexual relationships while suffering the intense and bewildering effects of dissociation during intimacy.

CORY: "Who Would Ever Want Sex?"

Cory summed up his pain when he laughingly but only half humorously said, "The trouble with sex is there's always someone in your face," and "I don't want any spontaneity in sex unless I know what's going to happen," and "If you really think about sex and all that happens in it, who would ever want it?"

When Cory was nineteen, a male dorm counselor tried to seduce him. Cory felt physically paralyzed and dissociated by mentally leaving the room. In adulthood, he continued to dissociate during sex: "Once I get things going in sex, I can just turn the machine on automatic and leave."

Cory worked hard to overcome his aversion to intimacy. He inadvertently discovered he'd gained a capacity to love when his wife suffered a miscarriage. In wonderment, he said, "I'd let myself love it. I didn't worry about the pain I feel now. And even though I cried all this week, I know now that I've opened up a big wonderful space in my heart where there had been a void—and I can love."

Sex Takes on Twisted Meanings

If you first felt arousal during betrayal and abuse, your sexuality may feel defective. Along with pleasurable physical sensations, you may associate sexuality with negatives such as:

- Coercion
- Putting out
- Giving in
- Defectiveness

- Violence
- Secrecy
- Shame
- Subservience
- Deviance
- Sissiness
- Victimhood
- Unmasculinity
- Evil
- Hypocrisy
- Powerlessness
- Manipulativeness
- Exploitation

If you experience these contradictory feelings, it's difficult to feel the joys and pleasures of sexuality. You may not even want to think of yourself as a sexual being because you associate sex with disgust, anxiety, or dread.

Ambivalence about sex can be troubling, confusing, and discouraging. It may make you think you're crazy, perverted, or hopelessly flawed. You don't have to stay stuck in this place, however.

The healing process involves a whole series of discoveries, insights, and realizations. It takes time to assimilate new perspectives and understandings of what happened and how it affected you.

LORENZO: Feeling My Abuser's Sexual Shame

Lorenzo, a gay man who had numerous supposedly heterosexual male abusers as a boy, explained what happened to his abusers' dissociated shame: "I realized one day that I was in the gym, looking around, admiring men's bodies, not coming on to them, but feeling attracted and yet terribly ashamed of my desires. It was crazy—I felt like a pedophile even though these men were my own age and I have no interest in children. I couldn't understand it, but then all of a sudden it hit me. The men who abused me had no shame about what they did. They invited me to come give them blow jobs when I was as young as eight or nine, and then I'd see them in church with their wives or on the street and they were totally casual, pillars of the community. Sometimes it was as though they hardly knew who I was. So I took on their shame! I took it in. They couldn't own it, so I did—and I still do! I walk around feeling my desire and feeling I'm terrible for having desire, that desire itself is abusive. I feel the shame they should have felt but never did!"

HUGO: Mourning Manhood

Hugo's series of molestations by older male cousins ended when he was seventeen. "I was trying to express my anger at the way I was being treated, so I willed myself not to have an erection, and I succeeded. I only meant for that night! But the result was I could never again have a spontaneous erection with anyone I cared about."

A gay man in his forties, Hugo spent years feeling defective in comparison with men to whom he was attracted. Not until Viagra came on the market was he able to achieve erections regularly when he felt aroused. Only then did he realize how deeply his sense of masculinity and power had been affected by his impotence.

He was overwhelmed, flooded by his suffering. He went through a mourning period for the years he couldn't perform sexually. The effects on his self-image and relationships slowly, sadly sank in.

Hugo grieved for his youthful sense of manliness. The anguish passed for him, and it can for you.

VICTOR: Bad Pleasure

Victor put his dilemma in a nutshell: "All pleasure is bad. It's bad that my father is touching my penis. His touching my penis gives me pleasure. Therefore, it's bad to have pleasure."

He elaborated: "I hated when my father talked to me while he touched me. He'd say, 'You're so big, you're so hard, you know Daddy loves you, and that's why he does this.' But I don't think I ever believed him. I felt like a hooker when he said that. I'd rather he would have just touched me and kept quiet. At least it felt good and I didn't have to think about it being my father who was doing it. When he touched me, he'd open my pajamas, and by the time I woke up, he'd have fished my dick out and it would be hard. I'd let him touch it for a while, then I'd get upset and I'd turn over. He'd beg me to turn back. He'd croon to me about how much he loved me, how handsome I was, what a big, strong man I'd become. He said he was doing this to me out of love, out of admiration of my beauty. I usually pretended to be asleep. It was both exciting and revolting. I was scared to let myself have an orgasm. If I was close, I rolled over. Sometimes he'd sigh and say, 'Okay, if that's how you want it,' and I'd feel guilty. I wasn't doing what a good son would do. So I'd turn around again and let him continue, and he'd be so grateful."

He had one forlorn victory: "At least I never came with him—I always made him stop before I came."

Differentiating between Abusive and Healthy Ways of Relating

If you were sexually abused, you may have trouble distinguishing between sex, love, nurturance, affection, and abuse. All these were lumped together when you were a boy, and now that you're an adult, the differences may be fuzzy.

Scott Heim chillingly conveys how this confusion develops in his main character in *Mysterious Skin*. Ten years after he was abused at age eight by the baseball coach he idolized, he describes the many emotions he felt during his abuse:

> He had chosen me, you know? Out of all the boys on the team, he'd picked me. Like I'd been blessed or something. He taught me things no other boy on the team or at school could know. *I was his.* . . . Coach took me to the movies, told me I was his star player. He stuffed me full of candy and let me win a trillion video games. And then he was there, on top of me on the kitchen floor, rubbing his dick against my bare belly. [emphasis added]

For this lonely boy, the affection, nurturance, and love he felt with his coach became indelibly identified with sexuality, abuse, and exploitation.

Explaining his phobia about emotion, Keith, who we first met in chapter 3, said, "For me, violation means intimacy, and intimacy means violation. Someone has an emotional flare-up and I want to dive into it. I *fuck* it, I become one with it, I feel those raw emotions again, like I did with my mother. Then I wind up being the caretaker of the person with all the emotions."

Abe's words further illustrate how sexuality, love, nurturance, affection, and abuse get confused. (His story is told in chapter 8.) His mother had verbally abused him and subjected him to exceptionally seductive stimulation. In despair, he said, "No one will ever love me unless I'm completely their servant. So I bring gifts to people who have abused me. I allow sadistic sex. I don't yet know to what lengths I'll go to feel loved. I keep returning to that wonderful cozy nest of abuse and incest. It's a sewer, and yet it's my spiritual home. Why do I continue to allow abuse as an adult? Because when I'm being abused, someone's attention is completely focused on me. I know that's not love, but it really feels like love." Any friendliness, even a benign dinner invitation, was highly suspect to Abe. Attention felt sexual and abusive, erotic and violating.

Sexuality as Currency

You may believe your sexuality is your only value as a human being. Early on, you learned that sex can be a kind of interpersonal currency. You can use it to get what you need, bond to authorities, or manipulate others. For some men, this turns into an unconscious feeling that they're entitled to whatever they want—a belief that the world owes them.

Since it's valuable to others, your sexuality becomes the basis of your self-worth. Then it permeates all interpersonal encounters. The only way to feel intimate (or seemingly intimate) with *anyone*, regardless of the relationship, is to make relating erotic.

You're probably hungry for contact with others, so you have a dilemma: you believe you're valuable only as a sexual object, but when you have sex it feels like abuse.

One solution is to engage in frequent and indiscriminate sexual encounters. These aren't free, joyous expressions of lusty sensuality. Rather, they're part of an endless cycle. You pursue sex incessantly while achieving little intimacy. You keep yourself distant from partners because couplings are anonymous or impulsive. And your anxiety stays low because if necessary you can dissociate during sex.

Casual sex isn't necessarily bad, but it's not intimate. If it involves seeking partners compulsively, you're seeking sexual release to allay anxiety rather than because of sexual interest or arousal.

Fleeting sex may momentarily make you feel loved or soothed. This works like other compulsive or addictive behaviors such as drinking, taking drugs, or overeating. Once the sex act is over, though, you probably don't feel loved anymore. You may feel empty and lonely, but pursuing a complete relationship risks repeating your abuse history.

It's easy to get abused or exploited in this situation. Because you're starved for love and intimacy, you may plunge so deeply into a relationship that you feel incapable of independent thought or are anxious about being abandoned. Maybe you go back and forth between compulsive sexual behavior and looking urgently for love.

RAMON: Looks Can Get You Through

Ramon felt his worth and power derived from his sexuality. At forty, he was for the first time starting a career, following years of drug addiction, drug dealing, jail, psychiatric hospitalizations, and rehab treatment.

A likable man with traces of the good looks that attracted many adults' desire earlier in his life, Ramon stuttered and cried as he talked about his first molestation. Ravaging childhood memories engulfed him. He'd never talked to anyone about them but realized he had no choice: not talking about his memories no longer kept them out of consciousness.

Ramon's physically abusive father deserted the family when Ramon was six. Ramon fended for himself while his mother worked. At eight, he encountered Sam, a neighbor who delighted children with impromptu sidewalk puppet shows. Sam invited him to his apartment. Amusing Ramon with his puppetry, he began to caress and undress him, then penetrated him anally. That night, Ramon bled profusely, and he stuffed tissues inside his shorts to stanch the blood.

Sam abused Ramon for two years, always in a "loving" manner. Ramon yearned to spend more and more time with Sam, the only seemingly caring and kindhearted adult in his life.

At forty, Ramon was ambivalent about Sam. Although ashamed and depressed about their relationship, he felt the old desire to be with him. Under the surface, however, he was enraged. He'd once seen Sam on the street and got so infuriated that he considered buying a gun to kill him.

After Sam moved away, Ramon allowed himself to be picked up by numerous men and women who engaged him in sex, often giving him money or expensive gifts. Ramon worried about getting too old to be physically attractive to these adults, feeling he was too stupid to be appealing on any other level. He said that in a way he didn't care whether he was with a man or a woman as long as his partner didn't leave. "They always left," he said, "even though they seemed to care so much about me. Every time I was with someone, I figured, I've got this one, they're really attracted, they'll stay. But they always left."

What was most important was a sense of being cared about and supported. Ramon's desperation about being abandoned was central to all his relationships. As he left the session when he laid this out, he sadly whispered as he passed me at the door, "I hope you don't get tired of me."

Ramon's early experiences left him confused, feeling that his worth was based on his body. He never felt that he had anything else to offer the world. "I know how to make men or women happy in bed, but that's all I know." It was a major step for him to embark on an educational program. It took him years to learn he had value, but he did learn it, and his world changed.

Exploitative Relationships

If you felt controlled during your abuse, you may try to overcome that feeling by exerting control in your adult relationships. This may help you feel that you have control over yourself and your fate. However, this may also make you predatory.

In a moment, we'll talk about men who abuse others, but you can also be predatory more subtly. Exploitativeness doesn't have to be overt, and it doesn't always have sexual overtones. Sexual abuse can be replayed as nonsexual exploitation, with one person maintaining power over another. This can happen in everyday relationships. Sometimes an abused man hardly recognizes how he exploits others because what he's doing is disguised and seems harmless. Sexual abuse victims know better than anyone that people shouldn't exploit others, however. The recovery process may involve seeing when you're being hurtful by repeating the past in some way.

KEITH: Seductive Manipulation

Keith was unaware that he treated colleagues hurtfully. He worked freelance in an industry in which people get partially involved in a number of projects simultaneously, knowing only some will materialize into paying work. People frequently juggle these business ventures, occasionally having to back out after doing a lot of work on a project.

Keith was surprised by the bitterness of people whose projects he'd withdrawn from. They felt he'd made a personal commitment to them and had then deceived and betrayed them. Their sense of treachery went far beyond what's usual in a business situation.

Initially, Keith was perplexed, but he conceded that he seduced potential work partners into wanting to work with him. "I feel they won't want me on the basis of my skills, so I pull out all stops. I show them how incredibly I understand their needs. I make sure they bond to me. Then if I pull out of a commitment for reasons that are totally understandable from a career point of view, they feel personally betrayed. I never understand why, and I never get it that I'm hurting them. And if I do get it, I don't care. I'm always the victim—I can't imagine anyone else being victimized and certainly not that I'm doing the victimizing."

OWEN: Expecting and Finding Exploitation

At sixty-eight, Owen felt too old to ever establish a positive relationship. But he came in one day agitated and ashen-faced, saying he was afraid he'd be considered a child molester. He'd met a teenager, Jimi, who initiated an encounter and followed Owen home.

A seventeen-year-old high school student, Jimi came from a poor third world country and had immigrated to the United States with his family five years earlier. He aggressively pursued Owen, who was astounded, frightened, and intrigued. Why would Jimi be interested in a man fifty years his senior? Was Owen being suckered by a young hustler? But then Owen wondered if it would be illegal to be sexually involved with someone Jimi's age. So who was exploiting whom?

Jimi was over the age of consent in New York State, so there was no question of Owen being in legal trouble if he and Jimi had a relationship. We talked about its potential psychological meaning. When Owen was twelve, twenty-nine-year-old Calvin started an "affair" with him. The parallel between a relationship with Jimi and Owen's relationship with Calvin was unmistakable.

Jimi came from a culture that venerated older people, which Owen couldn't comprehend. Jimi also seemed instinctively to see Owen as a mentor who would introduce him to an Americanized culture totally foreign to Jimi's parents, who spoke no English and worked long hours at menial jobs.

As their relationship progressed, Owen felt invaded by Jimi, who often arrived at Owen's home early in the morning, expecting to spend all day with him. Owen wanted Jimi to understand his needs for privacy and interpersonal space. They also had widely different interests in music, movies, and food, and had to negotiate how to spend their time. Having a hard time maintaining interpersonal boundaries, Owen found it difficult to tell Jimi how he felt.

Owen, who considered himself ugly and undesirable, was both flattered and suspicious of Jimi's attentions. He worried about being exploited for his money. He did spend a lot of money on Jimi, who had virtually none. He paid for tutoring, meals, and sports equipment, and felt both generous and foolish for doing so.

Jimi did seem to genuinely care for Owen. He profited from the relationship but gave a lot to it. He was an eager sexual partner and an ever-present companion. Owen had sought a lover like this all his adult life, but he learned to his surprise that he didn't always welcome companionship and sex. Maybe, he thought, he'd never had a successful relationship with a man because he really preferred being alone.

He reconsidered his relationships with Calvin and with his parents. He suddenly recognized that Calvin had exploited his youth and vulnerability. And his parents had allowed the affair to go on, even benefiting from it. A lifelong pattern began in which Owen learned to expect exploitation and to automatically comply with others' needs. In many relationships, and again with Jimi, Owen was afraid he'd lose the love of anyone whose needs he didn't satisfy. This was intolerable, so he'd usually allowed himself to be exploited rather than lose the interest of someone he cared about.

Abused Men May Become Abusers

Research suggests that although many male abusers were sexually victimized as boys only a small minority of these boys goes on to become sexual predators. Still, if this happens even once, it's very serious. The abuser betrays, hurts, and traumatizes another person. He may also induce guilt and shame in himself that can become a barrier to his own recovery.

I haven't treated many adult men who abused children. However, I've worked with men who as children or adolescents sexually abused other children.

FELIX: Nurturer and Abuser

Felix's parents married as teenagers, and he was born a year later. They divorced when he was twelve, the oldest of six children. Felix's premature erotic experience consisted of walking in on his mother and her lover in bed when he unexpectedly came home from school for lunch at age eleven. They saw him as he slammed the bedroom door shut, overwhelmed by so much at once: seeing a sex act, seeing his own mother in a sex act, feeling his own sexual arousal, seeing his mother betraying his father, and therefore the family and him.

Shortly afterward, Felix once touched and caressed his sleeping five-year-old sister's vagina. He believes she slept through the molestation and has never had any indication that she knew it happened. When he shamefacedly related this incident to me twenty-six years later, it was the first time he'd told anyone his guilty secret.

Felix described how he often acted as his younger siblings' parent. His mother was competent and well-meaning but was preoccupied and beleaguered by working while raising six children. Felix became caretaker for his brothers and sisters.

They came to appreciate this. As an adult, the sister he abused once said to him, "I always think I should send two cards on Mother's Day, one to Mom and the big one to you." Telling me this, he cried as he described again how he'd abused her, betraying the trust everyone had in him.

His own loneliness and the crushing burden of being both caretaker to his siblings and the carrier of the secret of his mother's infidelity had all contributed to Felix's deep yearnings for any close human contact. This explains why he abused his sister, but, as he repeated over and over to me, it doesn't excuse his behavior.

With time, Felix gained some perspective on both his abusiveness and his own overstimulation and emotional neglect. It was inappropriate for him to be asked to be his younger siblings' caregiver. While he didn't forgive himself for his abusive act, he began to see it in context: as part of a life in which he'd been forced to know and do things that ought to be left to adults. Seeing his sexual abusiveness within this larger picture, he allowed it to recede in importance and went on with his life.

WILLEM: Clinging to Human Contact through Sexual Abuse

Following earlier abuse by his mother's lovers and husbands, Willem molested his two-year-younger sister. After their mother died suddenly, he and his sister lived with their intimidating maternal grandparents. With guilty pain, he said he had sexual intercourse with his sister in his grandparents' home. He explained this as his way of clinging to the only human relationship he treasured, but he admitted his sister hadn't participated willingly. He was so remorseful and ashamed that he came to this country at the age of twenty to escape his memories.

When we first met, Willem hadn't spoken to his sister since then. He felt totally isolated without any family or friends and with hardly any childhood memories. He finally contacted his sister, who was eager to reestablish a relationship with him. He proceeded very slowly on this path, knowing his tendency to pull back suddenly when overwhelmed by previously dissociated memories and feelings. He continued to write and phone her, however, knowing he'd eventually have to talk to her about the abuse if he were ever to regain her as a sister.

Sadistic and Masochistic Relationships

If you received both pain and pleasure at the hands of a sexual abuser, maybe you grew up associating one with the other in sexual relationships. Your sexual desire may have gotten intertwined with wishes to inflict pain, receive it, or both.

Taking pleasure in causing pain or abuse, especially if there's a sexual component, is called *sadism*. Welcoming pain or abuse is called *masochism*. Since a sadist requires a masochist to fulfill his desires and vice versa, these opposite sexual interests are often grouped together as the single word *sadomasochism*, also known as S&M. A form of sadomasochism, *bondage and discipline*, often abbreviated as B&D, involves one partner tying up the other so that he's helpless and must surrender to discipline, which may or may not involve physical pain.

There's an established subculture of men and women who defend sadomasochism as a credible, natural, and harmless lifestyle. I'm not interested in passing judgment on the private and consensual acts of adults. Nor do I necessarily believe that everyone into S&M or B&D was sexually abused as a child. However, if an adult is suffering and unhappy after childhood abuse and also engages in sadomasochistic fantasies or behaviors, it's important to investigate how he came to associate pain with sexual pleasure.

Some men sexually abused as boys have sadistic fantasies without acting on them. For example, Victor had frequent fantasies of tying men up and either tickling them until they screamed or bringing them nearly to orgasm without allowing orgasm to occur. He'd never considered the possible connection between these fantasies and his own abuse. But it became very clear how his past affected him: his grandparents tickled him mercilessly as part of a sexual game, and later while being abused Victor kept himself from reaching orgasm to frustrate his father.

ABE: Abuse Became "Home"

Continually searching for and finding abusive situations that felt like home, Abe spent his life allowing exploitation, hurt, and abuse. Abe's father was neglectful and abusive. He couldn't deal with his wife's "scenes" and told Abe quite plainly that he was to take care of her hysterical outbursts. On several occasions, Abe walked in on his father masturbating the family dog and encouraging the dog to lick the father's penis.

But Abe's alcoholic and pill-addicted mother was the center of his world. Beautiful, sensuous, fascinating, and demanding, she had multiple affairs until she died in her seventies. She was extraordinarily self-involved and negligent about the impact of what she did. For example, she masturbated with candles, then left them around the house for Abe to find.

Abe's relationship with his mother was overstimulating, exciting, and arousing. He was never bored when he was with her and never stopped trying to keep her happy. Only when he sobered up as an adult did he recognize that his vivacious, charming mother was also vicious, vindictive, deeply depressed, and incapable of thinking about him, his needs, and his identity as separate from hers.

By age twelve, Abe was regularly looking to be picked up by older men. These men were cold and physically hurtful to Abe during sexual encounters. But Abe felt good about being chosen by them. It didn't occur to him for decades that these encounters were repetitions of his abuse at home. These pedophiles were abusing, exploiting, and intentionally harming him. They were criminal offenders who took advantage of his neediness. They began a long line of sadistic abusers he was drawn to. He craved the love of these parent substitutes even though he chose them exactly because they were incapable of giving it.

Abe felt especially masochistic right after feeling capable or pleased with himself. Once, after a particularly successful day, he suddenly longed to be beaten physically. He said, "Feeling good is a betrayal of my mother, so being humiliated and in pain is an act of loyalty to her. It's amazing—after all this time, I still feel that if I'm happy, I'll lose her support and love even though I know I never had it."

As an adult, Abe felt ashamed of his body and his sexuality. He engaged in sadomasochistic and dangerous sexual behaviors, including being tied up and anally fisted during casual encounters. When sexually involved with others, it was mostly in anonymous, compulsive, and unpleasurable encounters, or short, intense affairs with extraordinarily inappropriate and uncaring men. One man broke things off by saying he was disturbed by how much Abe wanted to be hurt and how much he had grown to want to hurt Abe.

High on drugs and alcohol, Abe once found himself being choked during a sadomasochistic sexual encounter. After he sobered up, he suddenly realized he liked being choked this way. This worried him so much that he decided to stop his substance abuse, realizing that while high he'd be more likely to pursue cravings for dangerous behavior to their furthest, life-threatening extremes. Later, he decided to seek treatment specifically for sexual abuse.

As therapy progressed, Abe began to have his greatest success professionally and was more assertive than in the past. Yet he experienced success as if he were still a boy, placating his mother, keeping her rages in check, waiting for the other shoe to drop. When people were abusive or cold, he was inappropriately friendly. He brought flowers or gifts to people he felt had abused him. He accepted the blame when he did not cause the problem. Occasionally he even compromised his work to appease an exploitative colleague.

Passionately talking about this, Abe cried out, "I have to get them to recognize my worth! They become my mother and father, people who have no capacity to see beyond themselves, who care nothing for me, who don't even think about me when I'm not there. But I keep hoping they'll turn around and say, 'Abe really has something there. We were wrong about him. Look—he's terrific!' And, even as I see that there is zero chance that they will do that, I also can't give up on the possibility! I see it all, but it does no good—I can't stop myself from repeating it yet again!"

His work was praised, but Abe couldn't feel pleasure: "I search for my parents among those who look at my work. I look for abuse and dismissal. There can be 198 people who like my work and two who don't. I'll listen to those two. For me, the abusive people are the only important ones there."

After six years of therapy, Abe finally began to address his masochism directly. He saw he wanted to be in pain after any sort of success. He felt he *should* feel pain rather than good feelings about his accomplishments. But he wanted to feel a more defined pain than the foggy suffering he experienced after good feedback about his work. Sadomasochistic sex fit that bill. Since he chose when to be in pain, how it would happen, and even when it would stop, he felt in control of it rather than lost in its chaos.

Abe began to leave behind his overly sensitive alertness to abuse. "I carry my abuse around with me. Whether or not abuse is really taking place, I'm going to see it there, because that's what I bring to every relationship." This perception helped him disentangle himself from his people-pleasing mode of relating when he felt anxiety, depression, and despair because confrontation was in the air.

After seven years of treatment, Abe noted that his attempts to stand up for himself in the world were no longer solely fueled by fury but rather from a capacity and wish to assert himself. Reflecting on his life and his treatment, Abe declared, "I'm still scared, inhibited, ashamed of my body. But I'm expressive, more than I ever, ever, ever, ever thought I could be. I don't consider myself unlucky at all."

Achieving Intimacy

Every man in this book struggled to understand and experience intimacy. Each endured years of difficult work and problematic relationships in order to achieve some closeness with another person.

With difficulty, most were able to look back at their childhoods with compassion, sometimes for their abusers but more importantly for themselves. Only then were they able to make connections between their past and current lives.

They were often surprised when they discovered that they were once normal children needy of affection from adults who either denied it or gave it to them only in return for sex. But an inner drive to have more fulfilling relationships kept these men going. They may not have felt this drive every minute of every day, but over the long run it was there.

You probably don't always know how to get close to others. You may not always know if you want to be intimate. But knowing how early trauma destroyed the possibility of intimacy can paradoxically allow you some freedom in pursuing it. That doesn't mean you'll always attain interpersonal closeness, but you'll know whether you want it. That's the first step toward achieving it.

PART TWO

MOVING BEYOND
BETRAYAL

Lance, a gay man molested on separate occasions by his father, his mother, and his sister, spent years overcoming the effects these violations had on him: "The last hurdle for me is dating. A lot of male survivors struggle with relationships. And that makes me angry. It's bad enough that our perpetrators leave us a legacy of self-hate. But to also be cut off from the renewing life energy that's possible in a relationship is even worse."

Miles, a man with multiple abusers at his boarding school, said, "I carried the secret with me everywhere. I kept it hidden away like something in my pocket, constantly checking, feeling to make sure it remained out of view. The secret stayed inside me—a weasel screaming into emptiness, a thick fog, a hunger, a howling wind that only I heard, making me do and think such awful things. Telling the secret has been very hard. The men who molested me put it into my head that I couldn't tell, that I'd die if I told. In my therapist's office, they kept telling me to refuse to speak, to not answer, to sleep. But, little by little, the secret was exposed."

Santo is a straight Hispanic man who was sexually assaulted by multiple family members. His parents often had sex in his bed while he was present. He talked about the effects of abuse and of the therapy he bravely sought: "Abuses need darkness and concealment to grow. The best healing for sexual abuse is getting it out in the open. The more it's covered up, the more it grows and the more damage it does. I placed all the blame

151

on myself and sank deeper and deeper into despair. I used to replay the bad experiences over and over in my head. The more I did, the worse and more hopeless I felt. Marriage and kids were out of the question. I didn't want to bring a human being into this world and make it suffer as I did. Since I've been in therapy, this has changed. A bad experience may come up, but I don't indulge in self-pity. I look at it, feel the pain, and then it dissipates. It's no longer a scary monster. I even think about marriage and having kids. The fact that I'm thinking about it, and it doesn't scare me like it did, gives me great hope."

Steve, who was abused by his Cub Scout leader/neighbor/barber, talked about his psychotherapy: "It took me a very long time to trust the intimacy of this engagement. It's essential that my therapist knows the complex, confusing, and subtle energies of childhood male sexual abuse and understands its language and nuance. I've learned to trust him, an adult male, with my most fragile, most intimate, most sacred self. Through our work together, I trust him to hold the tension of that room for me—hold up the walls, keep the door guarded, watch the windows, respect the sanctity of the place. I can go into the dark well of memory, pain, and grief and return safely—renewed, welcomed, and encouraged."

10

Taking Charge

If you were sexually abused as a boy and you're reading this book, then you already know what it means to take charge. You're doing it! You've already begun to take responsibility for helping yourself.

It would be great if you could simply wake up one morning and will yourself into a happier existence. But you know by now that's impossible. You've already tried it.

Healing requires teaching your brain to respond differently to the world. Your brain's neurons didn't establish their millions of connections overnight. Rewiring them takes time, willpower, and faith.

You're already on your way, however. There's no single beginning point except the one you've already passed. There's no road map except the one you create. There's no specific destination you must arrive at in order to feel healed. With every word you read in this book, with every thought you have about your healing, with every reflection, decision, and feeling you have about it, you're changing.

In overcoming your childhood trauma, you'll learn new ways to interact with the world. You'll gain greater mastery over your own mind. You'll take charge of how you act. You'll prevail over the terrible, confusing impulses you may now feel. You'll be in greater control of your inner states. You'll see the world anew.

Changing Perspective

You have a choice about how you see and define yourself. You can look back at your abuse and say, "I *am* a victim," or you can look back at what happened and say, "I *was* victimized in the past, but I won't allow that to define who I am."

The first perspective, *being* a victim, may be how you feel most of the time now. And no wonder! Your feelings and experiences left you thinking this way. After all, victims hurt, victims are angry, victims are confused, victims despair, and victims want to blame others. But you can also decide your past victimhood will neither define who you are nor who you will become.

Your abuse will never go away. It happened. But your abuse can eventually take its place alongside other hurts and disappointments in your life. For example, if you once failed an important test, chances are you don't spend your life reflecting on what happened or defining your entire existence around the event. Old traumas such as these will also never go away. They, too, happened. But you no longer think much about them.

You'll get to a point where what happened to you is such a small part of who you are that you might not even consider describing yourself as a survivor of child sexual abuse. You'll simply think of yourself as a normal human being: a computer programmer, a salesman, a manager, a designer, a fisherman, a soldier, a husband, a lover, a father, a son, a brother, a Christian, a Jew, a Muslim—a man.

This is possible. Picture a man who gets out of bed one day, looks down at his knee, and rediscovers a scar from a childhood injury long ago. He hasn't thought about that scar in twenty years. For a moment, he remembers how he got it. He remembers exactly what he was doing, how another boy pushed him, and how he fell on a sharp rock. He remembers the smell of the air and the blue sky above him, and the blood, and how he cried.

At the moment it happened, the injury and the boy who pushed him were the biggest things in his life. But the trauma passed. Just as the scar grew fainter, so did his memory of the experience as he moved on in life.

There's no question in his mind that he was really injured. There's also no question that the pain is gone. The gash has disappeared, the scar is small, the wound is healed, and the skin is strong again. Scar tissue is tough.

It may seem impossible that you'll ever view your past this way. It may feel like your body is one vast badly healed wound, like you live within an infected laceration with a scab barely forming over it.

If that's how you feel, healing will involve breaking through the scab, releasing the pus, shedding the old skin, and allowing a clean scar to form. This is how you will emerge as a fully mature person.

It will be wonderful to leave the world of victimhood, confusion, pain, and fear. And it's possible. First you must deal with your trauma through the perspective of a responsible adult. You must take charge.

Try the following exercise. On a piece of paper, write down the numbers 1 through 5. After each number, write a word that describes who you are. Write down any word that conveys a sense of the kind of person you are. Don't try to stop and think about it—just write down the words.

When you've finished, put the list aside and continue reading this chapter. We'll come back to the list later and talk about it.

Your Automatic Reactions

Many of your responses to the world are automatic. When you have an itch, you usually scratch it. When someone rudely shoves you, you get angry. You learned most of your responses early in life. If you were betrayed as a boy, especially if it was a repeated betrayal, you may have been programmed to expect betrayal as a natural part of life. You don't even think about it.

Your brain has to register an event as unique and different from other events in order to respond to it differently. Only when you respond with consciousness to the current world around you right now do you act from your own impulses, thoughts, and feelings. Otherwise, you're responding as you did long ago.

Your old responses may include unwanted impulses, feelings, and inner experiences. With all these inputs telling you that you're being betrayed, you'll have a hard time thinking rationally, knowing what to believe, relaxing, enjoying, and nourishing your relationships.

All the men in this book struggled with this challenge. They wanted one thing. Their minds' automatic reactions gave them another. This is like a plane flying on autopilot through strong winds. It's going in a certain direction, at a certain speed and altitude, and will keep flying this way regardless of the treacherous winds that try to push it in another direction. It's a dangerous way to fly—unless the pilot takes charge.

Taking charge isn't easy, however, especially if you've been abused. It's a struggle. It's tricky to lead a happier, more satisfied life when your mind won't cooperate.

How do you develop a life and maintain relationships when you're beleaguered by confusing feelings, intense dread, incapacitating rage, or deadening numbness? You have to retool your autopilot.

Your autopilot was calibrated when you were younger. It succeeded in flying you through the storms of your childhood with only one mission in mind: keeping you alive and sane. It had to do this when you were simultaneously dependent on adults and abused by at least one of them. So the calibrations were set in very specific ways to overcome highly dangerous conditions.

You're still flying with that same autopilot on. You're still calibrated for danger, as though the conditions were still the same, even though they're probably very different now.

Taking Charge of Your Actions

It's common for survivors to feel they can't control actions that get them in trouble. Perhaps you have a substance abuse problem. Whether you're an alcoholic or a drug addict, your intake may stop you from proceeding with your life. If so, you must take charge of your actions. You must get these habits under control. Consider going to a twelve-step program (see chapter 12) or otherwise hearing how people cope with alcohol or drug problems.

Perhaps you're saying, "Wait a minute, I can stop any time I want to! I don't need to take that kind of step!" That's fine, if you can. But if you can stop, why haven't you? Or why haven't you wanted to?

I'm not saying drinking or some drug use is bad for everyone in every situation. But if you smoke pot or have a six-pack instead of looking for a job, spending time with friends, or helping your children with their homework, then you have a problem. You're no longer in charge.

Similarly, if you run up credit-card bills, gamble money you can't spare, or borrow from one friend to pay another, then you have a problem with money. Take charge. Make a budget and see if you can stick to it. Go to your accountant and draw up a master plan or even have the accountant pay your bills. Go to a twelve-step program or a debt consolidation service. Take charge.

Perhaps you spend more time than you know is good for you viewing pornography, looking for casual sex partners, masturbating, or finding massage parlors, prostitutes, and escorts. Think through what this means. Take charge. There's nothing wrong with sexuality, masturbation, or pleasurable erotic desire. But do you masturbate when you feel aroused? Or when you're worried? Do you look at Internet pornography when you want to have some fun? Or when you don't want to be with your partner, write that paper, or figure out how to pay the bills? Or maybe you do it when you're just all-around anxious. If this sounds like you much of the time, then it's no longer about sex. It's about distracting and soothing yourself. You're no longer in charge.

If your autopilot engages you in actions and behaviors that stop you from getting what you want and deserve in life, then take charge. Do whatever you must to get yourself out of the rut you've been in for years. Maybe it was helpful once to live this way, but is this how you want to continue living? In chapter 12, we'll talk more about going for outside help if you can't change your programmed behaviors on your own.

Taking Charge of Your Responsibilities

Part of recovery is sorting out what you are and aren't responsible for. Equally important is looking back to your childhood and seeing what you were and weren't responsible for then. When you were a child, you were dependent on others for your survival. Adults were responsible for you. But you didn't have the life experience and emotional maturity to understand this. Maybe it felt like you were responsible for whatever happened to you. Those feelings may still remain now that you're an adult. You may still feel you caused your own abuse.

Look at an angry parent jerking a small child by the arm. You'll be reminded of the immense, overwhelming power adults have over children. You were once a child like that. Have compassion for the child you were. See if you can remember. Feel what it was like to be him.

As an adult, you know a child cannot stop you from doing what you want. Relieve yourself of feelings that you were the cause of any abuse you suffered at the hands of adults. Release yourself from the disturbing belief that you should have known better or been strong enough to resist.

Imagine this if you believe you instigated the abuse: A child wants to play in traffic. An adult doesn't stop him. Who's responsible for the child being hit by a car? Is it the child because he wanted to play out there? Of course not! The adult should have acted to protect the child from his own desires. All children are curious about sex and the need for affection, but it's up to adults to behave in children's best interests, not in pursuit of their own sexual desires.

Recognizing you're not responsible for what happened to you as a boy in itself doesn't repair the damage from years of believing you were to blame. The recognition is merely a doorway into looking at how your autopilot made you act and feel for years as though you were in constant danger. You'll see how you made choices limiting your ability to feel free, trusting, or spontaneous. From there, you'll do painstaking work to change your outlook.

The fact that you're reading this book is a good sign that you're already taking power away from the adults who abused you. You're regaining it for yourself. In adulthood, you may sometimes still be dependent on other adults, but you have greater flexibility about choosing the adults upon whom you're dependent. You also have the life experience to take care of yourself and become responsible for your well-being, your relationships, and your recovery.

Taking Charge of Your Belief System

We all have beliefs that frame the world for us. We may not think about our belief systems often, but they help us make sense of everything we experience. Belief systems create a moral compass that allows us to navigate life.

Religions developed over the millennia constitute one form of belief system. Other forms are based on science, a philosophy of logic or of the mind, or perhaps some blend of all of these.

Abuse is a major betrayal of a boy's belief system. Your beliefs probably led you to trust that authority figures would take care of you. When this confidence was betrayed, you may have concluded your whole belief system was a sham, along with everyone involved in it. Remember in chapter 5 how Dr. X bitterly talked about the "lie in the world"? This is a horrible way to see life. You have to disavow either one part of yourself or the other—either the part that has faith in your belief system or the part that thinks it's a fraud.

People with one set of beliefs often reject and criticize people with different ones. Both ancient and modern history demonstrate how people become so deeply attached to their belief systems that they're prepared to annihilate anyone who believes differently.

Yet for many people, belief systems, especially religious ones, are precious and life-sustaining. They keep them centered, ethical, and able to overcome whatever obstacles they encounter.

If your religion teaches homosexuality is wrong, you may feel rejected or humiliated if you're gay, or if you're straight but a man abused you. You may feel ashamed you were part of same-sex sexual situations as a boy. Whether you're straight or gay, you may be confused and disturbed from a religious point of view about any sexual feelings and desires you now feel for other men.

If your abusers were clergy or religious parents or caregivers, you may have developed extreme negative feelings about the religion of your childhood and the people who practice it. Perhaps your religion was once a source of comfort and strength for you. But if you now have very negative views of the religion you were taught as a child, it's important to resolve them, even if you never believe in a religion again.

As you recover, you may define and redefine your belief system. You may seek out others who believe as you do, you may become an activist for change, or you may create a new belief system that works for you.

Some people find an alternate religion or a more liberal sect within their own religion with which they can feel comfortable identifying. Others grow up with nebulous ideas about how the world works. If this describes you, then it's important to decide what you believe—to be aware of a coherent psychological, philosophical, ethical, religious, scientific, or mystic formulation that helps you navigate the world.

Without a belief system, you're a candle in the wind. Without purpose or reason, you'll be either passive or impulsive. Either way, you may leave yourself open to revictimization.

The solution won't come easily. You may push yourself through uncomfortable, lonely landscapes. You may abandon what you once believed and find something new. Or you may decide to remain with the religion of your childhood but develop a different understanding of its teachings, perhaps by choosing a different sect, church, congregation, or synagogue.

Even if you completely discard religion, even if you decide that you're an atheist or an agnostic or that you're a spiritual person without an organized religion, you'll still have a belief system. You have opinions about how the world works.

Your philosophy may not always seem coherent or obvious to you, but it's there. The more you put into words its most important principles, the better you'll feel. You'll strengthen and clarify your beliefs. You'll use them throughout life to make the world understandable and guide you through ethical and moral dilemmas.

Taking Charge of Your Recovery

Recovery must be deliberate. You must decide you want to get better, and you must be willing to work toward that goal. Recovery won't happen on its own. If you seek professional help, which I urge you to do if it's in any way possible, your therapy won't succeed unless you work with your therapist.

Recovery doesn't happen just from listening to someone else, or having someone listen to you, or even reading books like this one. Remember, you're rewiring your brain, making new connections to old, split-off feelings and memories. The only way the brain can be rewired is through *experience*. You will learn by *living* and *doing*.

The doing part should be as big as you can make it. Sometimes it requires making yourself behave in ways that don't feel like you. For example, you may sometimes have to force yourself to move out of your depressions by doing things that feel awkward or unfeasible but that counter your dark, disheartened mood—things like taking a walk, going to a movie, calling a friend, or writing a poem.

Doing means actively, willfully pursuing your recovery. Finding ways to keep therapy appointments rather than finding ways to break them. Taking medication if you and your therapist believe it might help you. Developing an attitude that you're going to get better. Seeing setbacks as just setbacks. The road to recovery is uphill. Few journeys worth the effort take place on level ground.

You'll learn to accept you cannot always control the contents of your mind. Being human means experiencing feelings, impulses, and memories. Your emotional self may fill you with desires your rational brain won't allow. You can't stop having these impulses and feelings, but you can decide whether you'll act on them or even worry about them.

You can improve your reaction to unwanted dissociated feelings or memories through understanding, insight, and a positive attitude. As you learn to accept them, you'll probably find you experience them less frequently.

Taking charge—really taking charge—does *not* mean becoming totally obsessed with yourself and your recovery twenty-four hours a day. Just as you need to sleep at night to rest your mind and body, you need to have times when you're doing something other than focusing on your boyhood betrayal and your recovery from it. Sometimes you'll be so exhausted after making a breakthrough that you'll want, need, and deserve a break. Vacations are good for everyone.

Highways, after all, have rest stops and off-roads. So does life.

You may not see the world in color very often, but now and then you may be surprised. When it happens, stop for a moment. Enjoy it. Rejuvenate yourself. Then you'll be ready to get back on the road.

The reward isn't one big prize at the end of your journey. The reward is a new way of experiencing and living life. The reward is loving the journey itself.

Taking Charge of Your Trust

Taking charge doesn't mean you can be in total command of the world. Airline pilots are at the controls of the plane, but they must trust the workers who built the plane, the mechanics who service it, and the crew. They don't blindly trust these people, but they learn from experience how to judge them and their work.

If you were abused as a child, trusting others is very difficult. You weren't able to control your abuser or your world. Maybe you grew up trying to compensate for this, exerting as much control as you could over everything from your friendships to your environment.

There's another side to this need for control: you may resent others who attempt to control you or whom you believe would control you if they could.

Taking charge can be the opposite of trying to be in total control. Taking charge requires taking risks. To take risks, you must trust. But whom do you trust? How do you know when to trust?

Make judgments using adult perceptions rather than a betrayed boy's beliefs. Recognize times when you're reacting as a victim, not as an adult who's taken charge. The experience, confidence, and knowledge you gain as you recover will put you in a better position to discern when to trust.

Taking Charge of How You Relate to Others

By taking charge, you'll become a person who others respect. This won't happen, however, if you try to control every aspect of your environment and relationships.

Nor will you recover if your mission is to exact revenge. Only victims and people who think of themselves as victims want revenge. Powerful people don't need revenge. Powerful people allow others (and themselves) to make mistakes, to be human. After all, no one's perfect. Everyone sometimes fails to say or do the right thing. Even people with whom we have loving relationships occasionally do things that upset us.

Taking charge of your relationships doesn't mean you'll never again be upset with others. It does mean you'll have resilience. It means you can recover from upsets more quickly, with less pain, guilt, and intensity, and with more self-assurance.

If you tend to dissociate, it may seem impossible to simply shrug off your dissociative experiences. It's impossible to even look at them objectively. You may emerge from dissociative episodes with little or no memory of your behaviors, thoughts, or feelings.

If you're dissociating because of the presence or behavior of others, it may be equally impossible to view them from a healthy and mature perspective. You may experience your relationship with them with the eyes and heart of a hurting, angry, powerless child.

It seems like you're boxed in, but you're not. There are ways out. Taking charge means learning to be objective when others upset you. It means seeing a relationship in the larger scheme of things and recognizing it isn't useful to try to smooth some things out. For example, if a stranger upsets you, you may conclude that setting things straight isn't worth your time or energy. You'll understand that every insult and skirmish doesn't deserve a war—even when the other guy is completely wrong.

If you're in a loving relationship with someone who repeatedly does something that disturbs you, however, address the issue. Otherwise, the relationship will deteriorate. Good relationships are precious, but they're like complex machines: they need attention and tune-ups to run smoothly.

Expectations, Limitations, and Goals

The world inevitably throws the unexpected at us. We're constantly faced with problems we can't solve. Taking charge doesn't mean we can fix everything or everyone. We have to accept not only our own limitations but those of others. Learning to accept life as unpredictable and realizing fallibility are basic to human nature. They are necessary parts of maturing emotionally and intellectually.

One limitation you don't have to accept, though, is a future filled with the past's pain and confusion. If you're suffering now, you don't have to accept that you'll always be limited to your current mental state. You can control your decisions and make your life choices. If you decide to get better—and stick to that decision—then it's more likely that you will. It's good to have expectations about what you'll be like after recovering from child abuse, but it's equally important to have realistic expectations.

As we discussed in chapter 2, popular culture bombards us with images of the ideal man. There are fundamental qualities every man should possess, such as honesty and respect for others. Otherwise the meaning of ideal changes drastically in different contexts. Over decades and across expanses of geography—even from one neighborhood to another—the ideal man can change from, for example, the cowboy, to the free-spirited artist, to the hard-hitting businessman, to the sensitive husband. Regardless of what time and place you live in, you've assimilated expectations about how to be. Taking charge doesn't mean you have to meet superficial, fashionable expectations. Being adaptable in your expectations—being willing to make minor adjustments in your goals and even adjust the nature of your goals—is critical as you recover from child abuse.

This is important to remember if you're seeing a therapist. A therapist isn't there to tell you who to be or even to describe the ideal man. A good therapist is like a good sports coach: The coach doesn't tell you what sport to play, but once you've decided you want to win a hundred-meter race, he'll help you achieve your goal. In the process, you may decide you're better at long-distance running, or you'd rather play basketball, or your real interest is sports medicine or reporting for the sports pages. A good coach will help you come to that decision and make the change. A good therapist will help you spell out your goals and then attain them.

Acknowledgment and Acceptance

Acknowledging what happened means more than saying you were abused. It involves something far greater and more difficult. It requires seeing how the abuse affected you and your life.

It means seeing how you interpreted the abuse as a child and how you understood it as you grew up. It means seeing how you felt about the abuse and how you then felt about yourself. It means seeing how you handled it, or denied it, or acted out your anger about it, or got depressed over it, or tried to be rescued from it, or a hundred other reactions you may have had to it.

Acknowledging what happened eventually leads to acceptance of what happened. What's the difference?

Acknowledgment is looking at something and saying, "It's there." When you acknowledge what happened, you can be angry about it, you can feel pain, and you can still feel the urge to forget it, turn away from it, and destroy it.

Acceptance is more internal and more complete. Its overarching quality is a feeling of peace and wholeness. It comes easier to some people than to others. It requires that you not only see what happened but see it while freeing yourself from pain, anger, disgust, and sorrow.

Acceptance means you allow the past to *have happened*. It occurs when mind, body, and soul no longer wish to deny or fight the past and all it meant to you from the time it first happened until now. Accepting what happened means fully absorbing the truth into your consciousness, knowing it affected you, and leaving behind your most intense negative feelings about it.

The word *accept* comes from a Latin word meaning "receive." You can't receive something well if you're angry at it. Nor can you happily receive something that causes pain. Pain pushes things away; anger destroys.

Receiving something requires being willing and able to hold on to it. Child abuse isn't something anyone deserves or wants to accept, but if it happened to you and you want to get better, there's no choice. Refusal to accept it rejects part of your own self. That can't happen without damaging consequences. You can only move your abuse to the corners of your life where it belongs if you accept that it's there to begin with.

How do you acknowledge and accept what happened? There is no single or simple method for accomplishing this. There are many possible paths, and in the rest of this chapter and the chapters that follow we'll discuss some of them.

Letting Your Victim Identity Recede

Pull out the list you made in the first part of this chapter. You wrote down words that describe you. Did you use the word *victim*? If so, where is it on your list? Did you describe yourself with any other words that convey the image of a person who is somehow broken, sick, or weak?

If you did, consider what these words say about your self-image. Do the descriptions play self-fulfilling roles? For some men who were abused, they do.

If you think of yourself as weak, you may not recognize opportunities to get stronger. It may be hard to go through life expecting anything besides more victimization. If you think of yourself as damaged goods, it's hard to feel hope, to feel peace, to enjoy your accomplishments, and to take pleasure in a loving relationship.

But if you suffer much of the time, how can you *not* say you're a victim? You must learn to think in new ways. Learn to distinguish between the past and the present. You were a victim as a child. Even yesterday, an acquaintance, a store clerk, or a criminal may have victimized you. That doesn't mean that at this moment you're still a victim or that you'll be one tomorrow.

It may not be easy to change your thinking. You can probably say without much difficulty that, yes, your abuse happened in the past. Your challenge comes from feelings and memories about the abuse that continue right now in your current life, because if you still have these mental experiences, you continue to feel like a victim.

It becomes a vicious cycle: You feel like a victim. You behave like a victim. You establish and maintain relationships in which you are victimized (or in which you only see victimization, regardless of reality). Your original feelings are validated, and the cycle begins again.

Leaving behind your victim identity can be grueling. On the one hand, if you're going to get better, you'll have to acknowledge your childhood victimization and accept it fully. That means making connections between the memories and feelings you experienced then and continue to experience now. Accomplishing this can take a long time.

On the other hand, after you've acknowledged and accepted the past, you mustn't hold on to it as if it's who you still are. It isn't. It may feel like it is, because acknowledging and accepting trauma can be an overwhelming challenge. It may be the biggest thing a sexually abused man accomplishes in his life. So it's natural to hold on to your accomplishment, just as the winner of a race holds on to his trophy.

But this is one trophy you want to leave behind. Its importance must diminish in your current life. It must recede into the background. It must become smaller than you.

If you do this, you'll eventually be able to make a list of words that describe you and none of them will convey the sense that you're damaged, or a victim. When you can do that, you'll know you've left the past behind: past trauma, past hurts, even past accomplishments that are no longer relevant to your life.

Whom Should You Tell?

If you were abused and kept it a secret until now, you may find yourself wanting to tell someone. This is a natural and healthy desire. It can be a tremendously relieving thing to do. It's also a very powerful thing to do. Therefore, you should think carefully before choosing whether to tell, whom to tell, and when.

Even though you may want to talk about your abuse, you may also be reluctant to tell because of fear or shame. These negative feelings have probably been with you since you were abused, when telling could have resulted in punishment or other serious consequences.

There may be negative consequences now if the person you tell reacts in hurtful ways. What if people don't accept what you say? What if they get angry? What if they say you're making it up? All these things can happen. They have happened countless times to other men.

Perhaps the first question you should consider is what would be the purpose in telling a particular person. Is it for moral support? Is it because you feel this person will understand? Is it because you're angry with someone who knew what was happening but didn't protect you? Is it because you need someone to confirm that the foggy memories are real and the abuse actually occurred? Is it because you want to express your anger directly to the person who abused you?

Understand what you expect before you tell someone. Be prepared for disappointment. This is especially likely if you confront your abuser or people still dependent on him or her, or if your abuser belongs to a social, professional, or religious group that's more dedicated to preserving the group's identity than acknowledging truth. (We'll talk about confronting abusers in chapter 11.)

How and When to Tell

Initially it's best to tell only those people you are certain will be supportive. Be selective. Take your time. You'll know in your gut who these people are. Even so, be prepared for letdowns. Not everyone can handle what you have to say. For example, if they themselves suffered from child abuse and haven't dealt with it, they may not be as receptive as you hoped.

Know what you want out of the disclosure when you make it. Be prepared to tell other people what they can do if they ask how they can help. Sometimes just being there and listening is enough. If that's what you want, say so. Sometimes, though, a sibling or a good childhood friend can help you solve puzzles, serving as a sort of memory bank to help you fill in parts of your life that you can't remember well.

It's not helpful to make an announcement about your abuse to the world at large, at least not initially. People are often uncomfortable hearing about someone else's personal tragedy, especially if they're not intimately involved with the victim. Some people just don't like to hear anyone—especially a man—say, "I'm a victim." They're subject to the same feelings and perceptions about manhood that have stood in your way as you've tried to face your abuse. So not everyone is going to rush to your side to offer sympathy and support.

After you've reached a good level of confidence in your inner strength, if you feel you need to make a public political statement, then do it. The world needs to know that boys are sexually abused. Just be sure you feel secure enough about yourself that you can stay balanced no matter what reaction you get. It's probably best to make your statement while involved with a therapist or with a sympathetic group of some kind. That way, if and when you get negative reactions or nonreactions, the support you need will be right there for you.

Telling what happened, putting the unutterable into words, is a large part of healing. As you tell other people, you're also telling yourself. You're putting together the full story of your life. The most important person who needs to know that story is you. So let's start!

11

Safely Experiencing Emotions

Emotions are the *feeling* parts of consciousness. They move you away from the blank state you're in when you can only feel numb. Emotions tell you that you're alive. They move you to act.

It's not a coincidence that the words *motion* and *emotion* share the same root. They both involve movement. You experience emotions mentally, but they also affect you physically. So while an emotion involves mental sensation (for example, when your feelings are hurt), emotions may also push you to take physical action such as crying.

You can still see the "motion" of emotion by looking at children. An unhappy child acts on his feelings by crying, throwing a tantrum, running away, or hurting someone. Only as he grows up and learns the consequences of fully expressing his emotions does he begin to manage them. As an adult, you may have learned to manage emotions by thinking rather than acting.

Reclaim Your Emotions

To *reclaim* means to take back ownership, to make something yours again. That's what you must do to heal. You must take back the total experience of your life. Make it yours, both the good and the bad. This means reclaiming emotions you couldn't feel or express when you were a boy.

But if you were molested, why would you want to reclaim something so profoundly upsetting? Because *until you take charge of your emotions*—remembered and unremembered—*they'll be in charge of you.*

When there's a fire, no firefighter would pretend it doesn't exist. He doesn't look away, or say it's an impossible task, or it's too dangerous, or it's someone else's responsibility. He doesn't just hope it will go away and then go party.

Nor does he approach the fire with the belief that it will control him. The firefighter asserts control over the fire. Even if he can't put it out right away, even if he has to extinguish one blazing brush fire after another, he never gives up.

The emotions of your betrayed childhood are the fires you must now control. How do you do it? By recognizing that they exist and that they are yours. You must reclaim your past experiences, memories, and emotions as your own. When you were a boy, you weren't given the right to have them, even though they existed and were part of you.

Reclaim what you couldn't have as a boy. It's yours.

Handling Emotions, Then and Now

We all sometimes have feelings pushing us to do something not in our best interest. If you were abused, your betrayal produced and may still produce such overwhelmingly strong emotions that you can't express yourself physically without disastrous consequences.

If you had acted on what you truly felt when you were betrayed, the consequences might have been worse than the betrayal itself. You could have physically hurt yourself or someone else. You could have been punished or exiled from your family. You could have hurt someone you loved. You may even have worried that disclosing your abuse would mean the end of your family.

So what were you to do? We talked in chapter 4 about how dissociation froze your emotions so that they wouldn't overwhelm you. When your instincts said you couldn't survive if you experienced those feelings, you put them in cold storage where they've remained ever since.

Even now, your instincts may tell you that you can't survive if you experience these feelings. But they are leftover child instincts. They're the ones that first told you to freeze your feelings. They themselves are frozen and haven't grown up with the rest of you. These instincts don't "know" that you're far more capable of learning to cope with overwhelming emotion now than when you were as a boy.

What if you're afraid the process of recovery will unleash such powerful emotions that you'll lose control and hurt yourself or someone else? This, of course, happens in some cases. Paradoxically, your asking the question makes it far less likely.

Your fear means you're enough in control to monitor things and make sure that nothing terrible happens. It means you have the maturity, intellectual capacity, and moral development to understand that acting on some emotions would be harmful. Having anxieties actually proves your mental strength. It means you know how to go for help if you feel overwhelmed or out of control.

Having navigated adulthood as well as you have—even if there have been some very bad times along the way—proves you're capable of having very strong feelings without acting on them. You didn't attack your girlfriend when she broke up with you even though your anger pushed you in that direction. You didn't steal the Porsche from your boss's driveway even though you envied him and coveted his beautiful car. So you know you can have strong emotions without acting on them to your detriment.

If you're overwhelmed by raw feelings of betrayal, you can recover. Your emotions don't have to remain in control of your actions, and you can use your mental abilities and life experience to ensure that they won't. In this chapter and the one that follows, we'll talk about managing strong feelings.

Will you make mistakes? Yes. Will it go smoothly? No. In the end will it be worth all the risk and the work? Absolutely.

Emotions of Betrayal

At times, almost everyone who has been betrayed feels the following negative, intense, and conflicting emotions:

• Anger	• Jealousy
• Rage	• Envy
• Resentment	• Contempt
• Frustration	• Disgust
• Indignation	• Hatred

- Fear
- Dread
- Anxiety
- Loneliness
- Embarrassment
- Guilt
- Shame
- Pain

- Regret
- Sadness
- Remorse
- Depression
- Despair
- Indifference
- Numbness
- Paralysis

If you were betrayed by someone close to you, however, many feelings you have (and remember) about the relationship may be positive. Men and women who molest boys often live outwardly decent, sometimes even admirable, lives. They're teachers, coaches, clergy, uncles and aunts, grandparents, mentors, brothers and sisters, fathers and mothers. Often they even do good things for the boys they're also betraying. So any of these painful relationships may simultaneously evoke some positive feelings. Let's say you were betrayed by someone you cared about and who seemed to or did care about you. Right alongside your negative feelings you may feel the following positive emotions:

- Love
- Friendship
- Sexual attraction
- Respect
- Duty
- Loyalty
- Gratitude

- Idolization
- Idealization
- Pride
- Innocence
- Excitement
- Hope
- Joy

Learn the Different Emotions

If you dissociate your emotions, you may be unfamiliar with them. Having trained yourself to put them in the deep freeze and not experience them, you may not be aware of the subtle differences among them.

It's important for you to think about all the different emotions you feel about your betrayal. If you consider them carefully, you'll be less likely to be surprised if they creep up on you and you start to feel them. Instead, you'll gradually allow them into awareness, learn to feel them, manage them, and become familiar with them.

It's much easier to be in charge of your life when you have a grasp on your emotions. They communicate what's going on inside you. Understanding what they say helps you understand their effect on you and prepares you to manage them. You become better equipped to recover and get back your whole self.

This chapter will help you gain perspective on feelings by articulating them. Emotions become much more manageable when you put them into words or express them through other outlets, rather than being at their mercy as they course through you.

Exercise: Defining Your Emotions

It's best to do this exercise over a period of days. Take as long as you need.

Get a small notebook. On the first page, write down one of the emotions listed previously. Then write down words that describe how that emotion feels. If you can't think of words to describe an emotion, look it up in a dictionary and write down a brief description of it.

Once you've written your description, think of a time when you felt that emotion as a child. Write down the occasion in the notebook. Think of other times in childhood when you felt it, and write them down, too. Then think of occasions when you've experienced it as an adult. Write them down as well.

Go on to another emotion, and on a new page do the same with it. Think about how one emotion differs from the next. This may be harder than it sounds. They may seem similar, but they're all at least slightly different.

Add to your descriptions in days that follow if you think of new words that capture the emotion's meaning or other occasions when you've felt it. Return to the exercise whenever you feel it might help you.

Do your descriptions become richer the more you think about an emotion? Are some emotions easier to locate than others? Which are easiest to manage? Which give you trouble? Which do you feel seldom or never? Do you have cause to feel emotions that you nevertheless rarely feel? If so, why do you think you don't experience them very much?

These kinds of questions will help you trace your feelings as they unfold. The more you know about them, the less they'll surprise you, the less afraid of them you'll be, and the fuller and more satisfying your emotional life will become.

Managing Your Emotions

The more you understand emotions, the more you can identify what you feel. You may not be very aware of emotions at all, or you may be mostly aware of negative feelings. You may start to notice that the positive emotions are either absent in your life or in very short supply.

The emotions you believe you *ought* to feel but don't are your dissociated emotions—the ones you've put into cold storage. As you slowly allow yourself to feel them, you may feel uncomfortable or even frightened. You may start to dissociate and sometimes find yourself not in the room. You may believe you can't manage these feelings, but you can.

Or at least you can learn to. You can use your new knowledge of emotions to keep them from overwhelming you. You can say to yourself, for example, "I'm sad right now, but that doesn't mean I feel despair or depression." If you are depressed, you can say, "This feels terrible. I recognize that, and I know something about where these feelings came from. But just because I feel this bad now doesn't mean I'll always feel like this. I need to think about how to get myself out of this state."

Some men didn't dissociate their feelings enough when they were betrayed. They may often feel overwhelmed and wish they could dissociate better. Feeling emotions so intensely can be disabling in a way different from not feeling them at all.

If this sounds like you, you'll want to reinterpret what we just talked about. You need to put feelings out of mind when necessary. In a way, you're a step ahead of the man who needs to get in touch with emotions.

When you're deeply depressed, it's hard to think that you can or will ever get out of it. The rest of this chapter will give you ideas about how to get in touch with emotions, manage them, and put disabling ones like depression aside so that there's more room for positive feelings and growth.

The pathways in this chapter can help both the man wanting to get in touch with his emotions and the one who feels intruded upon and overwhelmed by feeling. In chapter 12, we'll talk about ways to manage overwhelming feelings, such as practicing meditation and yoga.

Completing Your Story

Betrayal forces a boy to struggle with himself. His thoughts tell him one thing about the world, but his feelings tell him something very different. Neither side gives in easily.

No one survives this way for long without consequences. It's like when an electrical grid overloads. Something will break down.

What is likely to break are the connections between feelings and knowledge. Perhaps you repressed your feelings or your memories after your molestation, or dissociated during it so that your knowledge and feelings never interconnected. If so, your life story wasn't really available to you. If you wrote down the story of your life, it would be incomplete, missing certain words, pages, or even entire chapters.

You may know facts about your life but not know how you feel about them. Or you may know how you feel but have no idea why. You may even know two completely contradictory "facts" and not realize they don't fit together.

You may, therefore, draw wrong conclusions about yourself. For example, if you remember once playing a cruel trick on a schoolmate, you might conclude you're fundamentally mean. But if you also remember what happened to you the night before when you were sexually betrayed, you may start to see yourself with more compassion and understanding. You'll be able to do this as your life story becomes more complete. You'll make connections.

Recovery requires picking up the pieces of your past so that you can see yourself more completely than you ever have. If you don't know how you came to be who you are, your view of yourself will be distorted. You'll feel unfinished, yearning for something but not knowing what. If you see yourself more completely, however, you'll see the world more completely. Most important, you'll feel you fit into your life.

Why remember unhappy events and feelings? Why not just focus on the positive and decide to be happier and less anxious and depressed?

In order to see yourself and live your life more completely, you must experience your emotional past. The less you understand your past, the less you can understand and live the present and the future.

Allowing yourself to know your history allows you to become whole again. Piecing together the fragments of your traumatized life, you can reclaim it and become complete. Then you'll be able to see and acknowledge the pain, anger, and fear that you may have known little or nothing about. But remember, this also frees you up to feel joy, love, and exhilaration.

Rediscovering the splintered emotions of your past establishes pathways in your brain that were abandoned long ago or were never constructed. When you build these pathways, you restore your life story. It becomes familiar territory. The isolated feelings of your past fade. They recede to the corners of your memory, and most of the time they'll remain there. This is how you'll take charge of them.

Try to locate an inner child within yourself, the little boy you once were. If you do this, it doesn't mean that you have multiple personality disorder. It's simply a way your mind can organize things to allow you entry into your past.

Imagine the child you were who is still living inside you. He knows all about how it felt during your betrayal. Allow that child to speak, express himself, and become your friend.

And you should become *his* friend. Remember, he's probably a scared little guy. He needs help. You can be the grown-up who calms and soothes him and makes him feel safe.

In fact, you can help one another. You need him to reconnect to your past and to understand why you are frightened, angry, or sexually compulsive. He needs you because he's never had a grown-up he could count on—someone he could trust with all his fears, worries, and terrors. As you explore the paths in the next section, make sure the boy inside you comes along.

Seven Ways to Regain and Manage Emotions

In this section, we'll explore methods you can use to get in touch with the feelings that may be eluding you. Use them to find the lost emotions of your childhood. This may seem like too vast a task, but just work one step at a time. Don't forget to keep the little boy inside you close at hand. You'll need his help, just like he needs yours.

1. Keep a Journal

Find a quiet time and place every day where you can be undisturbed. Write down your thoughts, feelings, experiences, setbacks, victories, and questions. Write about your day or about the past if it comes to you. Allow yourself to remember. Describe what you see in your mind's eye as you recall your childhood, both the good and the bad. If you feel there's a boy inside you who wants to say something, let him have his say, even if it feels silly or awkward. Don't plan what you'll write. Keep your pen moving on the page. Write down every word or phrase as it comes to you, no matter how meaningless it seems. Just keep writing, even if you don't write complete thoughts or sentences. Don't worry about spelling or grammar or whether anyone reading your journal would understand what you say or approve of it. This exercise may seem odd at first or make you feel self-conscious, but it will become easier if you do it regularly. As time goes on, occasionally go back through your journal. See how your words make you feel.

2. Express Yourself with Art

Paint, sculpt, or perform—find your own art form and explore expressing yourself through it. Join a class or do it on your own. Don't try to make things perfect. Don't worry about whether you're a "real" artist, sculptor, or performer. If the boy inside you wants to express himself, let him. Don't feel that everything he comes up with has to be negative. Let him be happy, mischievous, or fantastical—whatever he wants to be as long as he doesn't hurt anyone in the process. Be aware of all of your feelings as you express yourself through your art. Allow yourself to be present as you and your inner boy create it.

3. Write Letters

It's important to put things into words. Write letters that help you talk about what's going on inside you. You don't have to send these letters. In fact, when you write them, assume you won't send them. That way you won't hold anything back. If you decide you really do want to send one of the letters later on, you can. Then, if you wish, you can edit it as necessary. For the moment, though, let all your feelings come through.

1. Write a letter to your betrayer. Talk directly to him. Say exactly how you feel now and how the boy within you felt then. Say what you felt when you still trusted her and the rest of the world. Say how things changed, if they did. Tell your abuser off if you want.

Say absolutely anything that you need to say. This is your letter and you can put anything into it that you need to. Write one every week if you want. See if there are any changes in what you write.

2. Write to your boy self. Comfort him. Let him know you're his friend and can protect him. Tell him it wasn't his fault even if he thinks it was. Explain why it wasn't his fault. Explain that his betrayer was older, more experienced, and more powerful. Explain that all boys need the attention of older people and try to please them if they can. Explain that boys' hormones can arouse them even in sexual encounters they don't want or aren't in their best interests. Explain how adults should know not to participate in acts that can harm children even if children want them to.

3. Write letters from your boy self. Be him and let him tell you how he felt then, how he feels now, what he felt about his betrayer or anyone else. Be him and let him tell you how he feels about *you*. Be him and let him ask you anything he wants to know. Be him and let him tell you what frightens him, excites him, challenges him, or discourages him. Be him at different ages, and at each age write more. Let yourself hear from the boy you were.

4. Write letters to other people from your past: The people in your life who you expected to protect you but didn't. The people who did try to protect you. The people who didn't know. The people who did know. The people who made you feel worse. The people who made you feel better. The people who labeled or teased you. The people you isolated yourself from because of your shame, anger, or fear. Tell them everything you need them to know.

4. Visualize Advising a Victim's Parent

Picture a person close to you—perhaps a sibling, coworker, or friend—with a young son the same age you were when your abuse began. Imagine that the perpetrator who betrayed you abused this boy instead. Imagine the parent coming to you, telling you that he or she doesn't know what to do. What you would say to the parent.? If you could sit down and talk with the boy, what would you say to him? Write these thoughts down.

5. Visualize Yourself as a Child

Imagine this younger self coming to you now and telling you about being abused. He says he blames himself for what happened. If only he were different! If only he'd fought back! If only he hadn't wanted the attention! He feels guilty for ruining your life. What would you say to him? Console him. Offer to watch over him. Let him know you love him. Allow him to look into your eyes as you offer him protection and reassurance. What do you see in his eyes?

6. Look Carefully at Children

If you're having difficulty letting yourself off the hook for your role in your abuse or you can't connect with yourself as a child, go someplace where you can observe children the same age you were when you were abused. Watch them. Listen. See how small they are. Notice how naive and powerless they can be. Watch what happens when an adult gets their attention. Can they be easily led? See if you can spot a child who reminds you of yourself at that age. Let yourself feel for him. Imagine what it would be like to be him. Consider how compassionate you would feel about him if you knew he were hurt. If you were a teenager when you were abused, take a close look at teenagers that age. They're older than very young children, and often at first glance they look like they know how to take care of themselves. Do they? Observe one who reminds you of yourself. Does he look like he could manage a scary situation like betrayal? Think about whether he'd be responsible if an adult he cared about pressed him into sexuality.

7. Argue with Yourself about Yourself

Write down whatever positive feelings or beliefs you have about yourself. Then allow first yourself, and then your boy self, to disagree, explaining why these feelings are baseless or these beliefs are untrue. Write down whatever negative feelings or beliefs this second self has about you. Respond with a rebuttal. Go back and forth until you run out of disagreements. You don't have to do this all at once. It can be an ongoing dialogue. You'll find your answers in time.

Triggers of Negative Behavior

Negative cycles of behavior can seem to take on a life of their own. Self-damaging and self-defeating addictions and compulsions may seem to come out of nowhere. Over time, though, you'll identify cyclical patterns. You can empower yourself to break these patterns if you recognize them as they develop.

Triggers are reminders of past traumatic events. When you are triggered, you may feel overwhelming emotions like the ones you felt when you were abused. Some triggers are obviously connected to the original trauma. For example, seeing a photo of your abuser may trigger anxiety or anger. Other triggers are subtler. For example, if your abuser often approached you when you were feeling sad, then the feeling of sadness itself may trigger tremendous anxiety. Once triggered, you may feel a need to do anything you can to calm yourself.

Say you often binge on food to cope with stress. If you're unaware of emotional triggers that lead to overeating, you'll feel defeated in efforts to watch your consumption. But if you recognize that certain emotions—like feeling lonely, bored, or unappreciated—trigger overeating, you can anticipate unwanted behavior and reduce or eliminate it.

Everyone experiences negative feelings at times. They may be accompanied by exaggerated negative thoughts that feel true at the time. Say a friend promises to call but doesn't. You feel hurt, abandoned, betrayed, or insecure. You think people are undependable or maybe something's wrong with you. These thoughts and feelings seem to make sense, but when you consider them later in a better frame of mind, you see you were overreacting.

Sometimes strong negative thoughts and feelings lead to behaviors you don't want. Called *compensatory behaviors*, they cover up the painful feelings and thoughts. Compensatory behaviors directed against others or against property are called *acting out*. For example, if someone is angry, he may act out by verbally or physically abusing others or breaking things. Acting out temporarily makes you feel more powerful or discharges some frustration, but often you regret it afterward.

Turning trigger feelings or thoughts against yourself is called *acting in*. You might mentally beat up on yourself or physically hurt yourself by punching a wall, self-cutting, or another self-injurious behavior. Or you "forget" to pay a bill on time and incur interest charges.

Another way to compensate for unwanted feelings and thoughts is to *numb out*. This blocks feelings through doing things like drugs, drinking, overeating, excessively watching TV or playing video games, or being compulsively sexual.

Interventions

Alternatively, when experiencing trigger thoughts or feelings, you can choose to make an *intervention*. This is empowering rather than disempowering.

Think about a recent negative behavior of yours. Did it lead to regrets or guilty feelings? Was it something you'd told yourself you wouldn't do anymore? If it made you feel better, did you pay a price for it later? If you look back to the minutes, hours, or even days before, can you now see that you should have known it was coming?

Many people go through predictable cycles of negative behaviors. If you can recognize your trigger feelings, perceive that the accompanying thoughts aren't valid, and notice that your repetitive behaviors are neither empowering nor productive, you can intervene at any stage and get out of the cycle.

The cycle involves four phases:

1. *Buildup.* Let's say you've worked hard on a project but get critical responses from your supervisor. This triggers feelings of rejection or inadequacy coming from thoughts that you're incompetent or worthless. Current situations can trigger negative emotions so that current feelings become more significant than they deserve to be. You may say to yourself, "I never get anything right," or "My boss hates me," or "Nobody appreciates my efforts."

2. *Withdrawal.* This moves you into the withdrawal phase. You feel sorry for yourself and feel victimized by others. You isolate yourself. You only stay in this phase briefly because you feel you must get away from these intolerable feelings and thoughts.

3. *Prebehavior.* Through fantasies of drinking or food bingeing, hurting yourself, getting revenge, or other compensatory behaviors,

you gain a sense of power or control that overcomes your negative thoughts and feelings. Say you fantasize about overeating. Food can be like a drug that numbs feelings. Bingeing on ice cream, for example, temporarily makes you feel better. Unless you make an intervention to break out of your cycle, you'll enact behavior you don't want.

4. *Postbehavior*. Afterward, you experience remorse, guilt, or shame. You promise yourself to avoid doing this in the future. This completes the cycle, helping you feel a little better until the next round of buildup.

Recognizing Triggers

You have choices when dealing with unwanted, disturbing feelings. You can take things out on others, numb yourself, or use empowering interventions. The cycle continues unless you change the pattern.

You need to recognize your triggers. Look at the list of emotions earlier in this chapter. Some may be inconsequential for you. Others may be strong triggers for you, and still others may be really powerful. Rate each emotion, noting which have low, medium, and high negativity for you.

Write down ten feelings that are most likely to trigger your self-defeating cycle. Then write down some typical negative thoughts you have when triggered. For example, if your supervisor criticized your work, your feeling of worthlessness triggered the negative self-statement, "I never get anything right."

With each trigger feeling and accompanying thoughts, write the negative behavior you often do as compensation. For example:

Feeling: Rejected.

Thought: "Nobody cares about me."

Behavior: Isolate, overeat.

As you identify more trigger feelings, you'll see a pattern emerging. Pay attention to the thoughts. Are there overgeneralizations? Broad statements using words like *nobody*, *everybody*, *never*, and *always* constitute all-or-nothing, distorted, inaccurate thinking. With time, you'll probably look at yourself, the world, and your relationships differently.

In the cycle, negative emotions may trigger thoughts or negative thoughts may trigger emotions. It's not important which comes first. Once triggered, they intensify and you feel compelled to do a compensatory behavior to feel better.

You can bail out with an intervention that empowers you instead of resorting to familiar, disempowering compensatory behavior. Remember to substitute interventions for negative behaviors. Think about activites that would make you feel better if you were triggered. Some you can do by yourself, such as reading, journaling, taking a hot bath, meditating, or listening to music. Others involve people, like playing board games, going to an Alcoholics Anonymous meeting (if appropriate), or being around someone you trust.

Many men find it's easier to unwind from stress through physical activity rather than talking. Walking, running, shooting baskets, and working out can be invigorating and soothing. If you tend to rely solely on these, however, consider trying other types of interventions to give yourself more options.

There are no "correct" interventions. The only rule is that it should be a behavior that reduces negative feelings and thoughts without disempowering you. It's difficult to create interventions in the midst of struggling in your cycle, so you need to figure them out when you're not feeling triggered. Write three lists of intervention activities—behavior you know makes you feel better—using these headings: "Alone," "With Others," and "Physical." On each list, include multiple interventions you're familiar with and have the ability to use. The longer the lists, the more resources you'll have at your disposal. For example, if your only intervention is going for a walk, you won't have something available if you get triggered at 2:00 A.M. when the weather is bad or if you live in a high-crime neighborhood.

Use your lists to substitute interventions for behaviors you don't want to do anymore. This won't be easy. Keep at it. You'll slowly learn to use intervention behaviors habitually when you feel triggered.

Interventions aren't permanent solutions for triggers. They are a tool in your recovery that prevents unwanted behaviors while you work on the feelings and thoughts that elicit them.

Resolving Your Emotions
about Your Abuser

How can you resolve your emotions about the person who victimized you, what he did, and how you were affected?

Confrontation

In an ideal world, you'd confront the person who betrayed you and express your feelings. He would acknowledge the betrayal, accept full responsibility for it, and ask for forgiveness. You'd decide if a punishment is appropriate and whether to forgive him. It would all end satisfactorily.

Of course, we don't live in an ideal world. People who molest children are usually incapable of acknowledging, much less understanding, the damage they have done. Chances are your abuser will deny having molested you, minimize its importance, or even tell you that you were the one who seduced him.

People who sexually abuse children may move away or die. Some angrily deny all accusations. Some shrug off the abuse as a minor incident. Some remember the "affair" you two had. Some won't respond at all. Few would be willing to participate in any sort of mediated intervention. Few would be willing to go with you to talk to a therapist.

If your abuser's whereabouts are unknown or your abuser is dead, your recovery can still proceed. It's rare in any case that confrontations result in a sense of real reparation or redress, so the chances of finding satisfaction in one are small. Don't bet your recovery on it.

Luckily, it's not necessary. You're working to heal yourself, not your victimizer. Your recovery depends on *you*, not on the person who betrayed you. Although talking to your betrayer might help you fill in parts of your life story, don't depend on her to help you at all.

In his memoir *In My Father's Arms*, Walter de Milly described confronting his father as an adult about the father's abuse of him during his boyhood. Walter sensed his father had himself been molested as a boy. He's clear that he felt compassion for him and that all he wanted was to understand why the man who'd brought him into this world had also molested him. At the same time, he wanted his father to visibly express grief, sorrow, or regret for what he'd done to his own son. None of this happened. Disheartened, Walter wrote, "I wanted Dad to show me his injuries. I wanted him to beg for forgiveness, to cry in rage against his own malefactor, but his composure never disintegrated. I felt both frustrated and empty."

Confronting an abuser is often disappointing. It can make things worse if you dissociate in your abuser's presence, or if you're still swayed by her words, or if he still has some control over your life.

Furthermore, your abuser probably can't answer the question you most want answered: Why? Child molesters aren't apt to understand why they feel and act as they do. Even if they can face the question of why they did what they did, they don't have a response. They don't know.

So don't confront your abuser unless you're absolutely sure you need to do so in order to move on. If you do decide to confront him, plan it carefully and be mindful that there is little likelihood that things will end up as you believe they should.

In planning a confrontation, make sure *you* decide on the location. Make sure it's not on your abuser's turf. Choose a place where you feel safe and where you won't be completely alone with your abuser.

Think through what you want to say. Rehearse it with your therapist or a good friend. Take notes if you want so that you're sure you won't go blank or forget anything.

Do you want to describe what you remember and how you felt? Do you want to talk about the aftereffects as you grew up? Do you have questions about why he or she behaved that way, what was going through his mind, how she rationalized what was done? Are you making demands for an apology? For restitution? For public disclosure? For your abuser to go to therapy? Are you hoping for reconciliation? Under what conditions? If your abuser wants to reconcile, would you consider it? Again, under what conditions?

Make sure you have someone available with whom you can talk through your reactions afterward. Keep a journal about your feelings. Treat yourself well, and remember this: *Your healing is not going to come from your abuser*. Your healing will come from within you. The only reconciliation you need is with yourself. Only you can know the whole truth of your life.

Forgiveness

What about forgiveness? Can and should you forgive your betrayer? What does it really mean to forgive? *Webster's Third International*

Dictionary says that to forgive means "to stop feeling resentment for a wrong that was committed." It means giving up claim to retribution against an offender. It means "to absolve, to pardon."

That's a very, very tall order. Why do it anyway? Why grant your betrayer such bounty? *Because forgiveness is not for him. It's for you!*

What does forgiveness *not* mean? It doesn't mean the betrayal never happened. It's not a "delete" button for the past. It's not a "Get out of jail free" card for your betrayer. And it certainly doesn't say that what he or she did was fine.

No, forgiveness is something else. It's a decision on your part to no longer wish your betrayer harm. You probably weren't going to hurt her, anyway. So who benefits if you stop wanting to wound your betrayer? *You do!*

Forgiving means releasing the anger that's kept you wrapped up in knots all these years. Forgiveness benefits *you*. It really has nothing to do with your betrayer.

If you do decide to forgive, when do you do it? Not immediately. You can't forgive until you know what your betrayer has done to you. You have to regain emotions and learn from your history. To accomplish this, you have to acknowledge, evoke, and reexperience some dark, horrible moments.

Forgiveness allows you to have learned. It allows your betrayal to *have happened*. It allows you to recognize that it's now in the past. It allows you to know that someone did something unforgivable to you.

Yet you have the power to forgive anyway. If you forgive, you become larger, more human, more alive and passionate. You know that what happened was wrong, but you can control how it affects you. Forgiveness means giving up victimhood. That's what you want. And you can choose to give it to yourself.

12

Helping Yourself Heal

Addressing Your Problems

If you were sexually abused as a boy, chances are you may suffer from any number of symptoms, including

- Depression

- Anxiety

- Low self-esteem

- Shame

- Guilt

- Loneliness

- Social isolation

- Difficulty finding a relationship

- Finding yourself in one brief relationship after another

- Problems in relationships with your partner or spouse, your children, your parents, your boss or coworkers, or others with whom you have intimate contact

- Irrational fear that you will harm a child

- Drug or alcohol addiction

- Compulsive behavior such as overeating, overspending, chronic gambling, constant viewing of pornography, continually seeking anonymous sexual partners, uncontrollable masturbation, or incessant trips to massage parlors or prostitutes

- Workaholism

- Worries about being gay even though your fantasies are primarily about women

- Inability to feel good about being gay even though your fantasies are primarily about men

- Feeling you're not a man

- Finding yourself a victim again and again

- Flashbacks, nightmares, intrusive thoughts, or other signs of reliving a trauma

- Emotional numbness or constriction

- Hyperarousal—being vigilant, irritable, and jumpy much of the time

- Outbursts of rage

- Physical symptoms your doctor can't explain on physical grounds—rapid heartbeat, anorexia or bulimia, shortness of breath, dizziness, or constipation

- Sexual problems—lack of interest, inability to achieve or maintain an erection, premature ejaculation, inability to have satisfactory sex with someone you care about, disturbing masochistic or sadistic thoughts or behaviors, or relentless and intrusive sexual fantasies

- Fear of being around other men, especially in groups, locker rooms, or public rest rooms

- Obsessive thoughts about sexual acts or partners you usually wouldn't be interested in

- Trouble with sleep—insomnia or sleeping all the time

- Self-destructive behavior

- Urges to hurt someone physically or incidents when you do so

- Amnesia for certain periods of your life

- Losing time

Of course, everyone responds differently to childhood sexual abuse, and it's unlikely that you suffer from every one of these symptoms. But if you recognize yourself in this list, there are many things you can do on your own to help yourself recover. We'll talk about them later in this chapter. But sometimes the right decision is to get professional help.

Men and Psychotherapy

Because the prospect of therapy often provokes anxiety, many men come up with excuses not to pursue it. For example, you might say, "I can do this on my own," or "Only weaklings need a therapist," or "My problems aren't really so big," or "Therapy is a crutch—I don't want to get dependent on it," or "Medication is bad for me."

Are these excuses valid or are they the same kinds of ideas that gave you trouble to begin with? Do your excuses echo old ideas about what it means to be a man, of being totally self-reliant and refusing to acknowledge that you hurt and need help?

Everyone needs help at times. It's smart to get it when you need it. Is insulin a crutch for a diabetic? Should he say, "I can do it myself"? Certainly not! So why should you?

If you were building a house, would you say you don't need any contractors, plumbers, or electricians? Probably not. You might be able to build a house by simply reading a book, but think how much faster and better construction would go if you had the right help—someone you trusted who had the experience to help you through all the challenges and support you through the inevitable blunders and mistakes. Recovering from boyhood sexual abuse is no different. You need someone to talk to.

Going to therapy isn't like having an operation where you find an expert surgeon, lay down on an operating table, go to sleep, and wake up different but not totally understanding what happened while you were under anesthesia. In fact, therapy can't work unless you and your therapist are collaborators, figuring out together what happened to you, what effect it had on you, what's going on in your life now (both good and bad), what you want to change, and how to make those changes. The therapist can't do it alone any more than you could.

What Goes On in Psychotherapy?

A therapist's job is to help you put your life story back together. To accomplish this, he listens to you without judging you and helps you keep track of your self. He may also help you learn some of the techniques I talk about later in this chapter.

A therapist should create a nonjudgmental atmosphere that facilitates your telling your story in an organized way. In doing so, you'll identify, express, and reflect on your emotions, making links between parts of your life that seemed unconnected before.

Your therapist may talk to you about how to approach everyday problems differently. You may discover patterns of behavior—some of them learned in childhood—that stop you from getting what you want in relationships, at work, and elsewhere in your life. This will help you choose whether these patterns need revising and plan any changes you need.

Because your therapist is (or ought to be) knowledgeable about male sexual victimization, he can answer your questions about it and help you sort out the facts. He may help you locate the boy inside yourself and speak to that boy, creating a dialogue that keeps you in touch with the parts of you that still feel childlike. You may start to see how complicated your feelings are about your abuse and your abuser, especially if you have both negative and positive feelings about him or her.

A therapist may work with you directly to make you feel less anxious or afraid. For example, if you were abused in the woods, you may feel frightened of being in the woods, or in parks, or anywhere with trees or open spaces. A therapist may help you alleviate this kind of phobia by teaching you to relax while you think about what frightens you. This process is called *desensitization*.

Also, a therapist may interrupt your usual thought processes and offer you new ways of thinking. For example, if you obsess about some part of your story, such as why you went back to your abuser's house after you knew it was dangerous, the therapist may directly interrupt that flow of thinking, which serves you no good in the present. This will teach you to interrupt yourself when you begin to ruminate.

All of these processes are important, but most important of all is the relationship you have with your therapist. In the end, this is what will make the therapy successful.

Because of your early betrayal, you may have a very hard time trusting even the most seemingly responsive and compassionate of therapists. After all, you were betrayed in an important early relationship. You may be especially suspicious of relationships that seem loving, nurturing, and kind.

It's important that you find a way to establish a different kind of relationship with your therapist than you had with your abuser in which you experience understanding, trust, and empathy in a nonjudgmental atmosphere. Having this kind of relationship will take you a long way toward restoring your beliefs about what's possible in relationships.

Ideally, your experience with your therapist will give you tools to enable you to develop relationships with others. As you do, you can talk with your therapist about those relationships and get feedback about what's happening.

The *person* of the therapist is crucial, because your relationship with him or her may be the single most important component of your healing. When a therapeutic relationship is healing, it's because the therapist has integrity, is not exploitative, and is sensitive, empathic, consistent, and trustworthy. Assuming the therapist is well trained and licensed—issues we'll address in a moment—it's more important to consider who the therapist *is* than what he or she *does*.

Your therapist should be able to establish and maintain a protected place for you to come and safely think through things that have been out of your awareness or too scary to contemplate. This isn't easy to accomplish. It may take a long time before you feel secure enough with your therapist to share some of your darkest thoughts or memories.

It's certainly vital that you put your life story together as best as you can, but huge gaps may remain in your memory of your childhood betrayal. Even so, you'll heal if you experience a different, more positive relationship with your therapist than you had with your molester and with others who enabled abuse to occur. If therapy goes well, you and your therapist together will create a bond that will change your ideas about what's possible between two people.

For simplicity's sake, in the following sections therapists are referred to as "he" or "him," but many therapists who work with male survivors are female, and are likely to be as competent—or incompetent—as male therapists.

Locating a Therapist

You shouldn't simply pick a therapist at random out of the phone book. Do some research. Ask around. Get opinions. Interview potential therapists.

Sometimes you can locate good therapists familiar with male survivor issues through recommendations from other survivors. If you have a support group available to you—such as one for survivors or sexual addictions—you can ask who has a therapist to recommend. You can also call rape crisis hotlines or mental health agencies in your area and get a referral specifically for sexual abuse issues. Be aware, however, that some competent rape and sex abuse counselors are inexperienced with male survivor issues. Ask a lot of questions both before you go and when you meet the therapist.

Agencies can help if you need a sliding scale fee. However, many agencies are field placements for graduate students or interns. There's nothing wrong with having a therapist who is a graduate student if this person is well supervised, but be sure the intern and his supervisor know what they're doing, and ask how long the intern will be able to work with you before ending his placement.

Perhaps you're in recovery without the benefit of a male survivor support system from which to get referrals. You may live in an area with few mental health resources and be unable to find a therapist experienced with male survivors. If so, look for an otherwise qualified therapist with whom you can establish a good rapport. Show him the list of books about male survivors in the bibliography of this book. If he's open to learning about male survivor issues rather than saying his inexperience doesn't matter, you may have a very satisfying experience in therapy with him.

Web sites helpful in locating therapists who deal with sexual abuse include those maintained by MaleSurvivor: National Organization against Male Sexual Victimization (www.malesurvivor.org), RAINN: Rape, Abuse & Incest National Network (www.rainn.org), the Sidran Institute (www.sidran.org), and some of the links on these sites.

Interviewing a Therapist

When you interview a therapist, you should be able to get answers to the following questions:

- What is your academic degree?

- Are you licensed by a board? Which one?

- How many years have you been practicing therapy?

- What internships, special training, or workshops in sexual abuse or male sexual victimization have you attended or conducted? Where and when?

- How many sexual abuse cases do you treat each year? How many do you currently have? What percentage are men?

- Do you specialize in any area of sexual abuse (working with offenders, clergy abuse, ritual abuse, and so forth)?

- How much experience do you have working with gay men and gay survivors (if this is a consideration for you)?

- Is supervision/consultation available to you?

- Has a complaint ever been filed against you?

- What is your fee? What are your billing, payment, cancelation, no-show, and vacation policies?

- Do you charge for telephone consultation or calls between sessions?

- What is your policy on confidentiality?

If the therapist seems annoyed or puts you off when you ask, consider this person someone you don't want to see.

You can always ask for professional references, but don't expect the therapist to give you names of satisfied customers the way a painter might. That would be a breach of other people's confidentiality.

Try to find a therapist who has worked with other sexually abused men. Sometimes a therapist fails to acknowledge he doesn't have sufficient experience with male survivor issues. His experience may be limited to having attended a single workshop or having read a book on the subject. Or maybe he's only worked with female survivors. He may be sincerely interested in working with male survivors, but he may be learning on the job while you're paying.

A therapist's lack of awareness and respect for your boundaries is a big red flag. Everyone who's been sexually victimized has had boundaries ignored and violated. A therapist who gives hugs without an invitation from you to do so is crossing your boundaries. This can also include less personal (but unwanted) contact, such as shaking hands, sitting too close, or even intrusive eye contact. Your gut feeling is the best indicator of someone who doesn't respect your boundaries. If you feel uncomfortable when interviewing a potential therapist, trust your instincts.

If you're considering participating in group therapy, ask your therapist if he runs male survivor groups. If not, ask if he would refer you to a group and feel comfortable working with you while you participate in one.

Ask a potential therapist if he's read about sexual abuse, especially male sexual abuse. Look at the list in the bibliography of this book and ask if he has read any of those books or would be willing to read any.

Don't be afraid to give your therapist a copy of this book or of my book for professionals, *Betrayed as Boys: Psychodynamic Treatment of Sexually Abused Men*. In fact, don't hesitate to give your therapist *anything* you think might help him understand and help you.

All of these factors are important in choosing a therapist. Assuming a therapist is well trained, however, what matters most is how you relate to him. So monitor your own feelings during and after your initial contacts with a potential therapist. The therapeutic relationship is a partnership between you and your therapist. You're both responsible for how it goes, but you're the one who chooses him. Don't let it be a passive choice.

Professional Background and Credentials

It can be confusing to sort out the meaning of therapists' degrees and licenses. Therapists may be psychiatrists, psychologists, clinical social workers, or counselors with different degrees of training. There's no hard-and-fast rule that the higher the degree (for example, M.D. vs.

M.S.W.), the better the treatment. Therapists' competency has more to do with how much supervised training they've had doing therapy either before or after they got their degree. Ask therapists how much supervised experience they've had doing psychotherapy.

You have the right to know a potential therapist's qualifications and whether he meets the standards of your state or province to practice psychotherapy. Different states offer licenses to therapists according to different standards, although they all have licensing boards for psychiatrists, psychologists, social workers, and nurses. Ask whether the therapist has a license. There may be no license available to a particular therapist in your state if he has a background not in these professions. If he doesn't have a license, ask why, and question him about his clinical training. He may be well trained, skilled, and capable. However, one advantage of seeing a therapist with a license is that the state holds him responsible to uphold standards of clinical practice, which unlicensed therapists may or may not adhere to.

Psychiatrists (M.D.) are physicians who usually do mental status exams and prescribe medication. If you have depression, anxiety, or other problems that may require medication, a psychiatrist can evaluate this and prescribe something to alleviate the symptoms. A psychiatrist's time is expensive, however. If you want or need to see one for therapy (beyond medication or maintenance), it will be costly to you or your insurance plan. In addition, some psychiatrists don't have as much training doing psychotherapy as other professionals. Ask—you may decide to see another professional for therapy and occasionally see a psychiatrist for medication evaluations.

Psychologists (Ph.D. or Psy.D.) are trained to do psychological testing in addition to therapy. Unless you need testing done for some reason, however, you're looking for competent therapy from a qualified therapist. This may be a clinical or counseling psychologist or a clinical social worker (M.S.W., L.C.S.W., or A.C.S.W.) who has had supervised experience doing therapy. Certain nurses also have this training. Sometimes professionals get further psychotherapy training after receiving their professional degrees. Ask how much psychotherapy training this individual has had.

A psychoanalyst has specialized intensive training using psychoanalytic principles. There are several legitimate schools of psychoanalysis, including the interpersonal, relational, object relations, and classical Freudian schools. If a therapist has received a certificate from a psychoanalytic institute, he has had considerable supervised experience doing psychotherapy and psychoanalysis. Be careful, however, because in many states anyone can call himself a psychoanalyst. Check that this individual has credentials from a reputable analytic institute. (Note that a therapist's degree does not indicate whether he has a certificate in psychoanalysis.)

If someone advertises himself as a counselor or psychotherapist, you need to question what this means. Regulations change from state to state. There are a number of degrees, such as M.A., M.S., and L.M.F.T., whose practitioners are trained and may be licensed, depending on your location. In many (but not all) states, clinicians are licensed to use the letters L.P.C. or something similar after their names, which indicates this person has met licensing standards for that state. Find out what the initials after a therapist's name mean and whether he has a license.

Individuals in some states can legally call themselves a counselor or psychotherapist without meeting any training and educational criteria. These people *may* have had good training, but they may be totally untrained in clinical treatment or have had inadequate supervision. Be especially careful of a layperson counselor who may be working through his own issues or a pastoral counselor with a religious agenda but little clinical training.

Theoretical Background

Different therapists will emphasize different issues based on personal style, training, and the school of thought on which the treatment is based. For example, a cognitive-behavioral therapist will challenge some of your beliefs, such as, "I must be bad because my father treated me so badly," or "I'm not really a man because I allowed abuse," or "No woman will ever want me because I am a victim," or "I'm only gay because my abuser made me that way." Other therapists may put more emphasis on different aspects of your experience, such as your fantasy life, your family dynamics, or your relationships.

All therapists need to have a frame of reference for therapeutic work, so it's fine when a therapist subscribes to a legitimate school of thought. Be skeptical, however, of therapists who rigidly adhere to one school and ignore other aspects of your experience. An example would be a cognitive-behavioral therapist who *only* speaks to you about your beliefs and behaviors, dismissing talk about your emotions or family relationships.

A clue to identifying (and avoiding) a therapist with a theoretical bias is his *over*stressing an approach or technique (such as overemphasizing his analytic, cognitive-behavioral, or eye movement desensitization reprocessing training). These approaches can help, but an overemphasis on a specialty may indicate he will fit your issues and experience into his theoretical framework. Be sure he'll see you as the individual you are.

Therapists' Personal Characteristics

Think of the kind of person with whom you would feel comfortable and safe. Try to locate the boy inside of you. With whom would *he* feel most safe and comfortable? What kinds of things matter to you in a therapist? Male or female? Older or closer to your age? Businesslike and practical, or warm and empathic? Gay or straight?

Think carefully about why you want one characteristic or another in a therapist. For example, you might feel you need to see a male therapist because you'd be ashamed to reveal to a woman your "weakness" as a victim. Similarly, you might feel you must have a female therapist because you're ashamed to reveal your "weakness" to a man. Or you may feel that only a man could understand how painful it would be for a boy to be sexually violated. Or you may think that only a woman could comprehend this.

If you feel very strongly about the sex of your therapist, go with that feeling. As you examine the reasons for your preference, however, you may find your reasoning is flawed. After all, some men are empathic with a boy who has been raped and others aren't. Some women make it easy for a man to talk about victimization without shame and others don't. What matters is the individual and the atmosphere the two of you create.

Likewise, if you have questions about your own sexual orientation or gender identity, you may feel you must know your therapist's sexual orientation. Perhaps you feel it's essential to see an openly gay therapist because you think only a gay individual can understand your gender and orientation struggles. Or perhaps you feel you'd only be comfortable with a straight therapist because you worry a gay therapist will push you in the direction of being gay.

A good therapist—gay or straight—won't push you one way or the other about your sexual orientation but will help you figure things out for yourself. Many competent therapists don't disclose their sexual orientation, believing that any given individual may sometimes need to think of them as gay and sometimes as straight. Many people don't want to know their therapist's sexual orientation, feeling that the knowledge would distract or overstimulate them. How do *you* feel?

A well-trained therapist will be open to talking your concerns through with you. Maybe this will reassure you about his ability to work with you. You may change your mind about how important it is that he be exactly what you'd had in mind. Still, if you're very worried about an issue and feel strongly about it, then choose someone of the sex, age, or sexual orientation that you feel you need in a therapist.

Should My Therapist Be a Survivor?

The idea that a therapist's personal history of sexual victimization makes him a more effective helper is questionable. Therapists' effectiveness is determined by skill, not simply by life experience. Sometimes survivor therapists' personal experiences with sexual victimization help them understand what you went through. Being stuck in their own experience, however, handicaps others. They may be unhelpful to you.

Likewise, nonsurvivor therapists may or may not be effective. If they don't understand your trauma, they won't do you any good. If they're empathic, however, they may be useful because of their objectivity about the problem. So there's no clear rule of thumb about whether it's better to have therapist who's a survivor.

Talking about Sex

It's important that you be able to talk to your therapist frankly about sex. But watch out if he shows too much interest in "gory details." For example, describing what happened (as you are comfortable disclosing) is important. Or knowing that a particular assault involved your having an erection and orgasm may be a valid issue when you're talking about the self-blame you feel for "enjoying" the abuse. But if questioning gets into minute detail or feels like pornography, let the therapist know you feel uncomfortable.

In contrast, a therapist who avoids any discussion of sexual details and talks in generalities or euphemisms is probably uncomfortable with sexual abuse. You need someone who can address your questions about your experiences and feelings without feeling anxious when hearing them. There are plenty of other people in your life who are uncomfortable with sexual victimization to whom you can talk for free. Your therapist shouldn't be one of them.

You may discover you're attracted to your therapist, whether you're straight or gay, and whether the therapist is male, female, straight, or gay. Whatever your feelings, it's important to express them to your therapist. This should be safe. No ethical therapist would take advantage of hearing about your attraction. Bringing your feelings to light—even embarrassing or sexual ones—will help you recover. This is how to learn to deal with feelings rather than have them rule your life.

Questioning the Relationship

It should be okay to question your relationship with your therapist. Does he become defensive and cut off your questions, or does he listen to your reservations? Do you feel invited to explore your doubts in a collaborative way? At the end of the discussion, do you feel reassured? If so, why? What have you learned about the therapist and his capacity to be criticized? What have you learned about his perceptiveness about you? Do you feel understood?

In a therapeutic relationship, you're allowed to make mistakes that might disturb, or even end, a more traditional relationship. As you take risks with your therapist, there may be stormy times when you feel very angry. You may feel something inexcusable has happened. If your relationship has been a trusting one in the past, try to weather the storm. Talk about what's on your mind. Be angry if that's how you feel. A good therapist will listen to your anger and respond.

You may test your therapist many times, often without even knowing that's what you're doing. There may be moments when you have doubts that he's the right person to work with. You may be right, but bring up your doubts to him and see how the interchange goes. You'll develop and deepen your relationship with your therapist through these exchanges.

Rough Times in Therapy

As you talk about your early betrayal, you may go through bumpy periods. Old memories will regain their power. New memories may emerge. There may come a time when you actually feel worse as you see your betrayal in a new light or from another perspective. Things may click into place that throw you. You may need to have extra sessions or take medication for a while. Stay the course. As your capacity to endure and deal with this kind of pain increases, the pain itself will subside.

Be aware of what your therapist may represent to you. If you were betrayed by an authority figure, you may discover you feel hostile about his authority. Since you learned as a boy that primary relationships can be betrayed, you may expect him to betray you. If you feel this way, voice it. Don't hold anything back.

Or you may decide there has been a betrayal of some sort in the therapy. I'm not talking about a sexual transgression, which is completely unacceptable. But there may be something that falls in the tolerable range of human behavior even though it shouldn't have happened. Your therapist forgetting something you told him or misscheduling an appointment may trigger a rage reaction from you out of proportion to the misdeed. Use this as an opportunity to find out more about how you get triggered and how to negotiate with someone who treats you badly.

Evaluating Therapy

After you've been in therapy for a while, ask yourself these questions:

- Am I intimidated by this therapist?

- Does he listen to me?

- Do I feel I can disagree with him?

- How does he handle crisis and conflict?

- Is he comfortable with the feelings and content I bring out?

If your therapist isn't psychologically healthy, it's important to change. Some therapists get caught up in their own issues and project them onto survivors. Perhaps your issues trigger old unresolved areas in his life. Talk to him about this. See what he says. Remember, you're paying him. If he needs to work on personal issues, he should pay someone for his own therapy. Or perhaps a conversation with him will clear up your concerns.

A clue to a therapist's overinvolvement is his becoming too emotional about some aspect of your situation. Not that he should be impassive and cold, but if he seems uncharacteristically interested, avoidant, or upset about something you've said, be alert. Also, if he strongly wants you to do something, for example, confront or forgive a perpetrator, this might indicate a personal issue for him.

If he begins to disclose personal information that is more than you're interested in or are comfortable hearing, this may also indicate an unresolved area for him. It's all right to use personal anecdotes or experiences from time to time, for example, to illustrate a point or demonstrate that someone's behavior is perfectly normal. Talking about things like personal sexual, drug, alcohol, or similar problems, however, blurs the boundaries between you. Tell the therapist how you feel. If his response doesn't make you more comfortable, pay attention to that and act accordingly. If necessary, find a new therapist.

Beware of therapists with a mission. An example would be someone who wants to fit you into a group that's wrong for you or that you're not ready to join. Watch out for the dogmatically religious counselor or one who maintains you need to forgive your perpetrator to be truly healed. Likewise, beware of someone who wants you to confront your perpetrator before you're willing or ready. Confrontation—when appropriate—is a serious undertaking needing careful preparation and safety.

If the Therapy Seems Unhelpful

You may encounter misdirected, inadequate, or harmful therapy. What if you're already in treatment with a therapist you feel is incompetent, inexperienced, of a philosophical direction you don't see as helpful, not respectful of your boundaries, or just plain makes you feel uncomfortable? Fire the therapist!

Whoa! I can't do that, you might be thinking. He's an expert, a professional! Remember, *you* are the consumer of the therapist's services. Unless you're court ordered to be in therapy, you have the absolute right to enter and leave therapy when you want and with whom you want.

If you've been seeing a therapist for some time and feel the therapy isn't working out, talk it over with him. If you can't come to a resolution, you can leave. Don't stay just because you're worrying about your therapist's feelings. If he takes it personally, that's further evidence you're making the right decision. When you find a new therapist, tell him how and why the earlier relationship ended. Try to learn with the new therapist what you couldn't figure out with the first one.

It's a good idea, however, to first talk to your therapist about your problem with him. You may find this hard to do. Being assertive, saying what's on your mind, getting what's due you, and speaking up for your rights are frequently difficult for survivors. So when a survivor tells a therapist the therapy isn't working, he's taking a positive step in being assertive.

Remember you're the consumer. When you were being abused, you were in a situation you couldn't get away from. That doesn't have to happen in therapy. If the therapy or the therapist doesn't feel right, get out. You need help from the right person in your recovery work. Your therapist should be a trusted partner in your healing.

Group Therapy

It helps to have supportive friends. It is also useful to be in the company of people who've had experiences like yours. This helps you feel less alone and stranded.

At one time, male survivors of childhood sexual abuse could not find groups for sexually abused men or even mixed-sex groups. They now exist, at least in some areas.

There are several kinds of groups you might want to consider.

Facilitated Therapy or Support Groups

Therapists often put these groups together. With a small number of members, they usually meet about once a week. The therapist facilitates the group, meaning he acts as a sort of referee. Invariably, one of the group's rules will be confidentiality: "What's said here, stays here." Meeting with fellow survivors in the presence of a trained professional is an enormous help in recovering and in finding the parts of your own life story. Survivors often find help for feelings of shame and isolation in this type of setting. You can also be helped by hearing how someone else deals with problems like yours and by providing help to someone else in psychological pain.

Twelve-Step Groups

These groups are free, although a donation may be requested. They're based on the twelve-step program originally developed for alcoholics. Run by the participants, they provide support through people telling their recovery stories in a structured environment. Personal development is encouraged through the twelve steps of recovery that have been used for decades by Alcoholics Anonymous. In addition to AA groups directed to alcoholics, similar groups focus on incest and sexual abuse, while others focus on problems that often accompany betrayal. A partial list of twelve-step groups includes Survivors of Incest Anonymous, Sexual Compulsives Anonymous, Sex and Love Addicts Anonymous, Gamblers Anonymous, Debtors Anonymous, Al-Anon Family Groups, Narcotics Anonymous, and Overeaters Anonymous. In addition, in many areas there are non–twelve-step groups, such as those run by Recovery, Inc., which are free of twelve-step groups' religious framework.

Moderated Chat Rooms and Discussion Forums

Even the most geographically or psychologically isolated person can find company if he has access to the Internet. Some Web sites, such as MaleSurvivor's, run moderated chat rooms or discussion forums where you can meet other men. Your anonymity is preserved by a screen name, and you decide how self-revealing to be. Men frequently have positive experiences in this kind of forum, sometimes disclosing their sexual abuse for the first time. While not a substitute for therapy, these sites can provide meaningful connections to other survivors. However, occasionally predators come to sites like these. Be careful about deciding to meet in person anyone you encounter online.

Medication

Should you take medications while you are in therapy? Sometimes yes, and sometimes no. When medication is called for, it can be extremely helpful in stabilizing your mood, calming your anxiety, helping you sleep, or saving you from a very dark depression. If used when it's not called for or if prescribed in an inappropriate dose, it can mask your feelings, make them inaccessible, not give you sufficient therapeutic effect, or give you undesirable side effects.

When possible, a psychiatrist, preferably one who specializes in psychopharmacology—rather than another kind of physician—should prescribe medication. Psychiatrists are more familiar than other doctors with medications used to help psychological problems. They prescribe them to patients every day. Since psychiatry is their specialty, they're more likely than internists or general practitioners to be up-to-date on new psychiatric medications. They're also likely to be more sophisticated about combining medications, should that be called for.

I'm not a psychiatrist or a medical doctor and don't claim to be an expert in this area, but I'll make some general comments. Antidepressants can be very helpful when you're feeling extremely down, depressed, lethargic, irritable, or overly sensitive to rejection. Sometimes the signs of depression are subtle and sometimes they take over your life. You may be reacting to a specific hurdle or event. Or you might suffer from a biological depression in addition to your reaction to trauma. If so, the medication may take care of the biological part, giving you more energy to work on other issues. If you think you might be depressed, discuss it with your therapist or psychiatrist.

Most antidepressants need to be taken for a number of weeks before they take full effect. This is because they build up slowly in the blood until they reach a therapeutic level. So there's no point in taking them only when you're feeling down, and there's no point in stopping them in the beginning just because you don't feel better. Also, it may be dangerous to suddenly stop taking antidepressants. If you want to stop, discuss with your doctor the best way to taper off.

When antidepressants work, your mood gets much brighter. Also, men have told me that these medications establish a new floor below which their depression no longer drops. One man told me that it was as though he were a house, living in his top floor when he felt very good, his middle floor when he felt average, and his first floor when he felt down and mildly depressed. "But then there was this cellar. The first floor's flooring would suddenly buckle and I'd fall down to that dark cellar, unable to see light or find my way up again. With the antidepressants, I no longer fall through that floor." So antidepressants aren't "happy pills," but when they work, they ensure that you don't fall into deep depression.

Men who take antidepressants sometimes believe they're better and no longer need medication. Sometimes this is true, but sometimes the medication has facilitated a sense of well-being. Once they discontinue their antidepressants, they may plummet into severe depression. The problem intensifies if they're too embarrassed to admit their mistake.

You may also be prescribed medications that relieve anxiety or help you sleep. In both cases, there are addictive and nonaddictive drugs available. If possible, work with your doctor to find nonaddictive drugs that help you. If you do take drugs that can be addictive, be very careful about not taking more than the prescribed amount, especially if you've had a substance abuse problem.

Medication can be stabilizing and help you through difficult periods. Or it may be helpful to you over a longer time. Make your decision about taking it in consultation with the professionals with whom you work. Whatever your choice, remember that it's not unmanly to take medication.

Additional Therapies

In addition to traditional individual psychotherapy, group therapy, and medication, there are a number of other therapies that are helpful to some survivors.

Couples Therapy

It can be constructive to be seen jointly with your partner or spouse if your relationship has suffered because of the effects of your abuse. Sometimes even a brief intervention to help your partner understand what you're going through can be effective. Or a therapy that focuses specifically on sexual problems can help alleviate them. Usually, though, ongoing couples treatment will focus on how problems common to many male survivors—such as isolation, discomfort with intimacy, difficulty with sexuality, numbing of feelings, and emotional overreactions—affect relationships.

Family Therapy

Sometimes having the whole family or segments of it go to a family therapist can help the family heal. This is especially useful if some family members feel guilty or angry about a molestation, or disagree about what happened. Sometimes it's beneficial to have family sessions where a man confronts his abuser in the presence of a therapist, although this should be carefully discussed and planned with the therapist ahead of time.

Massage Therapy

A trauma that usually starts with inappropriate touch may have had lasting effects not only on your feelings about touch but also on how you actually hold your body. Massage therapy can be very scary to someone suffering from betrayal trauma, but if you're ready, it can be rewarding. It's essential, however, to find a massage therapist who is not only fully trained in massage but also has experience working with traumatized clients and is respectful of your boundaries. You need someone who can go as slowly as you need to go so that you have time to learn to trust this person's touch. The goal is to make you more comfortable with caring touch and help loosen you up from old body postures that you may have unknowingly adopted over the years.

If you try massage therapy, you may sometimes regain *body memories*. These are memories of old traumas that seem to be buried in the body's musculature. They may get triggered when you're touched in certain ways. These can be frightening, but just as more usual memories help you get your life story back, so will body memories.

Movement Therapy

Through a combination of postural exercises, breathing techniques, and movement, you can learn to move and feel differently in movement therapies. They resemble massage therapy in that their goal is to loosen up the body from old postures. Like massage therapy, these techniques can sometimes evoke old body memories. Movement therapists may have backgrounds in movement therapy, dance therapy, physical education, or other related fields.

Art Therapy

Expressive art therapy may help free you emotionally as you use art media to contact feelings you don't yet have words for. Art therapists are trained to help you express these emotions through painting, sculpting, or other art forms.

EMDR

EMDR, or eye movement desensitization reprocessing, is a relatively new treatment modality whose goal is to reprocess how traumatic memory is stored in the brain. During EMDR sessions, you alternately stimulate the right and left sides of your brain while talking about your trauma. You do this by moving your eyes back and forth from left to right, having your body alternately tapped in some fashion on the left and right sides, or being otherwise stimulated on one side and then the other. The theory behind EMDR is that this changes how a traumatic memory is stored, and as it's reprocessed it becomes less painful.

EMDR is usually brief and can be quickly effective with specific traumas. For someone who has had complex childhood traumas, however, I believe that EMDR is most effective when done in the context of a more traditional psychotherapy where you can process psychological connections while reprocessing the trauma. The point of EMDR is to make the memories less horrible to endure, not to help you in your relationships or otherwise get on with your life.

Other Aids to Recovery

There are other ways to help yourself that aren't therapies but are nevertheless therapeutic. Many of the following activities and ways of approaching life would be helpful to nearly everyone, whether they suffer from aftereffects of trauma, are depressed, or are simply interested in taking good care of themselves. They're sensible ways to live, but they're particularly recommended for people whose emotions and feelings destabilize them and make them feel vulnerable and insecure.

Poetry Therapy, Creative Writing, and Journaling

As we discussed in chapter 11, creative writing, whether through poetry, prose, or journaling, can help a man regain his inner emotional life. Writing about your inner experience and memories has the added advantage of helping you put unexpressed dissociative experiences into language.

Meditation and Yoga

Through various combinations of deep breathing, gentle movement, guided imagery, and other techniques borrowed from Eastern religions, these disciplines teach you to you calm yourself and live life at a steadier, less harried pace. They can lower your blood pressure and even the level of stress hormones in your body. Exercises used in meditation and yoga teach you how to empty your mind of stray thoughts and intrusive feelings. They're best learned and practiced in a class with an instructor. To do them well, you need to practice them on a regular basis.

Spiritual Practices

Whether you comfortably identify with an organized religion or don't subscribe to any of them, think about whether spiritual practices of one kind or another can have a place in your life. These may take the form of attendance at weekly services if that's meaningful to you, but they may also involve prayer meetings, groups like Quaker meetings involving a kind of group meditation, solitary contemplation, or any other organized time to stop and consider your spiritual world. What's important here is focusing on transcending your personal problems. This can be accomplished through such means as thinking through your belief system, consolidating your faith in a higher power, or deciding how you want to make a difference in the world.

Maintaining Physical Health

Taking care of your physical health is as important as tending to your mental health. This means seeing medical doctors and dentists when you need to. You may feel so bad about yourself that you don't think you're worth taking care of. Maybe you've allowed your health to deteriorate because you feel worthless or believe you deserve to lose your looks and good health. Maybe you get anxious when you see doctors and dentists. Knowing you'll be touched, examined, and even physically invaded may push you into dissociated states.

Few people enjoy having bodies their prodded or having instruments or fingers inserted into their mouths or other body orifices. Maybe you're squeamish about getting prostate exams, which require digital penetration through the rectum but are generally not painful. Yet to put off an exam that can help detect early prostate cancer can be life-threatening.

Being anxious isn't something to be embarrassed about. Allowing your health to decline is far worse.

Consider telling your therapist that you'll be having a medical exam or dental appointment and that you're worried about it. Possibly you'll be prescribed an antianxiety medication before you go. If you're anxious about an impending exam or are afraid that you'll dissociate in the presence of the doctor, try talking to your doctor or the nurse beforehand. Let them know that you're recovering from sexual abuse, or if that feels impossible, tell them you've suffered trauma in childhood that makes medical exams especially taxing for you. You don't need to go into detail.

Many medical professionals are trained to treat patients with histories of childhood trauma. If they understand your concerns, they'll try to make you comfortable. If they don't understand, feel free to get another doctor. The better you treat yourself physically, the easier it will be for you to recover from your past.

Exercise

Regular exercise is a good plan for everyone. Its benefits to physical health are well known (for example, strengthening muscle groups and lowering blood pressure). It also improves your mood and mental state. It's helpful in managing depression. It keeps your activation level high, countering the way depression lowers it. It releases hormones that elevate your mood and counteract stress. This effect can last for some time after the exercise period.

Exercise can also act like meditation, creating a mental space that slows you down, allowing you to clear your mind of unsettling thoughts and destabilizing feelings. It gets you out of your head, reconnecting you with your body. Cardiovascular exercise is often helpful to your psychological as well as physical well-being, especially if it's done at least three times a week with an aerobic component of about twenty-five minutes or more. In addition, exercise can help your self-esteem and your sense of self-discipline. Consult your physician before starting any exercise program.

Sleeping Right

This seems obvious, but it's crucial to get adequate sleep. When you get insufficient sleep, you become irritable, short-tempered, low in energy, and anxious. Better sleep patterns are easier to maintain if you avoid caffeine and tobacco and limit alcohol. Keep a diary of your sleep patterns if you suffer from insomnia. This may require a medical consultation. Aids to sleeping better include making sure you go to your bedroom (or onto your bed) only when you're ready for sleep, leaving the bedroom if you can't sleep, exercising about five hours before bedtime, using relaxation techniques, and even the old remedy of having a glass of warm milk before bedtime.

Diet

Like exercise, diet affects both mental and physical health. There's evidence that a diet helpful to your mood and psychological health includes vegetables, fruits, grains, and salads. It also includes foods that contain omega-3 fatty acids (fish like salmon and mackerel), tryptophan (bananas, milk, tofu, egg yolk, and peas), tyrosine (meat, dairy, and eggs), and complex B vitamins, particularly folic acid. Likewise, this diet avoids or limits fast foods, most fats, red meats, sugar, caffeine, and tobacco.

Alcohol is itself a depressant and can interfere with some antidepressant medications, although in sensible amounts it can relax tension. It should be consumed sparingly (except, of course, by those with alcohol problems, who must avoid it altogether). Lastly, a diet that keeps you at a reasonable weight will benefit your self-image and therefore your mood.

Keeping in Touch with Your Personal Support System

It's hard to stay in contact with friends and family when you're feeling stressed, depressed, or anxious. But the more isolated you are, the more stressed, depressed, and anxious you become. You may feel you don't want to bring loved ones into the darkness of your black moods. Or you may feel ashamed of yourself or that people will pass judgment on you. It's important to sort out who will be negative influences on you and who will be positive.

Some people in your network may be critical of you; demand too much of you; burden, overprotect, or nag you; or reinforce bad behaviors you're trying to give up (such as drinking, gambling, overeating, or compulsive sex). Contact with them will make you feel more stressed, depressed, and anxious. Try instead to stay in contact with those who are supportive, encouraging, and empathic, who engage in activities you feel are positive, who you can feel vulnerable with, and who feel safe to you. The last thing you want to do is reach out to people who will make you feel lonelier.

Helping Others

You may feel you can't possibly help someone else when you feel so bad yourself, but giving to others raises your own sense of well-being. If you feel useless, make yourself useful. Think about skills that make you unique and valuable.

Find an activity that feels right to you. If you feel your abuse issues are sufficiently under control, find a way to help other victims of abuse. If you like children and are at ease around them, consider being a Big Brother or volunteering in the pediatric section of a hospital. If you're an environmentalist, find an environmental cause that's meaningful to you and give time to a group that works on it. If you're politically minded, volunteer for a candidate who stands for issues you believe in. If you have computer skills, think of an organization that could use your help or offer to teach someone how to use a computer. If you want to stay closer to your current network, ask elderly neighbors if you can go to the market for them or shovel their path in a snowstorm. Volunteer to babysit for someone who could use a respite from child care.

If the activity you choose doesn't work for you, find another. Doing an activity that helps others, you'll find added energy, a sense of competence, and a feeling of connection with those you help.

13

Deciding Who You Are

Taking Charge of Who You Are

Who will you become? By now, you've begun to develop an understanding of the three masculine self-images we discussed in chapter 2:

- The man you know you are
- The man you want to be
- The man the world expects you to be

These images exist in your mind in the same way you might envision the ideal football team or the perfect lover. You have a relationship with these self-images. You have feelings about them, as all men do. If you're content with all three, you'll be happy. If you're uncomfortable with them, you'll be unhappy.

If you dislike your self-images, your challenge is to find a way to restore harmony among them. To do this, you must first have a good understanding of them as they are. Then you must actually change and reshape the images in ways that are acceptable to you. This may seem impossible, but you can do it.

Taking Charge of What You Desire

All humans have desires—too many to count! In the course of our lives, some of our desires are satisfied and some are not. Even when we try to be realistic about what we desire, however, we don't always get what we want. As a result, we suffer. We suffer because we can't always know which of our desires can be reasonably fulfilled and which ones cannot. We suffer because others expect things from us that we cannot or don't know how to provide.

Which of your desires weren't met as you grew up? What about other people's desires for you? Think about all the expectations, dreams, and demands that you placed on yourself and others placed on you. Maybe they weren't always compatible. Maybe they accumulated and intensified over the years, pushing and pulling you in opposite directions.

Even if you hadn't been betrayed as a boy, no doubt you would have gone through periods of confusion. In such mental states, it's hard to understand what to do: what's practical and realistic, what's a waste of time, what's hopeless, and what's achievable.

Your Masculine Self-images

Try this exercise. Take three sheets of paper and title them as follows:

- The Man I Am

- The Man I Want to Be

- The Man the World Expects Me to Be

For each of these men, write a short paragraph or just list words that describe him as accurately and honestly as you can. In chapter 10, you made a list of words that describe yourself, and you can use that list to help. Don't worry if some of the descriptions contain contradictions. When you're finished, visualize your descriptions as three separate men.

Now ask yourself these questions:

- How alike are these men?

- How different are they?

- Do men like this really exist?

- How would they feel about one another?

- Would they get along or would they fight?

- If you had to be just one of these men, which would you be? Why?

- If you could change any of these men, which would you change? How?

Choosing What to Accept

Two of the most difficult cultural rules for men betrayed as boys are that men can't be victims and men can't be penetrated. It may seem like you don't have much choice about these rules, but not only can you reject them, you can help change them.

Over the course of human history, cultural rules have allowed (and, in some parts of the world, still allow) slavery, torture, racial segregation, and religious persecution. Less than one hundred years ago, women in the United States were denied the right to vote, but that rule changed because ordinary people made the effort to change it.

Most men adhere at least partly to our cultural ideas about manhood. Even men who rationally think these ideas are unfair or inequitable may feel uneasy if they break the rules. This is why, for example, so many men find it difficult to ask for directions.

You may not always feel you measure up to the rules, but you probably feel there's nothing you can do about them. Perhaps you've accepted these rules as correct, just as you might absorb an advertisement's claims about an automobile's power, beauty, and speed.

At one time, the rules for men were practical. They served to perpetuate the tribe, protect it from harm by marauding enemies, and develop warriors who fought real battles with real spears and suffered mortal injuries. The rules worked in societies where all meaningful accomplishments were the result of physical effort and strength. If a man abided by them, he was rewarded with praise and often an appealing mate.

A man was measured by his capacity to inflict violence not only on animals but sometimes on other humans. The more imposing the enemy, the greater the glory for the man who vanquished him. As civilization advanced, these rules still applied. Two hundred years ago, a gentleman offended by an insult could challenge his foe to a duel.

But these rules don't work in a society where women have equal rights and where men who kill other men are punished, not praised. These rules don't work in an age when human life is valued. They don't work in a world where many roles for men and women are interchangeable.

They don't work in a world where sexual orientation and gender identity are often considered innate qualities rather than conscious moral decisions. And they don't work in a world where we aspire to love, understanding, and compassion rather than vengeance, brute strength, and retribution.

The human spirit has outpaced our rules. We've developed new guiding principles without bothering to toss out old ones that no longer work. We like to think of ourselves as enlightened, but most of us haven't been able to let go of old rituals and beliefs. So the message that men are tough and never victims continues to echo through the world.

A Man in Charge of Himself

One of the most compelling ideas you've absorbed throughout your life—at least in the United States—is that you're free. Specifically, you possess freedom of will. You're given the right to exert your will as you please and to determine your own future in socially condoned ways and within the law. If you want to accomplish something, you can decide to attempt it. If you want to follow a career, you can decide to pursue it. If you resolve to be autonomous, you can decide to be independent. You're free to choose whom you vote for, befriend, and marry or partner.

The powers of will and self-determination are part of your identity. Set a goal and concentrate on it; you have the right to try to get there.

The Core of Transformation

Freedom of will is a grand principle that is essential to democracy, but it's also at the core of transformation as you recover from your boyhood sexual betrayal. This doesn't make it easy. One problem with the idea of free will is that it's often misunderstood and misused. People who blame victims for being victims often distort the meaning of free will so that they can feel more powerful and secure. An ill-informed person resents a victim, especially an adult or male victim, because of a belief that the victim asked for the abuse or did something to deserve it.

Of course, this isn't true. We'll discuss later that a person with epilepsy cannot will himself not to have seizures. Epilepsy isn't a mental illness, but its symptoms come from atypical neurobiological functioning in the brain. Likewise, psychological trauma seems to involve physical changes in the brain that cause symptoms. Children whose brains are still developing seem to be more affected by psychological trauma than adults whose brains were well developed before they were traumatized.

Over the long term, psychological recovery is a matter of persistence, education, experience, and will. But just as people can't will a broken bone to heal, we can't instantly undo the neurological changes of betrayal trauma.

Human will can't always have its way. None of us has complete control over our lives. Paradoxically, however, once we accept that we can't control everything, we gain greater strength and wisdom.

Change the Rules, Change Yourself

To change yourself, you must change the rules that define yourself. It may sound dangerous to change the rules you live by, but as long as your personal rules fall within the range of the law and pertain to your ideas about what it means to be you, there's nothing wrong with changing them.

You don't have to change the rules others live by. Change them only for yourself, and change only the rules that don't work for you. (After changing yourself, however, you may be surprised at how other people change.)

The following steps may help you define and change rules:

1. *Reevaluate what it means to be a man.* Decide you will no longer passively accept all the cultural rules for men. Decide you will no longer passively accept other people's assessments of you. After all, you know yourself better than anyone else does. You may completely abandon some old cultural rules or even discard the notion that you have to be a man in the conventional sense of the word. You may decide you'd rather think of yourself as a spiritual being, or an artist, or a nurturer, or a gay man, or a computer programmer, or simply a human being. You may also decide to become a man by facing your past honestly and solving problems that were unfairly thrust upon you. This is what heroes do.

2. *Give yourself the power to change the rules.* You have free will. That's all it takes to make choices. Choose which rules about manhood make sense for you and which don't.

3. *Distinguish between past and present.* Yes, you were once a victim, but you don't have to be one now. Yes, you may have lasting psychological scars from what happened, but you also have the ability to be larger and stronger than those scars.

4. *Become an independent but practical thinker.* Challenge conventional wisdom. Don't passively accept what others say, especially if it's about you (even in this book!). Challenge ideas and expectations you don't agree with, but in doing so, carefully pick your fights. Only wrestle with troubles that really have an effect on your happiness. A sign of a healthy man is his ability to adapt to the world around him.

5. *Be prepared.* If you prepare for challenges and setbacks, you'll emerge from them in one piece. Be prepared for occasional lapses or failures in how you think about yourself. Know you'll continue to hear about expectations for yourself that you don't like. As you change, you may also discover that more people than you realized act in ways you don't like. This is especially likely if you've been a people-pleaser and you begin to stand up for your rights. As you do, however, you may discover that rather than losing friends and relationships, you get new respect from others as they see you stand tall. Remember, people who can't bear your self-sufficiency are probably not people you want in your life anyway.

6. *Be patient.* It took you years, perhaps decades, to arrive at the ideas you have about the man you are, the man you want to be, and the man the world expects you to be. Letting go of some of these ideas will also take time. You may go through a grieving process as you let go of some old but unrealistic images of yourself. Know that your grieving is merely a step in your self-transformation.

7. *Keep track and play catch.* Keep a journal as you go through the process of changing the rules you want to live by. Make a list of the rules you want to adopt. Make notes to keep track of when they are challenged and when you have defended them successfully. As they emerge, learn to catch all the messages you hear from yourself before they leave your consciousness. Set each one aside and deal with it when you're ready. When others thrust their expectations on you, set them aside as well. Decide which ones

matter, which conform to your own rules, and which don't. Don't
create a scene if people expect something you don't want to give
them. On the contrary, use your ability to reason and your freedom of will to assert yourself. Remember, you ultimately control
how you handle these messages.

8. *Understand the difference between justice and recovery.* Justice
   is for whoever betrayed you. Recovery is for you. Recovery
   doesn't mean bringing justice to your betrayer. You don't have to
   punish your betrayer in order to heal. If you did, then men whose
   betrayers have died or disappeared could never heal, and yet they
   do. Healing means bringing yourself fully into the world with
   goodness and fullness of heart.

Living in the World

At some point in your recovery, you'll realize it's time to move on. Not
that your life will be perfect. You'll move on because you've accepted
that you were betrayed, understood how it affected you and your relationships, felt what it meant and still means to you, learned better ways
to be in the world, and come to terms with your self-concepts.

Recovering from betrayal involves deciding who you are. It's not a
simple or easy task. Nobody loves to think deeply about matters that
make them anxious. You have had to reflect on the most painful experiences of your life. Regardless of how you see yourself as a man, if you've
lived through betrayal and have worked hard to bring yourself through
a process of recovery, then you've suffered bravely. You're a hero! And
that's the second greatest thing you can say about any human. What's
the greatest thing anyone could say about you? Well, that's a very personal matter. It's not for me to decide. Choose wisely!

PART THREE

BETRAYAL'S OTHER
VICTIMS

Miles's wife, Laura, talked about her own reactions, her sense of what happened to her husband at his boarding school, and her understanding of child abuse: "I've read many books on the subject of child sexual abuse, which has been helpful. But as the spouse of an abuse victim, I've discovered there is little or nothing out there directly addressing problems encountered by partners. There's never one victim in a child sexual abuse case. There's a domino effect that reaches across the victim's life and touches everyone in his life, creating countless victims of the abuse. As Miles began talking about his abuse, I felt a lightning bolt strike me. How could I not have recognized that he'd been sexually abused? But he hadn't mentioned the school since we were nineteen. I'd been concerned over his sexual turmoil but hadn't recognized the root. I felt I'd failed him as a partner. He didn't want to be a victim. This teacher, this perpetrator, this *pedophile* told him he was gay. And Miles believed him. As this man violated him day after day, one, two, and three times a day, the child believed him. As this manipulative man "shared" his young body with other staff and adult friends, Miles believed him. He was taught this is what homosexuals do. The perpetrators didn't teach him that they were pedophiles and this is what pedophiles do. And that Miles would suffer the lifelong consequences of their actions. As with those who survive war, the trauma resulting from child sexual abuse can rear its ugly head throughout the victim's life. But I truly believe you can get through it, if not over it. What doesn't kill you makes you stronger, more compassionate, more humane throughout your life. You must constantly remind yourself that you're a victim through no fault of your own. Though abuse's damage can bury it, your true core existence as a human being of substance, worth, and deservedness of goodness and happiness is your God-given birthright. You can reclaim it."

Zane's lover, Morgan, was abused by a music teacher. Zane spoke about its effects on Morgan and on their relationship: "The night we met, Morgan and I exchanged coming-out stories. He told me that as an eleven-year-old boy he suffered ongoing sexual abuse by a trusted adult. As a result, he'd been deprived of the traditional coming-out experience. The man who abused him was the one person in his life that Morgan hated, a sentiment he's repeated many times. As our relationship grew, the subject of Morgan's abuse came up often. Sometimes an event would trigger a memory, and he would cry in my arms. I was concerned that issues of abuse would affect our relationship, but I could never be sure which aspects of his life had been formed by the experience and how it was affecting us. When his story became the subject of a newspaper article, the reporter asked Morgan if he felt the abuse had an impact on his sexual orientation. I was surprised to hear him respond that he wasn't sure. I thought he believed, as I did, that orientation was genetic. Even though he might have been gay anyway, he could never be sure. This made me sad, because I love Morgan as a gay man, and I hate to think that our love may have stemmed from the abuse."

14

For Families and Loved Ones

If You Believe a Boy Has Been Molested

If you're reading this book because your son or another minor under your care was molested or because you think he may have been molested, you are no doubt in a deeply distressed psychological state. Your needs and the needs of the boy are immediate and go beyond the scope of this book. Contact the authorities immediately and seek the help of a mental health professional who specializes in this area. To find out where to go, you can call Childhelp (800-4-A-Child or 800-422-4453) or go to Internet Web sites like www.malesurvivor.org or www.rainn.org and look for information about how to report child abuse in your location and where to get professional help for the victim. If you've already taken these steps to protect the child, consider giving copies of this book or my book for professionals, *Betrayed as Boys: Psychodynamic Treatment of Sexually Abused Men*, to the professionals who will be helping him.

First Things First: Understanding Him

If you skipped directly to this chapter because of its title or because you feel the rest of this book doesn't apply to you, please read the book from the beginning. Although it's addressed to men who were sexually abused as boys, you'll learn a great deal.

Consider some of the topics covered in this book:

- Trust
- Betrayal
- Boundaries
- Relationships
- Types of families
- Dealing with authority
- Sexual relations
- Cultural expectations of men
- Sexual orientation
- Gender identity
- Male and female abusers
- Altering reality
- Giving up
- Fighting blindly
- Fighting reflectively
- Redefining masculinity
- Shame
- Secrecy
- Dissociation
- Intimacy
- Power
- Control
- Anger
- Compulsive behavior
- Relationships with therapists
- Taking responsibility for recovering
- Steps to recovery

These are all areas you need to know a lot about if you are to understand the man you love.

How Can I Talk to Him about His Sexual Betrayal?

Sexually abused boys and men often have trouble loving. The people they love and who love them get caught up in that trouble. If you have a relationship with a sexually abused boy or man, you may feel concerned and sympathetic but also at times confused, hurt, or angry at him.

How you're affected depends on the nature of your relationship with him. If you're a sibling of a brother who was sexually abused, you may be affected in different ways than if your spouse or partner was betrayed. If you are the parent of a boy who was abused—whether he's still a child or is now a grown man—you'll have a whole different set of feelings. Whatever your relationship is to the abused man or boy, you probably have questions, concerns, and complaints about your loved one.

When is it okay to talk to your loved one about sexual abuse? What if you're concerned about his behavior, or feeling angry with him, or feeling hurt because of his actions? These are complicated questions. Unfortunately, there are no all-purpose answers.

Your loved one may experience radically different feelings at different times. Sometimes he'll have periods when he seems to have no feelings at all or no specific memories of abuse. Or he may desperately need to talk about what's going on inside his head. Or he'll need to isolate himself. There will be periods when he doesn't want to think about any problems at all and others when he can't think about anything else.

It's important to be attuned to his emotional openness when you want to talk to him about his betrayal. Try to develop a sensitivity to his open and his shut-down periods. Sometimes he'll be back at the moment of his betrayal, internally reexperiencing his childhood feelings or memories. Or he may be "flat," completely out of touch with his feelings. When he's like this, you can't have a productive conversation with him about emotional issues.

Dissociated States and Emotional Breakthroughs

Because many men dealt with their childhood traumas by dissociating (see chapter 4), you'll need to become perceptive about your loved one's various states of consciousness and what prompts them. He himself may not know what triggers his feelings and frame of mind. We'll talk more about this in a moment.

If you're just learning about dissociation, start observing his emotional states. See if you discern differences among them. There's often no way to predict what he'll be like at any given time. Sometimes he may seem detached or in a trance. You may see a faraway or dull look in his eyes, an expression that seems out of character for the moment, or an angry reaction to a seemingly innocuous event.

He may be reexperiencing the original feelings he had during his betrayal, but he may not understand what they're about or why he's having them. He may not even know he's in an altered state, just as in the middle of the night you're not conscious of dreaming. Even if he is aware, especially if he's just emerged from a dissociated state, he may not be able to explain what he's gone through. And he may feel embarrassed about being observed in an odd, vulnerable state.

What can you do? If he's emotionally overreactive, try not to respond with the same emotional force that he has. Matching his level of intensity may ratchet your emotional exchange up to ever-higher levels. This will make things worse for you both. One or the other of you will snap, withdraw, or feel totally misunderstood.

Dissociative Triggers

Remember how Patrick described frightening images of "yellow roses all around me," eventually recalling that these were the roses on the wallpaper of the room where he was abused? Yellow roses of a certain type triggered dissociative reactions in him. This is the kind of seemingly innocuous trigger that can send sexually abused people into a dissociative state.

Let's say your loved one was abused by a scoutmaster on an overnight hike in piney woods. For him, the smell of pine may be inextricably linked to his betrayal experience. Let's say he goes into a bathroom with pine-scented soap and experiences an intense state of fear. Perhaps he's aware of the connection to his abuse and perhaps not. He no doubt knows the scent of pine isn't dangerous, but that knowledge alone may not be enough to stop him from feeling anxious whenever he smells it. And there may be different triggers for the same dissociated emotion. For example, your loved one may also remember the feel of the rough wool blanket under him while he was being abused. He may not consciously remember the blanket, but feeling rough wool on his back may also trigger anxiety.

Usually, people dissociate because of an external trigger—something they heard, saw, felt, smelled, or touched. However, sometimes your loved one's own thought process may produce a dissociated state, for example, if he unexpectedly remembers some aspect of his trauma.

If he's open to talking about it, ask him if he knows what triggered his reaction. Sometimes he'll know and sometimes he won't. Even if he's able to identify the trigger, his dissociative reaction may still recur. Progress doesn't come in neat, discernible steps. Over time he'll get more in tune with himself, and he'll be able to figure out how his triggers fit into his life story.

When He's Shut Down

It's difficult to talk to a man who is shut down, detached, apathetic, preoccupied, or depressed. It feels like he isn't there much of the time, and it's hard and frustrating to talk to someone when he's like that. Don't forget that he may have shut down because he started to experience overwhelming feelings such as rage, pain, or despair.

Remember, he didn't make a conscious decision to shut down. It was an automatic response beyond his active control. When he's in this state, he may not even be aware of it, and he may not emerge from it without bumping into emotions or memories that knock him off balance. Sometimes men are shut down like this for very long periods—days, months, years, even decades. The longer he's been dissociating, the more difficult it may be for him to emerge from it and the more earth-shaking it will be when he does.

Trying to talk to a man who is shut down is a tremendous challenge. Don't come on like gangbusters and demand that he relate to you better. That will only make him withdraw even more. Instead, focus on making it easier for him to open up. That usually means backing off a bit so that you're neither too threatening nor too intimate. He'll respond better when he's given space than when he feels cornered.

Psychoanalysts are experts at listening. They have discovered that people are more likely to express their deeper feelings and thoughts to those who are actively receptive but quiet rather than to those who try to engage a hurting person in conversation by asking too many questions and offering assorted observations. The knack for remaining silent can yield great results.

It takes discipline on your part to hold your peace and create an atmosphere in which your loved one feels safe to either talk or not. But in the long run this will be far more effective than trying to argue with him or communicate your own feelings before he can begin to communicate his or even articulate them to himself.

When You *Must* Talk

What about you? There will be times when you feel you must talk to him even if he doesn't feel like talking. After all, you have feelings, too. You're responsible for your part of the relationship. There may be times when you decide you and he must talk no matter how he feels at the moment.

If you've reached your limit or there's some urgent matter at hand, then by all means, try. Sometimes simple honesty works well. And sometimes the shock of being confronted may help him emerge from his deep freeze. Even so, it's important to think things through. You'll have to find the right time and the right approach.

Be prepared, however, for him to promptly shut down again if he experiences feelings that are too stimulating or terrifying. If he opens up at all, even for a moment, that's a sign he has the capacity to do so. It's just a matter of time before he'll learn to make smoother, more conscious transitions between being present and being shut down.

What Doesn't Work

There will be times when you want to help but don't know what to say. At other times, you'll feel you've had enough, or think he's obsessed with some aspect of his abuse and carries on about it more than you can bear.

At these moments, you may be tempted to tell him to let it go. You may want to advise him to toughen up, or, less kindly, to get over it, or even to stop being such a baby. As tempting as it may be to say these things, they won't work. When a boy is sexually betrayed, the trauma it causes isn't like a minor grudge or insult. His brain is a physical organ, and it was changed by the trauma. He can't help his feelings or his need to dissociate them. If he could stop through willpower, he would have done so long ago.

What does work is for him to find the pieces of his life story and put them together. This is why listening is often the best thing you can do for him. If he wants to talk, it doesn't mean that he's asking you for advice. He wants to be heard. Even if he does want you to tell him what to do, it's often best to let him come to his own conclusions.

It requires extraordinary maturity, steadfastness, and love to maintain a positive relationship with a man who was betrayed. Over time, though, your patience and compassion will pay off.

"Sometimes I Just Want to Shake Him Out of It!"

When you feel like shaking him out of it because he should just grow up, or behave himself, or get on with his life, think about an epileptic. You know it would do harm rather than good if you reproached him for having a seizure. And if you understand the situation, you would never think of reproaching him anyway—you know the seizure isn't under his control.

Like a seizure, a dissociative state isn't something a person has conscious control over. He often doesn't even know it's happening. If he's aware that he dissociates, your loved one probably feels bad enough. He may be even more confused and upset about it than you are. With time, however, a healing process will help him stay in the room with you psychologically much of the time, even when the two of you are talking about emotionally triggering issues.

Men who dissociate will react in a more positive and healthy way if they are neither embarrassed nor put on the defensive about their dissociative states. It may help to ask him gently something like, "Where were you just now?" or even "Were you dissociating?" when you feel the time is appropriate. If he's read this book and understands what dissociation is all about, then you can both have an agreement that it's okay for you to ask what's going on when he seems to blank out.

If he hasn't read this book or doesn't seem to understand dissociation, use simpler language. You might say something like, "Did you leave the room just now?" Hopefully, he'll come to understand that he leaves the room psychologically when he feels triggered by something—perhaps by something that seems benign, even to him—and gets emotionally overwhelmed.

Helping Him Make the Connections

No one, not even your loved one, has an internal map laying out his dissociated feelings, memories, and memory fragments. So there's no easy way for him to find his way out of his dissociated state when he's there. You can help him by being observant, being cool, being available, and letting him know you're there and will talk to him in a nonjudgmental way if he feels like talking.

In the beginning, it may be easier for him to refer to his dissociated states as if they were something that's "not him." For example, few grown men would want to admit that smelling pine soap terrifies them. Still, there's nothing wrong with him or you referring to how his triggers or his dissociative states come over him as if they were separate from him. Only later, as your loved one is mentally strong enough to fully incorporate the original trauma into his consciousness, will he feel his dissociative state is part of himself. This acknowledgment may be present for only a moment at a time, but the moment will be transformational.

Living with His Other Behaviors

Dissociation is common among men who were betrayed as boys, but it's not the only challenge you and your loved one may be dealing with. You may have a relationship with a man who sometimes mistrusts you. He may easily get angry, depressed, controlling, or obsessed with pornography. He may get into trouble at work or with the law. He may have affairs.

Consider some of the men in this book:

- Lewis always had to be in charge during lovemaking. If he felt his partner was in control—even for a moment—Lewis would throw him across the room.

- Abe was a people-pleaser. People-pleasing may help in casual, temporary relationships such as sales jobs, but it doesn't work in intimate, loving relationships that require honest communication. A man who always pleases others doesn't know who he is or how to stand up for himself. He often shows his anger in indirect ways.

- Quinn was constantly furious at the world, demanding that his victimhood be central to any relationship.

- Julian, Peter, Devin, Patrick, and others developed compulsions to view pornography, engage in casual or anonymous sex, or go to prostitutes or massage parlors.

- Keith, Devin, Abe, Patrick, Ramon, and others developed severe substance abuse problems.

These behaviors and others common to men with sexual abuse histories all interfere with intimate, honest, mutually supportive relationships. You may feel powerless to help, and your relationship may be threatened to the point that you feel like giving up.

Handle these behaviors by understanding where he's coming from but clearly communicating your own boundaries. Know what behaviors you refuse to endure. Choose the time to tell him what you will and will not tolerate and what you will or will not do if he pushes beyond your limits. This doesn't have to be a drastic ultimatum. A loving but determined and resolute approach may work better.

If the relationship with him puts you or anyone else in physical or emotional danger, you must protect yourself. If this means going to a friend's house when he is in a rage, do it. If this means taking your children and going to a shelter, do it. If this means going to Al-Anon meetings to help deal with his alcoholism, do it. If this ultimately means leaving, do it.

Hopefully things will not come to this. If you feel overwhelmed, I recommend you seek professional help. You and your therapist can work out your relationship's survival plan. This may mean adjusting your own vision and expectations for the relationship. If things deteriorate to the point where there is clearly no hope, then that is the time to consider other measures.

Sometimes the problems you have with your loved one will seem impossible to sort out. He may not be exhibiting the obvious behavior I have described, yet there may still be something wrong that you cannot put your finger on. It may come down to your not really knowing who he is. Men abused as boys sometimes even seem unfathomable. (No wonder—they are often unfamiliar with their own selves.)

If you conclude you don't really know your partner or spouse, this doesn't mean the relationship must end. You may learn to view things from a different perspective with patience and faith. You may even learn to see his impenetrability as a sort of hope chest: as he opens up, he may reveal appealing, admirable facets of a man you'll cherish even more. Men who have recovered from boyhood betrayal often develop a lust for life and extraordinary gifts of compassion, empathy, wisdom, and strength.

Your Stages of Grief and Acceptance

Learning that someone you love was abused begins a period of mourning. You'll likely go through a series of grief stages. In some ways, these are the same stages people go through when someone is dying. When you learn that someone you love was sexually betrayed, you learn that his childhood innocence died an unnatural, traumatic death. Like him, you may mourn that innocence as you go through these stages:

- *Denial*—refusal to believe what happened

- *Depression*—feeling sad, losing hope, even feeling numb

- *Anger*—directed at his abuser, at the world, at him, even at yourself

- *Bargaining*—wanting to believe that the problem isn't so bad after all

- *Acceptance*—realizing that what happened is true and cannot be changed

- *Peace*—able to enjoy life again, even after accepting what happened

Sometimes people go through the stages in this order, sometimes in a different order. Sometimes people seem to skip one of the stages or shift rapidly back and forth between them. As you work through them, you will approach inner peace. You'll accept life's realities, both harsh and heartening. Part of the harshness may be an irreparably damaged relationship with your loved one's abuser. But the heartening part will include a better and more fulfilling relationship with the man who was betrayed as a boy.

Abusers' Complex Motives and Effects

Because child molestation is often kept secret, the abuser may continue to maintain and nourish many good relationships for years and even decades with family, friends, and community. This may happen even as he or she is abusing other children. Many child abusers are attracted to careers and avocations that make them special in the eyes of the community. They may be teachers, clergy, scoutmasters, choirmasters, coaches, Big Brothers, child care workers, doctors or other health workers, or civic leaders. These positions can help an abuser gain access to children and serve as a cover for the abuse they commit. Serving in these roles can also be a form of insurance, so if they get caught, they'll have ample support and plenty of advocates to state unequivocally, "This person could never hurt a child."

Equally important, people who are or become predators may have some genuinely fine and altruistic qualities. These people may or may not be aware of wishes to prey on a child sexually when starting to do this kind of work. Abusers may not be clear about any dark reasons drawing them to a particular type of vocation, or they may believe they have their impulses well under control.

An abuser may be charismatic and deeply interested in a child's inner life, which can be a life-altering experience for that child. Someone who is drawn to help children may, for example, sincerely want to better their lives, teach them to read, learn a sport, find a creative outlet, or gain a spiritual life. A predator may have good effects on many children she doesn't abuse, in addition to destructive ones on those she victimizes. She may abuse children while in a dissociated state, unable at that moment to connect with the terrible damages she is doing. This in no way excuses her behavior, but it makes it more understandable that many people in the community would be shocked by what she did.

Even though the abuse is traumatic, the relationship may have positive aspects. Recall that the priest who abused Julian for several years also taught him about classical literature, interested him in his education, and in many ways saved him from his physically abusive family. This made Julian very ambivalent about the priest.

So if your loved one's abuser has positive qualities, your loved one may waver in his feelings about him or her. So may you. It will require effort on your part to sort these feelings out.

Who to Believe?

All of this makes your relationship with the abuser complex and difficult. Coming to terms with what happened can be heart-wrenching, even volatile. If the accused person denies or minimizes his guilt and the accuser can't offer factual evidence that abuse took place, you have a terrible dilemma. You have to make a decision that inevitably—no matter how you handle it—leaves you in an agonizing position. You may ultimately be estranged from either the accused or the accuser, perhaps even from both.

Unfortunately, there's no simple way to avoid pain under these circumstances. You'll have to endure it until you find a resolution that fits your specific situation. Seeing a therapist experienced in working with abuse situations, if only for a short time, may be very helpful to you.

It's human nature to not want to believe something horrible. Psychological denial is both real and common. The problem is figuring out the truth.

The fact that you're reading this book—and this chapter—indicates you're interested in learning about the truth. Understand, however, that you may never have absolute proof of what did or didn't happen. You weren't present, and it's likely that no one but the accuser and the accused were there when the abuse did or didn't take place, and they may tell very different versions of those events.

Does Anything Support the Allegations?

Sometimes, of course, there is corroborating, or at least supporting, evidence of one sort or another. Recall, for example, how Quinn's grandfather showed Quinn's sisters nearly nude photographs he'd taken of Quinn, crooning about what a beautiful boy Quinn was. While he never told them that he abused Quinn, he conveyed to them the nature of his attachment, and the sisters had no doubts when Quinn told them about his betrayal. Similarly, when Patrick got the courage to talk to his siblings about his abuse by their father, one of his sisters told him, to his surprise, that the father had also abused her. In neither of these situations was there absolute confirmation of the man's abuse, but there was certainly support for the accusations.

Sometimes there is support that is more definitive: A sibling may have witnessed part of the abuse, as in the case of Dr. X. There may be medical records confirming physical aspects of what happened, as in the case of Andreas, who located hospital records indicating his rectum had to be rebuilt during the period when he was abused.

Few people, and even fewer men, have an incentive to make up stories about having been sexually abused. It's not impossible for a man to see how his symptoms resemble those of sexual abuse victims, then decide this must be why he has the problems he has. Still, it's rare for a man to willingly go public about a sexual violation that never occurred. Even when there is a financial payoff at stake, few men would be willing to go through the enormous effort, personal sacrifice, and embarrassment that a legal battle requires in order to pursue a false allegation of sexual abuse.

If you're uncertain of the truth, one way to guide yourself is to read about all the abused men in this book and learn how men react to boyhood betrayal. Then, using your knowledge, consider your loved one's story. Does the allegation fit the picture? Do the pieces fall in place? Are there other persuasive reasons for your loved one to have the problems he has?

Taking a Position

Many people who don't understand betrayal believe such matters are best kept quiet. This is shortsighted. If everyone thought this way, pedophiles would go free and no abused man would receive the help he needs.

But boys *are* molested, and the typical pedophile is not a misshapen, half-human monster who lives under a bridge. Nearly all people who sexually victimize children are part of their family, institution, or community. Most sexual predators are known to their child victims.

When you believe someone who says he was molested, you may have to deal with some consequences. Possibly you'll estrange yourself from those who support the abuser. Your arguments with them may get very heated.

But after an initial period when people take sides against one another, it will probably serve no purpose to quarrel with those who don't accept what you believe. Your energies and dedication should be turned to your loved one. Let him know that his recovery is not dependent on an abuser's confession, jail sentence, or remorse.

Men can recover from boyhood betrayal whether their abusers confess, are identified, or are even alive. Men can recover without confronting their abusers. All a man needs for recovery is himself and a personal support system. If you are a friend or family member in your loved one's caring network, you can be proud of yourself for helping him.

Many men recover from boyhood sexual betrayal. When they do, they are stronger for it, often finding hidden gifts that make them more sensitive, resilient, and robust. Your loved one, as he recovers, may very well become someone you love even more.

Bibliography

This bibliography includes material written for the lay public as well as for professionals. Some are primarily about sexual victimization of boys and men (including several memoirs), as well as material intended for partners and loved ones. I have also included some general books about sexual abuse and trauma, as well as some about related areas such as sexual compulsion and masculinity. Finally, there are books of fiction and poetry.

Adams, Kenneth. 1991. *Silently Seduced*. Deerfield Beach, Fla.: Health Communications.

Bass, Ellen, and Davis, Laura. 1988. *The Courage to Heal: A Guide for Women Survivors of Child Sexual Abuse*. New York: Harper & Row.

Berendzen, Richard, and Palmer, L. 1993. *Come Here: A Man Overcomes the Tragic Aftermath of Childhood Sexual Abuse*. New York: Villard Books.

Bolton, Frank, Morris, Larry, and MacEachron, Ann. 1988. *Males at Risk: The Other Side of Child Sexual Abuse*. Newbury Park, Calif.: Sage.

Boyle, Patrick. 1994. *Scout's Honor: Sexual Abuse in America's Most Trusted Institution*. Rocklin, Calif.: Prima.

Briere, John. 1989. *Therapy for Adults Molested as Children*. New York: Springer Press.

Camino, Lisa. 1999. *Treating Sexually Abused Boys: A Practical Guide for Therapists and Counselors*. San Francisco: Jossey-Bass.

Carnes, Patrick. 1989. *Contrary to Love: Helping the Sexual Addict*. Minneapolis: Compcare.

———. 1991. *Don't Call It Love: Recovery from Sex Addiction*. New York: Bantam.

———. 1983. *Out of the Shadows: Understanding Sexual Addiction*. Minneapolis: Compcare.

————, and Adams, Kenneth, eds. 2002. *Clinical Management of Sex Addiction*. New York: Brunner-Routledge.

Cassese, James, ed. 2001. *Integrating the Shattered Self: Gay Men and Childhood Sexual Trauma*. New York: Haworth.

Courtois, Christine. 1988. *Healing the Incest Wound*. New York: Norton.

————. 1999. *Recollections of Sexual Abuse: Treatment Principles and Guidelines*. New York: Norton.

Crowder, Adrienne. 1995. *Opening the Door: A Treatment Model for Therapy with Male Survivors of Sexual Abuse*. New York: Brunner/Mazel.

Davies, Jody Messler, and Frawley, Mary Gail. 1994. *Treating the Adult Survivor of Childhood Sexual Abuse*. New York: Basic Books.

Davis, Laura. 1991. *Allies in Healing: When the Person You Love Was Sexually Abused as a Child*. New York: Harper Perennial.

————. 2002. *I Thought We'd Never Speak Again: The Road from Estrangement to Reconciliation*. New York: HarperCollins.

de Milly, Walter. 1999. *In My Father's Arms: A True Story of Incest*. Madison, Wisc.: University of Wisconsin Press.

Dolan, Yvonne. 1991. *Resolving Sexual Abuse*. New York: Norton.

Elliott, Michele, ed. 1994. *Female Sexual Abuse of Children*. New York: Guilford Press.

Estrada, Hank. 1990. *Recovery for Male Victims of Child Sexual Abuse*. Santa Fe, N.M.: Red Rabbit Press.

Finkelhor, David. 1984. *Child Sexual Abuse*. New York: Free Press.

Freyd, Jennifer. 1996. *Betrayal Trauma*. Cambridge, Mass.: Harvard University Press.

Friedrich, William. 1995. *Psychotherapy with Sexually Abused Boys*. Thousand Oaks, Calif.: Sage.

Gartner, Richard B. 1999. *Betrayed as Boys: Psychodynamic Treatment of Sexually Abused Men*. New York: Guilford Press.

Gil, Eliana. 1983. *Outgrowing the Pain: A Book for and about Adults Abused as Children*. San Francisco: Launch.

————. 1992. *Outgrowing the Pain: A Book for Spouses and Partners of Adults Abused as Children*. New York: Dell Publishing.

Gonsiorek, John, Bera, Walter, and LeTourneau, Don. 1994. *Male Sexual Abuse: A Trilogy of Intervention Strategies*. Thousand Oaks, Calif.: Sage.

Graber, Ken. 1991. *Ghosts in the Bedroom: A Guide for Partners of Incest Survivors*. Deerfield Beach, Fla.: Health Communications.

Grubman-Black, Stephen. 1990; 2nd ed., 2002. *Broken Boys/Mending Men*. Caldwell, N.J.: Blackburn Press.

Hansen, Paul. 1991. *Survivors and Partners: Healing the Relationships of Sexual Abuse Survivors*. Longmont, Colo.: Heron Hill.

Heim, Scott. 1995. *Mysterious Skin*. New York: HarperCollins.

Herman, Judith. 1992. *Trauma and Recovery*. New York: Basic Books.

Hoffman, Richard. 1995. *Half the House*. San Diego: Harcourt Brace.

Hope and Recovery: A 12-Step Guide for Healing from Compulsive Sexual Behavior. 1987. Center City, Minn.: Hazelden.

Hopkins, Brooke. 1993. "A Question of Child Abuse." *Raritan*, fall 1993, pp. 33–55.

Hunter, Mic. 1990. *Abused Boys: The Neglected Victims of Sexual Abuse*. Lexington, Mass.: Lexington Books.

Hunter, Mic, ed. 1990. *The Sexually Abused Male, Vols. 1 & 2*. Lexington, Mass.: Lexington Books.

King, Neal. 1995. *Speaking Our Truth*. New York: Harper Perennial.

Kuhn, Jill, ed. 2000. *In Cabin Six: An Anthology of Poetry by Male Survivors of Sexual Abuse*. Atascadero, Calif.: Impact Publishing.

Levine, Robert Barry. 1996. *When You Are the Partner of a Rape or Incest Survivor: A Workbook for You*. San Jose, Calif.: Resource Publications.

Lew, Mike. 2000. *Leaping upon the Mountains: Men Proclaiming Victory over Sexual Child Abuse*. Boston, Mass.: Small Wonder Books; Berkeley, Calif.: North Atlantic Books.

———. 1988; 2nd ed., 2004. *Victims No Longer: Men Recovering from Incest and Other Sexual Child Abuse*. New York: HarperCollins.

McEvoy, Alan, Brookings, Jeff, and Rollo, Debbie, eds. 1999. *If He Is Raped: A Guidebook for Parents, Mates, and Friends*. Holmes Beach, Fla.: Learning Publications.

McMullen, Richie. 1990. *Male Rape: Breaking the Silence on the Last Taboo*. London: The Gay Men's Press.

Mendel, Matthew. 1995. *The Male Survivor*. Thousand Oaks, Calif.: Sage.

Mezey, Gillian, and King, Michael, eds. 1992. *Male Victims of Sexual Assault*. Oxford, Eng.: Oxford University Press.

Miletski, Hana. 1997. *Mother–Son Incest: The Unthinkable Broken Taboo*. Brandon, Vt.: Safer Society Press.

Mura, David. 1987. *A Male Grief: Notes on Pornography and Addiction*. Minneapolis: Milkweed Editions.

Pollack, William. 1998. *Real Boys: Rescuing Our Sons from the Myths of Boyhood*. New York: Random House.

Porter, Eugene. 1986. *Treating the Young Male Victim of Sexual Assault*. Syracuse, N.Y.: Safer Society Press.

Preble, John M., and Groth, Nicholas. 2002. *Male Victims of Same-Sex Abuse: Addressing Their Sexual Response*. Baltimore: Sidran Press.

Real, Terrence. 1997. *I Don't Want to Talk about It: Overcoming the Secret Legacy of Male Depression*. New York: Scribner's.

Ryan, Michael. 1995. *Secret Life*. New York: Vintage.

Sanders, Timothy. 1991. *Male Survivors: Twelve-Step Recovery Program for Survivors of Childhood Sexual Abuse*. Freedom, Calif.: Crossing Press.

Scarce, Michael. 1997. *Male on Male Rape: The Hidden Toll of Stigma and Shame*. New York: Insight Books (Plenum Press).

Shengold, Leonard. 1989. *Soul Murder*. New York: Fawcett Columbine.

Sonkin, Daniel Jay. 1992. *Wounded Boys, Heroic Men: A Man's Guide to Recovering from Child Abuse*. Stamford, Conn.: Longmeadow Press.

Spiegel, Josef. 2003. *Sexual Abuse of Males: The SAM Model of Theory and Practice*. New York: Brunner-Routledge.

Thomas, T. 1989. *Men Surviving Incest: A Male Survivor Shares the Process of Recovery*. Walnut Creek, Calif.: Launch Press.

Tobin, Rod. 1999. *Alone and Forgotten: The Sexually Abused Man*. Carp, ON: Creative Bound.

van der Kolk, Bessel, McFarlane, Alexander, and Weisaeth, Lars, eds. 1996. *Traumatic Stress: The Effects of Overwhelming Experience on Mind, Body, and Society*. New York: The Guilford Press.

Wiehe, Vernon. 1996. *The Brother–Sister Hurt: Recognizing the Effects of Sibling Abuse*. Brandon, Vt.: Safer Society Press.

Wright, Leslie, Loiselle, Mindy, and Bear, Euan, eds. 1999. *Back on Track: Boys Dealing with Sexual Abuse*. Brandon, Vt.: Safer Society Press.

Index